EPORTFOLIO

WHAT WE KNOW, WHAT WE DON'T KNOW, AND EVERYTHING IN-BETWEEN

Practices & Possibilities

Series Editors: Mike Palmquist, Aimee McClure, Aleashia Walton, and Karen Moroski-Rigney

The Practices & Possibilities Series addresses the full range of practices within the field of Writing Studies, including teaching, learning, research, and theory. From Joseph Williams' reflections on problems to Richard E. Young's taxonomy of "small genres" to Adam Mackie's considerations of technology, the books in this series explore issues and ideas of interest to writers, teachers, researchers, and theorists who share an interest in improving existing practices and exploring new possibilities. The series includes both original and republished books. Works in the series are organized topically.

The WAC Clearinghouse, Colorado State University Open Press, and University Press of Colorado are collaborating so that these books will be widely available through free digital distribution and low-cost print editions. The publishers and the series editors are committed to the principle that knowledge should freely circulate. We see the opportunities that new technologies have for further democratizing knowledge. And we see that to share the power of writing is to share the means for all to articulate their needs, interests, and learning into the great experiment of literacy.

Other Books in the Series

Jo-Anne Kerr and Ann N. Amicucci (Eds.), *Stories from First-Year Composition: Pedagogies that Foster Student Agency and Writing Identity* (2020)

Patricia Freitag Ericsson, *Sexual Harassment and Cultural Change in Writing Studies* (2020)

Ryan J. Dippre, *Talk, Tools, and Texts: A Logic-in-Use for Studying Lifespan Literate Action Development* (2019)

Jessie Borgman and Casey McArdle, *Personal, Accessible, Responsive, Strategic: Resources and Strategies for Online Writing Instructors* (2019)

Cheryl Geisler & Jason Swarts, Coding *Streams of Language: Techniques for the Systematic Coding of Text, Talk, and Other Verbal Data* (2019)

Ellen C. Carillo, *A Guide to Mindful Reading* (2017)

Lillian Craton, Renée Love & Sean Barnette (Eds.), *Writing Pathways to Student Success* (2017)

Charles Bazerman, *Involved: Writing for College, Writing for Your Self* (2015)

Adam Mackie, *New Literacies Dictionary: Primer for the Twenty-first Century Learner* (2011)

Patricia A. Dunn, *Learning Re-abled: The Learning Disability Controversy and Composition Studies* (2011)

EPORTFOLIOS@EDU

WHAT WE KNOW, WHAT WE DON'T KNOW, AND EVERYTHING IN-BETWEEN

Edited by Mary Ann Dellinger and D. Alexis Hart

The WAC Clearinghouse
wac.colostate.edu
Fort Collins, Colorado

University Press of Colorado
upcolorado.com
Louisville, Colorado

The WAC Clearinghouse, Fort Collins, Colorado 80523

University Press of Colorado, Louisville, Colorado 80027

ISBN 978-1-64215-108-4 (PDF) | 978-1-64215-109-1 (ePub) | 978-1-64642-180-0 (pbk.)

DOI 10.37514/PRA-B.2020.1084

Produced in the United States of America

Library of Congress Cataloging-in-Publication Data

Names: Dellinger, Mary Ann, editor. | Hart, D. Alexis, editor.
Title: Eportfolios@edu : what we know, what we don't know, and everything in between / Edited by Mary Ann Dellinger and D. Alexis Hart.
Description: Fort Collins, Colorado : The WAC Clearinghouse; University Press of Colorado, [2020] | Series: Practices & possibilities | Includes bibliographical references.
Identifiers: LCCN 2020044327 (print) | LCCN 2020044328 (ebook) | ISBN 9781646421800 (paperback) | ISBN 9781642151084 (pdf) | ISBN 9781642151091 (epub)
Subjects: LCSH: Electronic portfolios in education. | Curriculum planning.
Classification: LCC LB1029.P67 E66 2020 (print) | LCC LB1029.P67 (ebook) | DDC 371.39—dc23
LC record available at https://lccn.loc.gov/2020044327
LC ebook record available at https://lccn.loc.gov/2020044328

Copyeditor: Don Donahue
Designer: Mike Palmquist
Cover Image: Malcolm Childers, "A Twilight, Way Over Par"
Series Editors: Mike Palmquist, Aimee McClure, Aleashia Walton, and Karen Moroski-Rigney

The WAC Clearinghouse supports teachers of writing across the disciplines. Hosted by Colorado State University, and supported by the Colorado State University Open Press, it brings together scholarly journals and book series as well as resources for teachers who use writing in their courses. This book is available in digital formats for free download at wac.colostate.edu.

Founded in 1965, the University Press of Colorado is a nonprofit cooperative publishing enterprise supported, in part, by Adams State University, Colorado State University, Fort Lewis College, Metropolitan State University of Denver, University of Colorado, University of Northern Colorado, University of Wyoming, Utah State University, and Western Colorado University. For more information, visit upcolorado.com.

We lovingly dedicate this collection to the memory of Dr. Christy Desmet (1954–2018): mentor, friend, teacher, scholar, and stalwart innovator and advocate of ePortfolio platforms and pedagogies.

Contents

Acknowledgments

First and foremost, we would like to thank all our authors for their contributions to ePortfolios@edu and for their patience over the years since we issued the "Call for Papers." Special mention goes to our invited scholar, Dr. Helen Chen, who penned the preface to this volume.

As well, our heartfelt thanks to the WAC Clearinghouse Editorial Board members, Mike Palmquist and Nick Carbone, whose critical eye and attention to detail have proved invaluable throughout the proposal-to-publication process. Aleashia Walton, co-editor for the WAC Clearinghouse Practices & Possibilities Series, also merits our note of appreciation for her part in the publication of this volume.

Without the support of our home institutions, Allegheny College and the Virginia Military Institute, this volume would not have been possible. The professional development opportunities vis-à-vis electronic portfolios and the time afforded us through sabbaticals and internal grants facilitated our work on this project, for which we remain most grateful. Thanks also to our students at Allegheny and cadets at VMI whose ePortfolios and reflective writing have fostered better understanding of what we two know and what we don't.

Last, but not least, we thank our families for their love and support, and especially their patience during the long hours we spent on FaceTime editing our manuscript. Our love to you all.

Preface

Helen L. Chen

STANFORD UNIVERSITY

Over the last two decades, the ePortfolio has progressed from being just another educational technology fad into a dedicated field of study. The ePortfolios@edu collection illustrates how the research and the practice of ePortfolios in higher education have become more nuanced, more rigorous, and more generalizable as a result of the evolution of pedagogical approaches, assessment methodologies, and the technology platforms underpinning these efforts.

Pedagogy

While it's easy to focus on the ePortfolio product, innovations in pedagogy incentivize and propel the creation of new features and technology platforms. Portfolios continue to have a strong presence in the traditional disciplines of writing and rhetoric, first-year composition, and teacher education. Yet, as a learner-centered orientation that incorporates reflective practice and integrative learning, ePortfolios have gained followers in academic areas ranging from international studies and language learning to undergraduate medical science and politics. The incorporation of ePortfolios as a key component of Texas Christian University's first-year seminar "Introduction to University Life" and in the School of Medical Sciences' honors program at the University of New South Wales (Australia) demonstrates its value as a mechanism to document growth over time and facilitate academic exploration through the formation of students' intellectual identities. Innovations in teaching and learning initiatives from individual course enhancements to programmatic, departmental, and institution-wide efforts have been introduced at multiple levels with varying levels of success, but with many insights gained and recommendations for what should be repeated and also what could be done differently in future iterations.

Assessment

One of the areas of greatest change is the emergence of ePortfolios as a focused area of research. This is seen in the *International Journal of ePortfolios* and the peer-reviewed research articles documented in the *Publications on ePortfolio: Archives of the Research Landscape* (PEARL) database sponsored by the Association of American Colleges and Universities (AAC&U). Evidence of the impact of ePortfolios has moved beyond anecdotal, one-off stories to detailed observations and findings that are contextualized within a cross-disciplinary body of

DOI: https://doi.org/10.37514/PRA-B.2020.1084.1.1

literature. The design of curricular and programmatic ePortfolio programs have been informed by a backward design approach at the Virginia Military Institute (VMI). Deakin University (Australia) has incorporated a standards-based assessment framework that relies on career development theories and other models to determine how graduate employability skills and work-related learning are measured. The adaptation of relevant theoretical traditions from other fields such as mapping of the conversational framework as a strategy to map pedagogical patterns in ePortfolios (Castaño & Novo, this collection) is an illustrative example of how the ePortfolio researchers are referencing the disciplinary traditions of other fields to create new applications and conceptualizations that are unique to ePortfolios.

The rising interest in and engagement with ePortfolio research are linked to a corresponding increase in rigor in study designs and data collection and analysis methodology which in turn, has improved teaching and learning practices and assessment strategies. The design and thoughtful implementation of rubrics with clearly articulated criteria at San Francisco State is one illustration. Carpenter and Labissiere's structured comparison of ePortfolio assessment practices at Portland State describes a research direction and a process that is generalizable on multiple levels and can be adapted to different types of institutions, student populations, and disciplines.

Technology

Today, we take the format of the electronic or digital "e" in ePortfolio as a given and as a result, the affordances of ePortfolio technology have moved beyond simply being online to features that provide greater security, interoperability with learning management systems, fine grained permissions, accessibility, personalization, and a more sophisticated user experience. We recognize that ePortfolio tools are not "one size fits all" and specific requirements vary depending on who the stakeholders are and what goals they have for their students. Our search for the minimally viable feature set for an ePortfolio is influenced by the feedback and perspectives of three critical stakeholders: individual learners who are incentivized by the portfolio's value beyond the specific experience or course; institutions and programs' emphasis on assessment and evaluation and desire to effectively demonstrate how learning outcomes are being met, and the faculty and instructors who prioritize instructional and pedagogical needs.

For example, EMMA, the University of Georgia's homegrown writing environment, was initially adapted for ePortfolios and is now potentially being transitioned to a vendor-hosted solution to address the changing demands of the campus. The process of ePortfolio platform selection at Embry-Riddle Aeronautical University identifies both challenges and opportunities that are emblematic of the broader political, financial, leadership, and cultural considerations related to supporting the teaching and learning ecosystem on campuses.

Sustainability

Our aspirations for long-term sustainability and stability for our ePortfolio initiatives require more than just funding and timing (or *Kairos*) as identified in San Francisco State University's framework for assessing institutional readiness for ePortfolio adoption, growth, and support. The historical perspective of Northern Illinois' ePortfolio initiative highlights personal qualities of persistence and a willingness to collaborate as necessary for scalability. Yet, increasing the number of ePortfolio users requires a parallel effort to reinforce the infrastructure and networks to assist students, staff, faculty, and instructors. Students who join VMI's Writing Center in a teacher-learner role and serve as peer consultants and portfolio ambassadors may come to think about ePortfolios differently due to their position of advocacy. At the same time, these students are well-situated to provide a meaningful perspective on the design and value of ePortfolios to key stakeholders, namely other students and faculty.

Connecting to a community of researchers and practitioners is essential to a strong infrastructure and the well-being of ePortfolio advocates and leaders, some of whom may be part of a small cohort of ePortfolio enthusiasts on their campus (or the only one). At some institutions, individuals appointed as ePortfolio directors and coordinators often involve colleagues in academic technology, centers for teaching and learning, and departments, programs, schools across campus such as the Electronic Portfolio Interest Group at the University of Georgia and regional networks such as the Illinois Regional ePortfolio Partnership. Nationally and internationally, conferences and thought leadership promoted by the Association of American Colleges and Universities, ePortfolios Australia, and the Association of Authentic, Experiential Evidence-Based Learning via in-person and online events, webinars, and Twitter chats provide engagement and networking opportunities to join a diverse and inclusive community of practice.

Looking to the Future

As we look to the future, the ePortfolios@edu collection highlights the maturation of ePortfolio research and practice in three areas. The first is a greater awareness and understanding of the needs and interests of the ePortfolio creator and their intended purpose and audience. The process of curation and the selection of relevant artifacts and evidence are guided by purpose and audience, especially as they relate to the formation of an online identity, demonstration of competencies and skills, or meeting the requirements of a project, course, or program. Similar to tailoring a resume or cover letter for a specific position, new platforms allow easy duplication and personalization of ePortfolios, expanding the possibility of a more expansive use of portfolios for different situations and contexts. With this mind, while "scaling up" ePortfolio use has typically referred to growing the number of students, there may also be an opportunity to "scale down" and to consider how portfolio pedagogies and models could be applied to a group project or course assignment.

The second area of focus underscores how ePortfolios are evolving in the higher education space and recognizes the knowledge and skills that are necessary for successful curation practices, such as digital literacy, authenticity, and visual rhetoric. As we ask students to share personal reflections, multimedia artifacts, and evidence of curricular and co-curricular experiences in online environments, some in public spaces and others inside learning and assessment management systems usually behind an institutional firewall, a growing number of questions and concerns about privacy and digital ethics in the short term and long term continue to arise.

Lastly, while the recognition of ePortfolios as a high impact practice prioritizes their independent value, they are at their best when coupled with other practices in order to expand, enhance, and foster greater student engagement. Integrative learning is a foundational principle of ePortfolios in the context of a lifelong and lifewide learning trajectory, moving beyond simply making connections among experiences inside and outside the classroom and paying explicit attention to the translation and transfer of learning from diverse contexts and experiences in order to enlighten future decisions about education, employment, and achieving a meaningful and purposeful life. Future ePortfolio research will continue to draw upon the findings and insights from the learning sciences, self-authorship, self-efficacy, career development theories, and other research traditions.

The ePortfolio@edu case studies, exemplar tools and practices, and emerging research are a rich and vibrant snapshot of not only where the ePortfolio field is today but also how far we've come. Yet, the foundation and core values of reflection and metacognition and the emphasis on pedagogical process over technological product remain unchanged. Integrative learning and synthesis have become even more important to ePortfolios as students, faculty, and administrators take a more holistic and comprehensive view of the design of the educational experience and who learners are when they set foot on our campuses as well as who they are becoming. The emergence of new practices, methods, research questions and directions exemplified in this collection will inform and guide researchers, practitioners, and learners in our ongoing ePortfolio journey.

EPORTFOLIOS@EDU

WHAT WE KNOW, WHAT WE DON'T KNOW, AND EVERYTHING IN-BETWEEN

Introduction

Mary Ann Dellinger
VIRGINIA MILITARY INSTITUTE

D. Alexis Hart
ALLEGHENY COLLEGE

A life accumulates a collection: of people, work, and perplexities.

We are all our own curators.

—*Richard Fortey*

This volume is a book of essays about teachers wrangling with ePortfolios. It's not about large theories of ePortfolios or broad trends, but rather a sampler of close instructional encounters that seeks to look at what those large trends mean at the course, program, and institutional levels. Representing four countries on as many continents, the authors identify challenges associated with different phases of program development and provide theory-informed, experience-based advice to administrators, program directors, and instructors at institutions of all sizes.

Multiple publications already on the market advance theory, research, and pedagogical approaches in the multiple facets of ePortfolios in higher education. We do not intend or even suggest that our book could replace any of them; rather, our aim is to complement the existing literature. While we share the same audience in general, the purpose of this book and our colleagues' publications vary discernibly from one to another. A critical collection such as ePortfolios@edu cannot offer the wealth of empirical evidence that Bret Eynon and Laura Gambino include in their book *High-Impact ePortfolio Practice: A Catalyst for Student, Faculty, and Institutional Learning* (2017). Nor can it replicate the scope of Field Guide to ePortfolio (AACU and AAEEBL, 2018), supported and created collaboratively by four professional organizations. Similarly, the purpose of this book differs from those publications and other more targeted studies ranging from the *meta-assessment*[1] of international models (Cambridge, 2012) to integrative practices in the classroom (Reynolds & Patton, 2014).

The main portion of the book is divided into three sections: Getting Started, Implementation, and Assessing Performance. Having designed the volume as a go-to manual for ePortfolio novices, seasoned practitioners, and curious explorers alike, we want readers to close the book and immediately be able to apply whatever information they found most appropriate for their course, program, and/or institution. Towards that end, authors embed screenshots and diagrams

---

1. We use **bold italic font** for terminology included in the glossary.

DOI: https://doi.org/10.37514/PRA-B.2020.1084.1.3

within their essays, and addend their chapters with relevant timelines, prompts, and *rubrics*.[2]

The essays in ePortfolios@edu center on qualitative evidence, although authors offer empirical evidence to support staked claims. Most importantly, however, readers will find that ePortfolios@edu mirrors ePortfolio publication in its presentation. We purposely use the active voice and include meaningful screenshots from students' ePortfolios as meta-evidence; the companion website ensures relevance and connections, both hallmarks of ePortfolio publication.

Part I. Getting Started/Lessons Learned

In Chapter 1, Ron Balthazor, Elizabeth Davis, and their co-authors discuss the strategies that they have used—and even been forced to use—for almost a decade in order to sustain two related ePortfolio capstone projects within the Department of English at the University of Georgia: First-Year Composition and the Writing Certificate Program. The authors discuss challenges in getting started with ePortfolio implementation on a large scale, beginning with software development and pedagogy. In addition, this chapter addresses a different set of challenges that arise at the other end of the historical process, including forming a succession plan as the original team of developers moves on; adjusting to changes in administrative policies at higher levels; moving away from open-source to proprietary platforms on an institutional level; and centralizing technological resources.

Expanding on the all-important question of ePortfolio software, Chapter 2 discusses the course and course corrections in the implementation of an ePortfolio program at Embry-Riddle Aeronautical University. The authors relate the step-by-step process from choosing a platform to launching and assessing the program, dedicating most of their chapter to the planning/pre-implementation phase, in particular the membership, role, and impact of an "ePortfolio Selection Committee." Throughout the chapter, the authors underscore the all-important concept that, as with any instructional technology, the platform must fit the pedagogy, not the other way around.

Part II. Implementation

In Chapter 3, Daniel Terry and David Whillock explain how Texas Christian University (TCU) created a large-scale, system-wide, sustainable ePortfolio initiative in a relatively short time via a unique first-year seminar course in which receiving

---

2. We understand that screenshots and instructional materials quickly become obsolete, due to the dynamics of instructional technology and growth rate of human knowledge. For this reason, our companion website aims to provide updated information from the authors and editors of *ePortfolios@edu* as well as revised and new materials for immediate use.

and building an ePortfolio is nested within larger conversations about the nature of college learning. The authors detail why and how TCU came to offer this first-year seminar in its present form, including the unique faculty/staff co-teaching model they adopted, the role of faculty/staff mentoring in promoting *folio thinking*, the use of peer coaches, and the adoption of a template portfolio to structure *reflection* and *artifact* collection.

Chapter 4 also addresses implementation of an institutional-wide ePortfolio program, offers a series of suggestions to colleges in the initial stages of program development, and presents a model for *back-end/front-end collaboration* designed to separate pedagogical questions from technical issues in order to better troubleshoot the latter, especially during the first years. As reflective as it is informational, this chapter centers on the "what we know" with examples of how perceptions of ownership can hinder the success of an ePortfolio program even before it is implemented.

Moving to program-level implementation in Chapter 5, Deidre Anne Evans Garriott considers the intersection of writing centers and ePortfolio pedagogy. Garriott discusses the successes and challenges of training undergraduate writing consultants to provide students and professors with ePortfolio technical know-how as well as "global" considerations regarding content, layout, and organization of the ePortfolios. In addition, Garriott ponders the implications of undergraduate writing consultants as ePortfolio "ambassadors."

Chapter 6 considers the role of ePortfolios in Deakin University's (Australia) recent course/program enhancement initiative, designed to offer anywhere, anytime learning to students. Detailing the course enhancement process, this chapter describes how the authors employed backward design in order to align course learning outcomes with evidence-based assessment and also facilitated learning through the development of related structures to scaffold instruction and better support learners.

Building on the foundational concepts of goal setting and reflection discussed in the previous chapter, Chapter 7 focuses on the explicit modelling and *scaffolding* of folio thinking skills: curation, composition, and creativity. The authors discuss the *outcome-based* learning and assessment design that they and their colleagues implemented in various medical science courses, in which they integrated both reflective practice and career development learning (CDL) as part of their ePortfolio pedagogy.

Chapter 8 proposes an ePortfolio model based on Diana Laurillard's theory of teaching and learning as design, specifically the principles of pedagogical patterns and the conversational framework. This chapter also describes common challenges in fostering students' "folio" skills (see Polly et al., this collection) towards meaningful documentation of both classroom and independent learning.

Within the context of pre-service teacher education, authors Ximena Castaño Sanchez and María Teresa Novo Molinero offer a complex but valuable model for capturing the relationships between teaching methods and learners' activity.

Part III. Assessing Performance

Chapter 9 addresses the necessity of scaling implementation and sustaining support for pedagogy and technological innovation after the successful adoption of an ePortfolio program. This chapter combines the perspectives and experiences of administrators, faculty, and students to demonstrate the importance of administrative advocacy and support; faculty programming and support; and meaningful, *authentic* purposes for students developing their ePortfolios.

Addressing the crucial issues of purpose and cohesiveness in student ePortfolios, Chapter 10 discusses the role of structured, scheduled reflective activities as part of a course for which students are asked to create a summative ePortfolio to demonstrate their learning. Like other authors in the collection, Howard B. Sanborn and Jenny Ramirez note that students are often unprepared to link artifacts, assignments, or other learning experiences as part of the case they make about their learning. Therefore, Sanborn and Ramirez argue in favor of structured reflection, required at discrete moments of the semester and aimed at encouraging students to think deeply about a specific assignment or artifact as both process and product.

In Chapter 11, Rowanna Carpenter and Yves Labissiere present research findings focused on five aspects of the ePortfolio assessment process and examine the pros and cons of national rubrics and other tools and approaches that have emerged in response to questions raised about the validity and reliability of ePortfolio-based assessment. The authors compare three different approaches to assessing digital portfolios at the program level in order to illustrate their ensuing discussion about the benefits and challenges of each approach as well as how programs might weigh the five factors when selecting an ePortfolio-assessment strategy.

In the final chapter, Michael Day describes the process and outcomes of Northern Illinois University's first-year composition electronic portfolio and discusses the intra-university consensus-building and stakeholder analysis needed to move to the next level: a longitudinal general education electronic portfolio. Further, he explains how intra-institutional work led to the creation of a regional inter-institutional partnership focused on using ePortfolios for articulation and transfer.

In the collaborative spirit of ePortfolio development and the targeted synergy between creator and author, ePortfolios@edu represents a contribution to the current scholarship in electronic portfolio research, building on parts of published research, complementing other work, and including experiences from other faculty and staff stakeholders who to date remain underrepresented in electronic portfolio research. We hope you, our reader, will find it useful, no matter where you fall on the what-we-know/what we-don't-know continuum.

References

Batson, T., Coleman, K. S., Chen, H. L., Watson, C. E., Rhodes, T. L. & Harver, A. (Eds.). (2017). *Field guide to eportfolio.* Association of American Colleges and Universities.

Cambridge, D. (Ed.). (2012). *Eportfolios and global diffusion: Solutions for collaborative education.* IGI Global.

Eynon, B. & Gambino, L. M. (2017). *High-impact ePortfolio practice: A catalyst for student, faculty, and institutional learning.* Stylus; AAC&U.

Reynolds, C. & Patton, J. (Eds.). (2014). *Leveraging the eportfolio for integrative learning: A faculty guide to classroom practices for transforming student learning.* Stylus.

Part 1. Getting Started

Chapter 1. What? So What? Now What? A Decade of Writing ePortfolios at the University of Georgia

Ron Balthazor
Elizabeth Davis
Christy Desmet
Deborah Church Miller
Sara Steger
THE UNIVERSITY OF GEORGIA

Two related programs at the University of Georgia have been using ePortfolios for individual and program *assessment* for over a decade. The first-year composition (FYC) program implemented electronic portfolios as a capstone project using EMMA, the department and program's in-house writing environment, in 2005. The use of ePortfolios was expanded to the Writing Certificate Program in 2008. Thus, within the English Department, ePortfolios are well established as a method of assessment. In this essay, we discuss the strategies that we have used—and even been forced to use—in order to sustain ePortfolio use at the curricular level. The challenges in the early part of the program have been discussed in the literature as well as in this collection, including questions of instructor and student buy-in, logistics of implementation on a large scale, user support, technological infrastructure, and software development and user studies. At the other end of the historical process, we face an entirely different set of challenges, including forming a succession plan as the original team of developers moves on; adapting to changes in administrative policies at higher levels; moving away from open-source to proprietary platforms on an institutional level; and dealing with the centralization of technological resources. This chapter focuses on programmatic connections—how to make connections between curricular efforts in a de-centralized institution—and the long-term arc of development over a decade, in response to and in resistance against educational trends and institutional practices. We hope our historical perspective will prove useful to institutions at different stages of ePortfolio development and curricular expansion.

The story of EMMA and the electronic portfolios that EMMA has made possible on a programmatic level began quietly, when Nelson Hilton, then Head of the English Department at the University of Georgia, sought a cadre of colleagues who might be interested in exploring his latest technological enthusiasm: markup languages, and more specifically, *XML*, or Extensible Markup Language. For one semester, we met regularly to learn abstractly about the potential of markup

DOI: https://doi.org/10.37514/PRA-B.2020.1084.2.01

languages for teaching and research, and more concretely, to learn and use XML. Like many digital humanities projects, this one started with a penchant for learning and playing with tools. For the simple reason that many participants were instructors in the first-year composition program, the project eventually found its home there, and the group began thinking about the potential for teaching writing with XML. As the project progressed, however, the emphasis was reversed, as pedagogy began to drive EMMA's technical development as a writing environment. The adoption of electronic portfolios within the first-year composition (FYC) program and their eventual migration to the Writing Certificate Program (WCP) is thoroughly intertwined with the development of EMMA, the integrated writing environment that was developed at the University of Georgia between 2001 and the present.

What?

What is EMMA, and how has it changed, been developed, and survived between 2002, the year we first piloted the application with a class, and the time of this writing? The changes have been many, the reasons varied. EMMA was "born" within the early days of Learning Management Systems (LMS). Still the dominant form of technological classroom support, LMS began as tools built to assist the delivery of information to students, and in many ways, they still are limited by this initial design imperative, a limitation that other programs have attempted to mitigate via LMS plug-ins for additional affordances (see Dellinger & Hanger, this collection). Composition instructors have long known delivery of information is less-than-central to the composition classroom. Well before user-generated web content was common and expected, the heart of composition pedagogy was the student document. Thus, some fifteen years ago, before Web 2.0 sparked a revolution in how we interact with texts and one another in digital environments, instructors and administrators in the Office of First-year Composition in the English Department at the University of Georgia (UGA) set out to imagine an electronic environment for the writing classroom.

Once the project had found a home within First-year Composition, development focused on pedagogy, for all of the developers were also instructors. As EMMA developed according to their pedagogical needs and requests, it aimed to facilitate collection of the various stages of the writing process—from generation through revision and review. The application, as the teacher-developers realized, should also support asynchronous exchange of students' documents for peer review. More globally, it should encourage a common vocabulary for writing pedagogy from rhetorical to mechanical issues, and as part of this community-building effort, it should make it easy to tag or mark-up any document to make more visible to students, their peers, and their instructors the formal aspects of writing (e.g., everything from "what actually is the thesis of this essay?" to "how many prepositions are in this paragraph?"). The writing environment that we created was initially named EMMA or the Electronic Markup and Management Application, in order to reflect the driving purpose at its inception. Though few remember or care what EMMA once stood for or why the name lived for a time in angle brackets (a nod, of course, to XML or eXtensible Markup Language, which was at the core of early development), the underlying pedagogy has matured, along with the software program developed to implement it.[1] To the core features dictated by these initial pedagogical imperatives, we added a variety of tools to provide space for low-stakes writing, tools that support integration of *multimodal* composition, and a portfolio composition and assessment piece to complete the suite of electronic writing possibilities.

Even though EMMA was initially designed to facilitate an established writing process and encourage pedagogy grounded in that process, writing itself is a technology, and it is a technology in the midst of dramatic changes catalyzed by the very same shift from paper to screen that we were making with EMMA. Thus EMMA's own evolution reflects some of the changes the application itself may have instigated in the way students and instructors write and the way they present and evaluate that writing, particularly in the culminating product of the ePortfolio.

Early Days with XML

We began naively, thinking that we could build our own writing application, a word processor of sorts that would meet the broader needs of the writing classroom. But quickly recognizing this project was in so many ways beyond us, we adopted an open-source code editor (jEdit) and began to modify and repurpose it in order to realize the markup dreams we had for student writing. We anticipated that eXtensible Markup Language (XML), as a language that is at once readable by people and machines, could help writers become more reflective, or self-conscious about their choices and processes. At the very least, marking one or more sentences as <thesis> would make a writer or peer reviewer think twice about what actually was a document's "center of gravity." On an even more mundane level, marking subjects and verbs within a sentence would confirm whether or not the writer/reader could identify these grammatical parts. Moving outward to more global issues, it was thought, would foster reflective practice without interrupting the flow of writing with revision or editorial concerns. Best of all, writers could literally see their documents in new and more intentional ways.

During the first year in which we implemented electronic portfolios as capstone projects through EMMA for FYC classes, documents were uploaded, marked up, and shared using jEdit as an XML editor. To the amazement of

---

1. XML is a protocol for marking the structure of documents, and is designed to store, transport, and exchange data (rather than display data, like *html*). XML is used for organizing data of any kind in a systematic manner by creating descriptive markup tags (e.g., an essay might include tags for marking paragraphs, sentences, introductions, thesis statements, etc.).

some (and the chagrin of many), we had all of our composition students actually tagging their work to produce well-formed XML documents. But in spite of the strengths of XML as an open, customizable text standard that could easily be manipulated to create information-rich displays on screen and mined for research and assessment purposes, the creation of Document Type Definitions (DTDs) and valid XML documents predicated on them proved a significant challenge and hindrance to students and instructors.

As an unintended—and undesirable—consequence of the complicated markup interface, the act of composing documents became largely divorced from preparing them for display in a web browser. Students basically wrote their essays in a traditional word processor, then copy-and-pasted their texts into the XML editor and marked them up with the appropriate tags for display (Figure 1.1). The results were clean and beautiful displays—that is, once the XML parser was satisfied that all of the code was well-formed and valid. One mistake was fatal and would produce only a blank document or an error code. Since markup took place at the end of the process, when an essay or final portfolio was due, the exacting nature of the markup became a source of added tension.

Those early years of EMMA, during the pilots in 2003 and 2004, and the big rollout year in 2005 garnered a problematic reputation that took several years to overcome, principally because all 6,000 students taking first-year composition were marking up their essays in order to turn work in to 90-some instructors. That period became a cautionary tale about finding a balance between the surface of digital text and the technological language that lies beneath, constructing the text. To provide a sense of the ambient level of technical expertise in the years EMMA was being introduced (2003–2005), we can look at a few examples. Up until 2004, the first-year composition's "computer support" consisted largely of a small group of teaching assistants dedicated to providing minor fixes to issues in the three computer lab rooms (e.g., removing stuck floppy disks with a wooden tongue depressor). Computer-support teaching assistants also made sure that the twenty-two new Dell desktops in each of three labs were booted up in the morning and shut down at night, cleared of renegade documents, desktop messages, and pictures. Because all FYC classes were required to spend two weeks each semester working on "digital communication & writing skills," support staff also oriented teachers and students to the computer use in labs and recommended computer-focused pedagogical approaches. In lab orientations, they covered skills such as opening, closing, and minimizing Windows; writing, copying, pasting, and saving documents in Microsoft Word; using the "Netscape" browser; and emailing using a dial up TelNet system. The support team also offered digital lesson plans. One such lesson was designed to teach the use of the main library's digital resources and databases. Another taught students to use fonts and highlights to "mark up" and edit documents. Overall, the general teaching and student population was still in digital toddlerhood; we were not far past giving instructions on how to operate a mouse.

Figure 1.1. Writing in the jEdit XML Editor.

Meanwhile, over in our EMMA development camp, a lively discussion about the theory of creating and using tags defining varieties of text (DTDs or "document type definitions") was taking place. The team discovered the jEdit text editor and saw it as a means to "increase students' awareness of the complexities of the writing process by requiring them to identify and tag various features of their texts using XML [extensible markup language—a form of text coding]" (Balthazor et al., 2013, p. 23). jEdit, compared to the other open source text editors the group had worked with, seemed incredibly accessible. Our developers foresaw great pedagogical possibilities: students would gain new rhetorical perspectives by having to deconstruct and name the function of each of the parts of their texts as part of the composing process. The parts of students' essays' structure and, more importantly, the definitions of those parts would become visible. EMMA developers imagined that classes would discuss and challenge those definitions, raising students' consciousness about the nature and structure of digital text. Once defined and tagged, a whole set of essay "parts" could be displayed together for class examination. An instructor might, for example, collect and display for discussion a whole set of theses or topic sentences. All of this should be done instantly and without difficulty, thanks to the development team's work.

The introduction of the jEdit version of EMMA took place over a little more than two years. In Academic Year 2003–2004 the development team ran a small test pilot with a handful of sections led by some of our most enthusiastic and tech-savvy instructors; response seemed very positive. Instructors from that pilot presented conference papers, published articles, and won awards for their innovative work teaching FYC with coding. In the following year, 2004–2005, we branched out to test run EMMA with our entire class of new teaching assistants, and this is where we encountered head winds and red flags began to appear. After a few initial EMMA training sessions, we asked for feedback. The comments, at best, damned the jEdit EMMA with faint praise, scaling up from there to annoyance, frustration, and subdued panic. For example, in one of the most positive comments, the instructor noted hopefully that "the experience itself was not, overall, particularly unpleasant. It is a logical process that, once learned, is not really a huge problem." At the same time, the commenter noted, more negatively, "while I am commenting in jEdit, I have trouble keeping my place and properly assessing the flow of the sentence/paragraph/paper." Another teacher frankly resisted, writing: "I honestly feel that the EMMA program is so young and so primitive that there is no way to make students and instructors use it successfully. About commenting, I hate it; it takes so long. It is almost impossible to read after a few comments in the student's paper." Other instructors were just panicky: "Basically, it took me an hour to enter the comments from one paper, and then I saved it to the A drive, which is apparently a cardinal sin. Miranda tried valiantly to save it, but ended up rebooting the system . . . I need to be drilled when it comes to this sort of thing. Just can't be turned loose yet—I'm concerned: will we be doing this full-time next semester? I am concerned that it will take longer than grading on paper & I am concerned about being expected to introduce EMMA to students."

As we moved to a program-wide introduction of the jEdit version of EMMA in 2005, we herded our instructors through the change with a number of pretty attractive carrots and one big stick. As carrots, we offered a series of concessions and adaptations to alleviate any felt or real teaching burdens. First, we expanded a voluntary program of workshops and opened a centralized help lab. We let instructors know that students struggling with coding and uploading could be outsourced to the "EMMA Lab" staff. Further, while we encouraged instructors to have students use EMMA to create documents throughout the semester, we required only a final portfolio of documents in the EMMA environment and again, instructors could refer students to the EMMA Lab for help with adding documents and images to their portfolios. We also appealed to our instructors' better educational angels by substituting these final EMMA course portfolios for the single, high stakes three-hour exam essay that was, at that time, determining 30% of every student's course grade, a grade based heavily on a timeworn model of "correctness." Finally, we reduced the required number of graded essays from five to four, and later down to three. The big stick we employed, since all of our teachers were either on teaching assistantships (about 75%) or were on semester-to-semester contracts at that time, was simply to make the use of EMMA a top-down requirement for the whole FYC program.

To provide a sense of the learning curve involved in the switch to EMMA's jEdit digital environment, two items come to mind. The first is the seven-point hand-out, "Steps for EMMA Introduction," that we used as an outline for instructors and computer support staff as they led students through the first steps of EMMA work. The handout outlined seven class meetings of introductory work and homework to accomplish the following: have students enroll in EMMA and log in, learn to navigate to course materials (syllabus, readings, and so forth), write a short response in a "journal" tool, install the text editor, tag and upload a document, access a digital portfolio template and add a document to it, tag a document for structure, insert an image into a document, and respond to a peer's work. By comparison, the tasks that then required more than two weeks of in- and out-of-class instruction and practice (plus many trips to the EMMA lab for code detangling) could now be accomplished during a fifteen-minute orientation. The second item was the handout for instructors, "How to Grade in EMMA"; it involved seventeen "easy" steps to get an essay downloaded, a *rubric* attached, comments and grades entered, and the document tagged, identified, re-uploaded, and made available in a display to the student. While we required the new teaching assistants to use this online grading interface for at least one set of essays, only a tiny group—perhaps five instructors out of 90—voluntarily used the jEdit version of EMMA to comment and grade a semester's worth of essays.

As we concluded that first year, and while students were fighting their way through tagging in code to upload documents, we made one further mistake by having all portfolios (ca. 6,000) due at the same minute on the same day. Ron Balthazor, who was in charge of the server, watched anxiously as the system hesitated, hiccupped, but never crashed. It became clear to even the most deeply committed EMMA developers that a change of direction was required. While the EMMA team had believed, along with XML promoters, that the benefits of seeing and controlling the underlying construction of text would win out over the WYSIWYG (what you see is what you get) surface of the familiar word processor's text, as program leaders later reflected, "They were wrong: students raised on Microsoft Word rebelled at the exertions required of writers working with visible XML in their texts. Furthermore, the visible XML tags continued to work against what is probably the most important process to writing instruction: revision" (Balthazor, et al., 2013, p. 25). A fortuitous switch to the Open Office word processing program, similar to MS Word and providing a familiar-looking writing environment for our students, came on the heels of the first year's broad experiment. EMMA would consistently evolve from that point on towards a simpler and more accessible user interface.

The Return of the Word Processor

OpenOffice offered the power of XML (which operated in the background of the word processor), retained many of the sophisticated display possibilities that we had with jEdit-created XML, and allowed for text creation and markup in an environment that was much friendlier. Open Document Format (ODF), an international standard for word processing documents, gave us a common ground for document creation and exchange that added no additional fees for students, as OpenOffice is free. For a time, we offered our students a portable version of OpenOffice on CDs and thumb drives (Figure 1.2). This put the focus back on writing and less on the technology of markup.

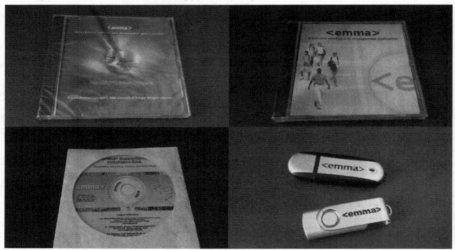

Figure 1.2. Media for delivering OpenOffice EMMA.

While OpenOffice allowed for a more familiar composing and revision environment, it too had drawbacks. Most obvious was the negative effect on presentation. Electronic texts have the advantage of being at once working documents and published ones. This is particularly true of the electronic portfolio, whose status as multimodal composition makes liberal use of the Web's spatial and visual affordances. Like all word processors, OpenOffice inserted extra, hidden codes that made control of the virtual page difficult. This Introductory Reflective essay to Charlotte Byram's portfolio in 2008–2009, where text and comic are spaced perfectly within the browser, is the exception that proves the rule (Figure 1.3). Most products appeared much less polished, sometimes even sloppy in presentation.

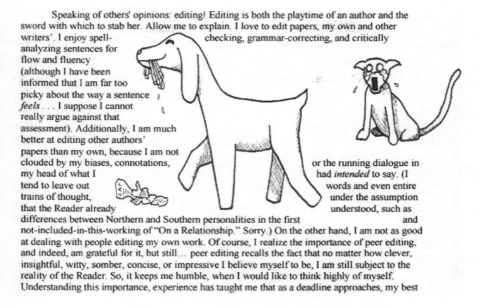

Speaking of others' opinions: editing! Editing is both the playtime of an author and the sword with which to stab her. Allow me to explain. I love to edit papers, my own and other writers'. I enjoy spell-checking, grammar-correcting, and critically analyzing sentences for flow and fluency (although I have been informed that I am far too picky about the way a sentence *feels* . . . I suppose I cannot really argue against that assessment). Additionally, I am much better at editing other authors' papers than my own, because I am not clouded by my biases, connotations, or the running dialogue in my head of what I had *intended* to say. (I tend to leave out words and even entire trains of thought, under the assumption that the Reader already understood, such as differences between Northern and Southern personalities in the first and not-included-in-this-working of "On a Relationship." Sorry.) On the other hand, I am not as good at dealing with people editing my own work. Of course, I realize the importance of peer editing, and indeed, am grateful for it, but still . . . peer editing recalls the fact that no matter how clever, insightful, witty, somber, concise, or impressive I believe myself to be, I am still subject to the reality of the Reader. So, it keeps me humble, when I would like to think highly of myself. Understanding this importance, experience has taught me that as a deadline approaches, my best

Figure 1.3. Charlotte Byram's introductory reflective essay.

As a result, teachers were asked to be lenient about formatting issues when grading capstone portfolios—in the browser, line spacing could vary, lineation could be ragged, and images moved out of place—and so we found ourselves in the uncomfortable position of accepting less professional productions than we would have liked. Some students resorted to using PDF documents, but these had to be downloaded before being read and evaluated, which added a burdensome amount of time for graders, each of whom assessed two classes of portfolios for each one they taught: for an instructor who taught four classes per semester, that could mean as many as 160 portfolios during the ten-day grading period at the end of a semester. In a program of this size and considering the working conditions under which U.S. composition instructors labor,[2] every technological choice has magnified consequences. Another drawback of PDF documents, discussed more fully below, is the inability to extract marked-up data from those documents for research and program assessment.

---

2. The "CCCC Statement on Working Conditions for Non-Tenure-Track Writing Faculty" (2016) notes the increasing numbers of non-tenure track faculty generally, and in composition classrooms in particular, in its call for changes to a variety of "practices and situations affecting NTT faculty and their efforts." The outcry in response to Arizona State University's 2014 effort to increase NTT composition instructors' course loads to 5/5 without increased compensation brought national attention to the widespread problem of workload and compensation for NTT composition faculty (see Flaherty, 2015).

Migrating to the Web

Because the lifespan of a technology generation is brief, EMMA would soon undergo another sea change. As wikis, Google Docs, and similar applications invited us all to move more and more of our work to the web-browser, EMMA, too, began moving the creation, sharing, marking, and evaluation of student-generated work to the Web. At the time of writing, most student work, including portfolio work, is submitted through a browser-based word processor (a customized version of the open-source CKEditor). Instructors and students can make comments on documents and provide feedback in the form of clickable markup tags (for example, "comma splice"). In the document, when students hover over text that has been tagged, they can see a brief description of the tag and have the option to click a link that provides additional feedback (see Figure 1.4).

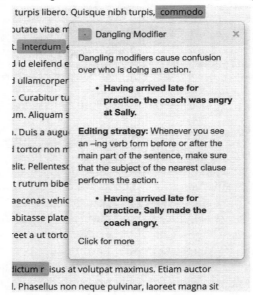

Figure 1.4. Student view of markup tag in EMMA.

We also have continued to develop tools for building multimodal texts and to provide tools for students to make choices about the appearance of their texts, encouraging them to think of themselves as writer/designers. These design options are particularly visible in the portfolios that students create as their final project in the semester.

Moving Outward: The Writing Certificate Program

While the first-year composition program at UGA provided students with a strong foundation based in best practices for writing instruction and EMMA facilitated a process and portfolio-based approach, there were indications that we were not building on that base as effectively as we should in order to give students consistent *scaffolding* and support for writing development across the curriculum. In 2003 and 2005, UGA participated in the National Survey of Student Engagement (NSSE), which surveys first-year students and seniors about their academic experiences. Responses to the NSSE showed that seniors felt they had not been asked to write very much beyond their first-year composition coursework and, yet, they felt that writing "clearly and effectively" was a crucial skill.

In 2007, a Writing Task Force was convened that developed a comprehensive plan for addressing concerns among faculty and administration about the amount and quality of writing done by undergraduate students. One of the key pieces of that plan was the interdisciplinary Writing Certificate Program (WCP), instituted at UGA in academic year 2008–2009. The WCP offers a way for students to develop their writing skills by taking a writing intensive program of coursework culminating in a capstone ePortfolio that showcases their work in the program and reflects on their writing experiences and accomplishments. Students in the program are required to take at least one course that is explicitly devoted to the subject of writing, the aim being to give them a foundation in how to approach writing in terms of process, rhetorical strategies, and working with peers to give and receive feedback during the development of projects. Students can select this course from a list that includes such approved writing courses as Advanced Composition, Technical and Professional Communication, Creative Writing, or Writing for the Web.

The rest of the coursework can be a mix of other writing courses, undergraduate research experiences, and writing intensive courses, such as those offered in the Franklin College of Arts and Sciences' Writing Intensive Program, or any course that has been approved for credit and carries a "W" suffix in the university's curriculum system. These courses are meant to help students learn about the research and writing practices in specific disciplines and a large part of a student's coursework for the program may take the form of writing intensive courses in their major field. The director of the program may also approve courses for certificate credit on a case-by-case basis by reviewing the syllabus and assignments and using the definition of writing intensive developed for the "W" suffix as a guide. For a course to have a "W" suffix in the university's curriculum system, it must demonstrate that

1. Writing is an ongoing activity throughout the course and is part of the process of learning content;

2. Writing assignments take a variety of forms appropriate to the course and the discipline; and

3. Students learn to write effectively by having opportunities to receive feedback from their instructors and peers in order to revise their writing as it progresses through a series of stages. ("W" Suffix)

Finally, WCP students take a one-hour ePortfolio Workshop, in which they compose the capstone portfolio. This course not only serves as the "exit" requirement for the certificate, but it also provides one final writing intensive experience for students. The portfolio itself must include one (or more) sample(s) of work from each course being counted for certificate credit, along with critical *reflection* on the work that describes and analyzes the ways in which portfolio *artifacts* demonstrate particular writing skills and/or how those skills have developed through the student's writing intensive courses and experiences. In that regard, the WCP capstone ePortfolio is similar to the FYC final course ePortfolio: both are meant to *showcase* writing done for the course or program and to demonstrate an ability to reflect critically on that work and the student's development as a writer.

Because the WCP is housed in the English Department and directed by an English Department faculty member with a specialization in rhetoric and composition, there is a strong cohesion between the ePortfolios for both programs. The FYC portfolio and rubric have strongly informed the pedagogical approach to the capstone workshop course and the assessment of the WCP portfolios (see Appendices A–C). The workshop's syllabus evokes the vocabulary of the FYC rubric and course goals, emphasizing coherence and engagement with process and reflection.

So What?

Looking back over EMMA's development over more than a decade, we feel strongly that the most important outcome has been the incorporation of electronic writing portfolios into the curriculum as a capstone project for both FYC and the WCP. In many ways, the advent and success of the portfolio programs at the University of Georgia have rested on the ever-increasing simplicity and flexibility of EMMA, the home-grown tool through which those portfolios are constructed. At the same time, the pedagogical imperatives that governed EMMA's development are also evident in the shape of its electronic portfolios.

The pedagogical advantages offered by electronic portfolios include support for synthesizing or linking together academic experiences; encouragement of reflection and meta-cognition as well as the ability to foster multimodal composition to an extent not possible in other, especially print, formats. Within the broad range of purposes for electronic portfolios, first-year composition ePortfolios fulfill several functions: as constructs "published" on the Web, albeit to a carefully limited audience, they are "showcase" portfolios; but given the position of these portfolio authors within the entire university structure, this function is less important than others. Since the ePortfolio functions as the FYC Program's capstone project, assessment is an important driver for the program. The FYC ePortfolio, substituting for the traditional final exam, counts for 30% of a student's final grade. Because the program conducts embedded program assessment at the portfolio-grading level, the assessment also works at the program level, a connection

Carpenter and Labissiere (this collection) explore further in their research on reliability and comparability in ePortfolio assessment. Finally, the FYC portfolio is structured to encourage reflection and demonstration of learning. The portfolio's landing page is a biography accompanied by an image of the student's choice; the task of composing and designing the landing page allows students to take ownership of and personalize their work. The next item is an introductory reflective essay, which extends and supplants the "introductory letter" of early portfolios. This assignment asks students to at once reflect on and present, in a thesis-driven manner, the "take-away" that they want the assessor to focus on in evaluating their portfolios. The showcase function of the ePortfolios is communicated through two revised essays from the course (which are presented as "best products") and a "wild card," the student's rhetorical choice to round out their image as a writer within the portfolio. The ePortfolio's function as a record of students' learning is communicated through two process exhibits responsive to their understanding of the writing process: the first is a demonstration of and reflection on the student's revision process, the second a demonstration of their peer revision process. As Polly et al. (this collection) likewise observe from a programmatic perspective, in a concrete sense, the portfolio's structure scaffolds desired pedagogical outcomes, in the case of our FYC courses by making revision and peer review central to the writing classroom. Both process pieces and the introductory essay also encourage reflection in action. The FYC ePortfolio's basic structure is shared by the WCP capstone portfolios. WCP ePortfolios also include a biography, an introductory reflective essay, various revised pieces, and "wild cards"—which, in the case of the capstone WCP portfolio, are artifacts that were produced outside the WCP curriculum, but that students may desire to include in the portfolio as demonstrations of writing skills or accomplishments (e.g., publications).

The second takeaway from our extended collaborative project is the value of program longevity and personal cooperation for ePortfolio programs over an entire institution. The long tenure of ePortfolios in the University of Georgia First-year Composition Program and then the Writing Certificate Program has created a certain degree of continuity in a university where, for purely contingent, historical reasons, writing programs have grown up in isolation from one another, and for financial and political reasons, they lack any good political or financial reason to try to merge with one another. On an institutional level, the consistent ePortfolio pedagogy across programs provides a suitable scaffold for future efforts to unite writing initiatives across the university. The use of EMMA by both the first-year composition and writing certificate programs has been a connecting thread that has had a significant impact on both the capstone workshop and the capstone portfolios themselves. Because the WCP uses EMMA as its ePortfolio platform and as its LMS for the ePortfolio Workshop, the emphasis remains on the writing process and peer review, both of which EMMA supports and facilitates extremely effectively. However, the final product of the workshop—the capstone ePortfolio itself—is constrained by the format of the EMMA portfolio tool, which was built more for the FYC portfolios and does not provide the multitude of options for organization, navigation, and multimodality that would be more ideal for capstone portfolios that include a wide variety and large number of artifacts created in many different courses and for many different rhetorical purposes. This constraint results in more homogeneous and, perhaps, less truly "electronic" portfolios in that they do not allow for the exploitation of the digital medium described by Yancey (2004), in which ePortfolio composers draw on such digital affordances as "text boxes, hyperlinking, visuals, audio texts, and design elements" to create a "Web-sensible" reading experience (pp. 745–746). And, ideally, the capstone portfolios should at least allow for the option of public presentation, an option precluded by EMMA's institutional login and course enrollment requirements.

Within the Writing Certificate Program, many students view their capstone portfolios as a collection of showcase writing samples, even if the portfolio is oriented around a reflective analysis of process and development, which means that they see the portfolio not only as an academic requirement, but also as a professional tool, functioning similarly to career development learning ePortfolios (Polly et al., this collection). The workshop asks students to, once again, put their rhetorical understanding to use as they establish purpose(s), audience(s), ethos, and context(s) for the portfolio and, often, they identify a primary audience outside the walls of academia. This decision can create a dissonance between the portfolio concept and the portfolio reality that will likely guide next steps in the development of EMMA as we consider a widening interest in portfolios campus-wide. Concomitantly, given the growth of research on transfer and writing skills development over the past two decades (see Bergmann & Zepernick, 2007; DePalma, 2015; Donahue, 2012; Foerstsch, 1995; Hagemann, 1995; Reiff & Bawarshi, 2011; Wardle, 2004, 2007; Yancey et al., 2014,), it would be salutary to project backwards from the curricular endpoints in programs using (or considering incorporating) ePortfolios at UGA—be that the Writing Certificate Program, engineering, education, or the law school—to consider ways in which the goals, constitution, and assessment of writing ePortfolios could be adjusted to foster better transfer of writing content knowledge (i.e., understanding various rhetorical situations, writing processes, the role of peer review) as our students move through the curriculum.

The final programmatic advantage offered by the University of Georgia ePortfolio programs is the ongoing potential for research and assessment. Even before the institution of ePortfolios as a program-wide requirement, EMMA functioned as a standing database under IRB permission. The rich cache of essays and portfolios has provided opportunities for studies of citation practices (Barratt et al., 2009) revision (Desmet et al., 2008), and program assessment (Desmet et al., 2009). For the FYC Program, the EMMA portfolios also provide a platform for embedded assessment on an ongoing basis, conducted through a web-based rating of learning objectives as part of regular portfolio grading.

Now What?

The current state of the university brings with it new opportunities and new challenges. First, the challenges. As with any software program, EMMA has to be periodically rewritten from the ground up, updated regularly, and adapted to conform to changing institutional policies, all with no additional funds. Both within institutions and on a national level, monies for digital humanities projects are generally directed toward start-up efforts. In 2011, we began the process of completely rewriting the EMMA code to update to the Symfony framework. The rebuild offered an opportunity to train new developers and reevaluate the whole web application to ensure we had forward-looking and *standards-based* code. In 2015, a change in policy within the College of Arts and Sciences at UGA involved phasing out departmental servers and consolidation of all websites centrally under the auspices of the College. This moment was nearly a breaking point for EMMA. The developers had attempted to establish a partnership with a hosting company that was providing EMMA access to other institutions, but that agreement would have involved a small cost to students, and UGA's Legal Department ruled that because EMMA was developed with University of Georgia funding, students could not be charged for using it. After negotiating with the College, the developer was able to move EMMA to the cloud for an amount of money that the Department of English could afford.

One of the great advantages of this long-term project is also its greatest liability. EMMA is the product of a small group of people working together for over a decade, and now we are faced with some changes and challenges that will influence and shape EMMA's future. In August 2018, our esteemed FYC Director and co-author of this article unexpectedly passed away. Christy was a champion for EMMA, and the loss of her leadership left much up in the air about the future and direction of the program. Deb Miller, another co-author of this article and Associate Director of FYC, retired in October 2019, and Ron Balthazor, our lead developer, in May 2020. Our small EMMA team is getting even smaller, so our plan moving forward is to likewise shape EMMA into a smaller project.

After a series of pilots of other digital platforms, we are now working on developing a version of the EMMA program, for now dubbed "Emma Lite," that allows us to keep some of the essential functionality for how we teach writing. We plan to integrate Emma Lite with UGA's online learning management system, which eases many of our concerns about security. Large-scale LMSs have many capabilities, but we found during pilots that one of the main limitations of the university's system was that sharing and marking up documents was onerous. Our plans are thus to start small so that Emma Lite will first be simply a tool for students to share their documents with each other and get feedback from their peers and their instructors.

Beyond that, much is still up in the air regarding the future of portfolios at UGA and Emma Lite's capabilities. We often refer to the "three Ps" of writing pedagogy upon which EMMA was built: process writing, peer review, and portfolios. Emma Lite will allow us to maintain the first two "Ps." Yet the third, portfolios, remains critical as a measure of assessment for the Writing Certificate Program. In the last three years, all degree and certificate granting programs at UGA have been required to develop assessment plans based on measurable student learning outcomes. For the WCP, that data comes almost exclusively from assessment of the capstone portfolios by faculty using a rubric developed from an Inter/National Coalition for ePortfolio Research-supported comparative portfolio study. In the experience of the WCP, portfolios have proven to provide quality measurable data in support of program outcomes. At this point, we don't know what role portfolios will play in the FYC Program moving forward, but we do know that technology and pedagogy will continue to inform and revise each other in both the FYC and Writing Certificate Programs.

References

Balthazor, R., Desmet, C., Steger S. & Wharton, R. (2013). <emma>: An Electronic Writing Space In Pullman G. & Baotong, G. (Eds.), *Designing Web-based Aplications for 21st Century Writing Classrooms*. Baywood Publishing.

Barratt, C. C., Nielsen, K., Desmet, C. & Balthazor, R. (2009) Collaboration is key: Librarians and composition instructors analyze student research and writing. *portal: Libraries and the Academy 9*(1), 37–56.

Bergmann, L. S. & Zepernick, J. S. (2007). Disciplinarity and transference: Students' perceptions of learning to write. *WPA: Writing Program Administration, 31*(1/2), 124–149.

CCCC statement on working conditions for non-tenure-track writing faculty (2016). CCCC: Conference on College Composition and Communication. https://cccc .ncte.org/cccc/resources/positions/working-conditions-ntt.

DePalma, M-J. (2015). Tracing transfer across media: Investigating writers' perceptions of cross-contextual and rhetorical reshaping in processes of remediation. *College Composition and Communication, 66*(4), 615–642.

Desmet, C., Miller, D. C., Griffin, J., Cummings, R. & Balthazor, R. (2009). Re-visioning revision with electronic portfolios in the University of Georgia first-year composition program. In D. Cambridge, B. Cambridge & K. Yancey (Eds.), *Electronic portfolios 2.0: Emergent findings and shared questions*. (pp. 155–163). Stylus Press.

Desmet, C., Miller, D. C., Griffin, J., Balthazor, R. & Cummings, R. E. (2008). Reflection, revision, and assessment in first-year composition. *Journal of General Education, 57*(1), 15–30.

Donahue, C. (2012). Transfer, portability, genrealization: (How) does composition expertise "carry"? In K. Ritter & P.K. Matsuda (Eds.), *Exploring composition studies* (pp. 145–166). Utah State University Press.

Flaherty, C. (2016,). Writing wrongs? Inside Higher Ed. http://insidehighered.com /news/2015/01/23/arizona-state-u-backs-down-some-details-controversial-plan -writing-instructors.

Foerstsch, J. (1995). Where cognitive psychology applies: How theories about memory and transfer can influence composition pedagogy. *Written Communication, 12*(3), 360–383.

Hagemann, J. (1995). Writing centers as sites for writing transfer research. In B. L. Stay, C. Murphy & E. Hobson (Eds.). Writing center perspectives (pp. 120–131). NWCA Press.

Reiff, M. J. & Bawarshi, A. (2011). Tracing discursive resources: How students use prior genre knowledge to negotiate new writing contexts in first-year composition. *Written Communication, 28*(3), 312–337.

Wardle, E. (2004). Can cross-disciplinary links help us teach 'academic discourse" in FYC? Across the Disciplines, 1. https://wac.colostate.edu/docs/atd/articles /wardle2004.pdf.

Wardle, E. (2007). Understanding transfer from FYC: Preliminary results of a longitudinal study. *WPA:Writing Program Administration, 31*(1/2), 65–85.

Yancey, K. B. (2004). Postmodernism, palimpsest, portfolios: Theoretical issues in the representation of student work. *College Composition and Communication, 55*(4), 738–761.

Yancey, K. B., Robertson, L. & Taczak, K. (2014). *Writing across contexts: Transfer, composition, and sites of writing.* Utah State University Press.

Appendix A: First-year Composition Essay Rubric

Student's Name _____ Teacher _____

Paper #_____ Special Assignment Requirements: _____

Competent/Credible/Complete

If you meet these first three standards, you are writing competently and you will earn a grade of "C." (70–79)

1. Unity

- ☐ Contains a center of gravity, a unifying and controlling purpose, a thesis or claim, which is maintained throughout the paper.
- ☐ Organizes writing around a thesis or according to the organizational requirements of the particular assignment (e.g., summary, narrative, argument, analysis, description, etc.)

2. Evidence/Development

- ☐ Develops appropriate, logical, and relevant supporting detail and/or evidence.
- ☐ Includes more specific, concrete evidence (or details) than opinion or abstract, general commentary.

3. Presentation and Design

- ☐ Follows SMH guidelines for Standard English grammar, punctuation, usage, and documentation.

☐ Meets your teacher's (or the MLA's) and the First-year Composition program's requirements for length and/or format.

Skillful/Persuasive

If you meet all of the competency standards above and, in addition, achieve coherence and exhibit audience awareness, you are writing skillfully and you will earn a grade of "B." (80–89)

4. Coherence

☐ Uses words and sentences, rhythm and phrasing, variations and transitions, concreteness, and specificity to *reveal and emphasize the relationship* between evidence and thesis.
☐ Explains how, why, or in what way the evidence/detail provided supports the claim/ point /thesis/topic ideas.
☐ Incorporates evidence from outside sources smoothly, appropriately, and responsibly.

5. Audience Awareness

☐ Demonstrates a sense that the writer knows what s/he's doing and is addressing real people.
☐ Reflects a respect for values that influence ethos (e.g., common ground, trustworthiness, careful research).

Distinctive

If you meet all of the competency standards, achieve coherence and exhibit audience awareness, and, in addition, demonstrate a mastery of one or more features of superior writing, you are writing *distinctively* and you will earn a grade of "A." (90–100)

Distinction

☐ Your writing stands out because of one or more of the following characteristics: complexity, originality, seamless coherence, extraordinary control, sophistication in thought, recognizable voice, compelling purpose, imagination, insight, thoroughness, and/or depth.

Essay Grade _____ **+/- Points for special assignment requirements** _____ =

Ineffective

If your paper does not meet competency standards, either because you have minor problems in all three competence areas (1–3 above) or major problems in one or two competence areas, you will earn a grade of "D" (60–69) or "F" (<60), and you should schedule a conference with your teacher.

Appendix B: FYC Portfolio Grading Rubric

Biography and Image

- Is present and complete;
- Is carefully proofread and edited, with very few errors of a grammatical, mechanical, or typographic nature.
  [CCC] _____
- Shows clear and appropriate awareness of audience;
- Gives a coherent picture of the writer.
  [SP] _____
- Is distinctive for its:
- imaginative quality;
- extraordinary and effective care in craftsmanship and presentation;
- prose style;
- compelling authorial voice;
- persuasive argumentation.
  [DIST]_____

Introductory Reflective Essay

- Is present and complete;
- Makes a clear and complete statement about the writer's ethos, development, and/or skill set that is more than an autobiographical narrative or list of exhibits (unity-thesis);
- Offers a clear rationale for the choice of exhibits and their order (unity-organization);
- Explains the role of each exhibit in the overall portfolio and in proving the thesis (evidence);
- Is carefully proofread and edited, with very few errors of a grammatical, mechanical, or typographic nature.
  [CCC] _____
- Offers a strong, and vivid understanding of the writer and writing (audience awareness);
- Is particularly persuasive about how exhibits contribute to the whole portfolio (coherence).
  [SP] _____
- Is distinctive for its:
- imaginative quality;
- extraordinary and effective care in craftsmanship and presentation;
- prose style;
- compelling authorial voice;
- persuasive argumentation.
  [DIST] _____

Two Revised Class Essays

- Are present and complete;
- At a minimum, meet the FYC Rubric qualifications for CCC;
- Are carefully proofread and edited, with very few errors of a grammatical, mechanical, or typographic nature.
  [CCC] _____
- At a minimum, meet the FYC Rubric qualifications for SP.
  [SP] _____
- At a minimum, meet the FYC Rubric qualifications for a DIST or a "high" SP that shows extraordinary thoughtfulness and care.
  [DIST] _____

Exhibit of Composing and/or Revision Process

- Is present and complete;
- Offers a clear and complete statement about and/or example of the composing and/or revision process (unity);
- Supports that thesis with specific examples (evidence);
- Presents the examples in a logical manner (unity-organization);
- Is carefully written, edited, and proofread, with essentially no distracting errors of a grammatical, mechanical, or typographic nature.
  [CCC] _____
- Offers strong and vivid examples of the writer and writing (audience awareness);
- Is particularly persuasive about how the examples support the thesis (coherence);
  [SP] _____
- Is distinctive for its:
- imaginative quality;
- extraordinary and effective care in craftsmanship and presentation;
- prose style;
- compelling authorial voice;
- persuasive argumentation.
  [DIST] _____

Exhibit of Peer Review Process

- Is present and complete;
- Offers a clear exhibit of a peer review (unity);
- Arranges one or more examples of peer review in a logical manner (unity-organization);
- Is carefully presented so that both the original and comments are easily seen. Errors in grammar or spelling don't interfere with conveying comments (presentation & design).

[CCC] _____
- Shows a strong, and vivid understanding of the writer and commentary (audience awareness);
- Is persuasive because comments show a clear understanding and response to the work (coherence).
  [SP] _____
- Is distinctive for its:
- imaginative quality;
- extraordinary and effective care in craftsmanship and presentation;
- prose style;
- compelling authorial voice;
- persuasive argumentation.
  [DIST] _____

Wild Card

- Is present and complete;
- Fits into the portfolio as a whole in a logical way that is described in the introductory reflective essay;
- Is carefully written, edited, and proofread, with few errors of a grammatical, mechanical, or typographic nature that distract from the purpose of the exhibit.
  [CCC] _____
- Offers a strong and vivid understanding of the writer and writing (audience awareness).
  [SP] _____
- Is distinctive for its:
- imaginative quality;
- extraordinary and effective care in craftsmanship and presentation;
- prose style;
- compelling authorial voice;
- persuasive argumentation.
  [DIST] _____

Appendix C: Writing Certificate Program Capstone ePortfolio Workshop Syllabus

ENGL 4834: E-Portfolio Workshop 2016–17

Required Text

Portfolio Keeping: A Guide for Students, Third Edition (Reynolds and Davis). Bedford/St. Martin's. ISBN: 978–1–4576–3285–3

Course Description

This course fulfills the capstone requirement for the University of Georgia Writing Certificate Program. Students will work with the instructor and one another in a workshop setting to construct the portfolio by composing, revising, and editing selected work produced in courses taken for the certificate program.

A capstone writing portfolio involves looking backward and forward as well as at the present moment. In this course, we will focus on constructing a cohesive story about your development as a writer, looking at the writing intensive program of coursework you have taken for the certificate, other writing experiences you have had during your undergraduate career, and your on-going professional goals. We want to think about how to make your skills as a writer clearly "visible" through showcase pieces, but also to help readers of your portfolio see how you think and work as a writer. The reflective components you will create to tell that "story." Reflection is the key to the portfolio, especially in a capstone portfolio that represents many semesters of coursework and a wide variety of artifacts and will unify them into a coherent and unified composition.

The goals of the workshop are to help you:

- understand the different rhetorical purposes and educational/professional functions of e-portfolios
- understand the nature of reflection for formative assessment and personal/professional development in electronic portfolios
- understand and practice principles of good e-portfolio design
- develop and publish an e-portfolio as an exit requirement for the Writing Certificate Program
- understand and engage in composing, peer review, revision, and editing practices in the develop of an e-portfolio

Course Requirements and Grading

Participation and Workshopping (50%)

Because of the workshop nature of this course, each student's success in this course is dependent on responsible cooperation and collaboration with other students in the course. I expect everyone to participate fully and have all work ready when it is due.

Final E-Portfolio (50%)

A complete, coherent, polished, and refined electronic portfolio will be the final product for this course. *One sample of writing from each course that counts for credit for the Writing Certificate must be included in the portfolio, and the portfolio must be framed by a reflective "introduction" that critically analyzes your own development as a writer through the courses you've taken for the WCP.* You may also include other pieces of writing done outside the certificate coursework if they serve a clear purpose in your portfolio.

Attendance

We'll run this class as a hybrid online and face-to-face class. During weeks scheduled for peer review of artifacts, we will not meet as a class, but you will be required to post your review feedback and any other materials by class time on those weeks. If you are unable to post an online assignment by the due date, please let me know as soon as possible. You must be able to provide acceptable documentation to support any legitimate circumstances that interfere with your timely submission of assigned work or scheduled meetings. If you miss more than three online assignments or class meetings before the withdrawal deadline, you may be dropped from the course. If you are in your final semester, being dropped from the workshop means you will be ineligible to receive the Writing Certificate.

Academic Honesty

All academic work must meet the standards contained in "A Culture of Honesty." All students are responsible for informing themselves about those standards. Please refer to http://www.uga.edu/honesty for further information.

Students will collaborate in a workshop setting and engage with one another in the peer review process, but the contents of each student's e-portfolio must be his/her own work. If you choose to include a project that was written collaboratively in your portfolio, you must obtain written permission from your collaborators on the project to do so. I expect you to be ethical in your representation of your own and others' contributions to any collaborative work and peer review contributions.

Access Policy

Students who require reasonable accommodations in order to fully participate in course activities or meet course requirements should contact the instructor during regular office hours or by appointment to discuss those needs and make specific arrangements. Make sure you review the resources available to you and register with UGA's Disability Resource Center.

Chapter 2. The ePortfolio Selection Committee—the Quest for the Perfect Platform

Tracey M. Richardson
Kelly Whealan George
Denise Bollenback
EMBRY-RIDDLE AERONAUTICAL UNIVERSITY

The portfolio has been used for decades in the fields of art, architecture, and photography as a *showcase* for a professional's growth and expression. Traditionally, the portfolio was a leather-bound jacket containing hard copies of one's work. Conceptually, the electronic portfolio (ePortfolio) grew out of the need to display one's professional accomplishments in a digital format through a platform that is current, portable, and instantaneously accessible by any reviewer with internet access.

The ePortfolio has been widely implemented in higher education as more institutions have recognized the multidimensional benefits of this *evidence-based* solution for collecting and assessing evidence of student achievement. An ePortfolio system embedded within the curriculum can prove especially helpful when educational programs are delivered in multiple locations across different modalities (see Coleman et al., this collection). Our institution, Embry-Riddle Aeronautical University (ERAU), is a private, not-for-profit university with three campuses: Daytona Beach, FL; Prescott, AZ; and the Worldwide Campus. The Daytona Beach and Prescott campuses are traditional brick and mortar with residential accommodations and nationally ranked engineering programs, whose target populations are full-time students. To the contrary, the Worldwide Campus includes over 120 geographically dispersed teaching sites in the United States, Asia, and Europe, and targets a working adult population.

This chapter chronicles ERAU's quest for the perfect ePortfolio platform and the process we employed for the evaluation and selection of suitable software. We discuss not only the key role of the ePortfolio Selection Committee and its membership, but also our stakeholder analysis, requirements list, and creation of a Platform Selection Scorecard, all of which we used to identify a short-list of suitable vendors. As we describe the process from the planning phase to the final selection, we include a review of the committee's Request for Proposals (RFP) and explain how the committee developed a scorecard to evaluate a series of vendor demonstrations leading to a platform selection. Finally, we reflect on the major lessons learned, from the 20/20 hindsight perspective of an implemented ePortfolio at our university.

DOI: https://doi.org/10.37514/PRA-B.2020.1084.2.02

Literature Review

While web-based technologies have enabled various forms of collecting and displaying student work in digital form, portfolios are nothing new in the educational industry. Understanding the evolution, use, and stakeholder perspectives within higher education will help develop a basis that informs the needs *assessment* and selection process that ultimately will maximize the portfolio's effectiveness in the institution.

The first use of student-developed portfolios dates back to the 1960s (Ehley, 2006). Up until the 1990s, students were asked to compile physical portfolios primarily for demonstration purposes (Chathan-Carpenter et al., 2009). With the advent and expansion of electronic platforms, the purpose of portfolios expanded from a showcasing tool into an instrument to measure learning and to conduct assessment (Barrett, 2007). Even though the formats and organization may have changed over the past five decades, the primary purpose remains the same: to communicate something about students' performance. The ePortfolio not only leverages technology to organize, showcase, and contain student work (Barrett, 2001; Mehlenbacher & Kelly, 2015), but also allows students to select their ePortfolio *artifacts*, reflect on their work, and share that work with internal and external audiences.

With respect to higher education, many studies that document faculty and students' perspectives on the creation and use of electronic portfolios consistently underscore non-negotiable factors for the success of ePortfolio-based assessment. Like other researchers before us, we assert that communicating the ePortfolio's purpose to all stakeholders is critical to the success of its implementation and ultimately its success in achieving the desired outcome (Barrett, 2001; Barrett & Knezek, 2003; McKenna et al., 2017) (see Dellinger & Hanger, this collection). Secondly, we concur that for optimal use of ePortfolios in an educational setting, the interface difficulty level must not impede creation, *reflection*, or evaluation (Tsai et al., 2004). Fortunately, training can alleviate suboptimal use, especially if the university has already adopted an electronic portfolio system (Herner-Patnode & Lee, 2009; Jun et al., 2007).

In other words, an inaugural adoption of an electronic portfolio system requires much more than evaluating software options. A successful ePortfolio system adoption requires curriculum alignment and standards, faculty buy-in, assessment, evaluation, communication, leadership, implementation plans, and change management procedures before students even begin to create their portfolios (McNeill et al., 2014; Mills, 2013; Wilhelm et al., 2006).

While such faculty and staff considerations are vitally important, consideration of student voices should not be minimized, since they are the ultimate end users of the ePortfolio. For example, Wetzel and Studler (2008) analyzed student perceptions in six programs and concluded that understanding student perceptions of their experiences can lead to improved practices and policies with regard to ePortfolios (see Dellinger & Hanger, this collection). They specifically found that students' ePortfolio experience benefited from greater opportunities to reflect about the holistic nature of their classes, the organization and architecture of their academic and professional documents, the development of a new technological skill set, and a better understanding of evaluation standards, while students' experience with the ePortfolio was negatively impacted by the costs, reliability, and time and energy the ePortfolio technology demanded (Wetzel & Studler, 2008). Ehley (2006) also collected student criticisms of ePortfolios and identified the difficulty of software functionality, the lack of communication about the ePortfolio's purpose, and a lack of faculty support throughout the curriculum as top frustrations for students. Not surprisingly, students and faculty alike were more apt to use an ePortfolio tool if it was easy to use. Reinforcing Ehley's (2006) conclusions, Javed Yusuf and Pita Tuisawau (2011) also found that a majority of students view ePortfolios as a useful tool and an important method of assessing their performance in a course. Students also believe that the more they use an ePortfolio tool, the more effective the ePortfolio can be for their learning experience (Schuessler, 2010). Therefore, implementing an ePortfolio tool within a curriculum should be complete and inclusive from a "faculty-staff-student" perspective to maximize the tool's effectiveness.

Since the selection and implementation planning process is a critical element to ePortfolio success in a university system (Butler et al., 2006; Slade et al., 2017), stakeholders' needs and engagement commitment levels should be assessed throughout the process of procuring, implementing, and operationalizing the ePortfolio system. Stakeholders include, in no specific order: faculty, institutional technology, the center for teaching and learning, institutional research, and the student body (Barrett, 1998; Reynolds & Pirie, 2016). These stakeholders' power hierarchy can vary from institution to institution depending on the leadership structure, change management culture, controlling bodies, and, ultimately, the initiative's sponsorship (Slade et al., 2017). If the technological stakeholders demonstrate the technical competencies required for implementing and operationalizing ePortfolios, they can amplify their influence in the selection process. As the literature emphasizes, implementing an inclusive approach to identifying ePortfolio stakeholders along with institutional requirements and extramural considerations during the planning stage and committing to a holistic assessment of stakeholders' needs throughout the process will ideally ensure that learning and the assessment of learning drive the technology, not vice-versa.

Embry-Riddle Aeronautical University's Needs Assessment

Institutionally, Embry-Riddle Aeronautical University (ERAU) recognized the value an electronic portfolio would bring to the students' experience. Students were already producing extensive digital collections of assignments, reflections, and other academic artifacts documenting their learning, but we lacked an efficient solution for providing access to multiple reviewers. As an institution, we knew the platform had to be user-friendly so that students could focus their efforts on framing and reflecting on their growth as learners rather than being hampered by technological barriers, but we also required a detailed reporting function to meet our institutional assessment requirements. In sum, our needs assessment had to take into account the perspectives and realities of all ERAU ePortfolio stakeholders, as described below:

> *Student perspective*: Students sought a single repository to collect and catalog their academic growth by highlighting selected academic assignments as learning evidence. Additionally, students wanted the ePortfolio to help them document their critical reflection, by which they could confirm the integration of their educational journey. The students expected their ePortfolio experience to culminate with a self-selected collection of artifacts to share with professors, peers, and potential employers.

> *Faculty perspective*: Faculty sought a single source to assess a student's application of specific course content related to the student's professional goals, course outcomes, and program of study.

> *Program perspective*: Program directors sought a single source for longitudinal assessment by multiple reviewers. They desired software that included a query schema that could produce reports based on multiple criteria: specific course learning outcomes; specific program outcomes; location-specific results; professor-specific results; and customized reporting, as such reports would help them identify exemplary work as well as areas for improvement.

> *Department perspective*: Department chairs sought a source for evidence-based evaluation that would add another data point to the evaluation of a faculty member's teaching success during the annual appraisal cycle.

> *Institutional perspective*: Institutionally, administrators sought a central source for evidence-based evaluation of academic programs and candidates for promotion and/or tenure and for preparation for visits from external accrediting bodies.

> *Accreditors' perspective:* The accreditors sought a comprehensive source of evidence-based reporting of student learning. They wanted to have a means by which site visit teams could "see" the proof of program goals through a "show and know" by accessing not only the reports, but also the direct student work as evidence.

To tackle the challenge of meeting all of these stakeholders' needs, the chancellor charted a selection committee, chaired by the chief information officer (CIO). The selection committee consisted of ten voting faculty members representing each of the three campuses and a host of non-voting support agencies to critically evaluate the vendors. The committee's non-voting members included representatives from Academic Assessment, Instructional Design and Development, Academic Technology, Information Technology, Educational Technology, and the Center for Teaching and Learning Excellence.

Stakeholder Analysis: The Academic Perspective

Curriculum demands in the Master of Science in Project Management degree originally drove the need for an ePortfolio system at ERAU. However, the thrust behind the project to search for a perfect ePortfolio platform really gained importance when it was connected to the university's Quality Enhancement Plan (QEP) required by our regional accreditor, the Southern Association of Colleges and Schools (SACS).

To support the university's mission and vision, ERAU implemented the Ignite Initiative as its QEP. "Ignite" sought to create an *active learning* environment dedicated to systematic inquiry as a way to solve problems or to advance knowledge. Ignite's goals were two-fold: 1) to ensure faculty and staff were engaging students in scholarly activities and facilitating student research through curricular or co-curricular learning opportunities; and 2) to ensure students were obtaining the skills to investigate hypotheses, solve problems, and advance knowledge utilizing various disciplinary methods. This research-supportive curriculum was designed to provide undergraduates with a learning experience rooted in the process of discovery through research and inquiry. Implementation focused on ensuring that undergraduates followed a tiered plan of activities that first introduced them to research skills, then allowed them to practice and eventually to master those research skills. The enhanced research culture included course-based research and curricular/co-curricular research and academic support services.

Ignite developed six student learning outcomes (SLOs) to encompass the basic principles of research in every discipline. Infusing the SLOs into the curriculum enables students to graduate with a strong foundation in research principles. The Ignite SLOs are:

- Define and/or articulate a research problem;
- Design a course of action to solve a research problem using appropriate multidisciplinary principles;
- Apply ethical principles in research;
- Conduct research independently and/or collaboratively;
- Reach decisions or conclusions based on the analysis and synthesis of evidence; and
- Communicate research results.

As a result of this initiative, the institution needed an ePortfolio platform that would enable students to build a non-discipline-specific portfolio of work that could be archived and, more importantly, assessed by secondary evaluators to build longitudinal data about the trend of competency levels demonstrated in each student's artifacts. With both a program and a broader university need, the selection of and funding for an ePortfolio system that could serve the university and had the promise of growth and evolution was elevated to the university administration's strategic acquisition list.

Stakeholder Analysis: The Institutional Support Perspective

ERAU conducted an internal analysis of the instructional systems previously used for building digital portfolios. The available options had multiple flaws, including invalid files and links, poor arrangement of ePortfolio artifacts, constrained storage, inadequate content editing and spacing preferences, and confusing instructions for both students and faculty. Therefore, students expected a solution that would allow them the flexibility to create their own digital portfolio designs, consistent with various course and assessment requirements. In addition to analyzing current instructional systems, ERAU also looked at the feasibility of building an organic ePortfolio system. Given our limited time and resources, as well as the cost requirements and the middle-ware requirement to integrate with other instructional systems, ERAU's leadership decided the best option would be to search for a third-party vendor. By bridging the university's legacy systems with an improved third-party ePortfolio option, the opportunity to meet every need within a reasonable timeline seemed more likely.

It became apparent that a Software as a Service (SaaS) model would inform several important aspects of the software vendor selection. Using a third-party vendor would provide ERAU with several benefits, including minimizing maintenance costs as well as reducing the need for IT staff, software licensing, and hardware. A SaaS option would also provide a lower total cost of ownership and a smoother conversion of capital expenses to operating expenses, which would allow for an easier implementation. Additionally, third-party partnering would facilitate the ease of upgrading, increased scalability, greater utilization of resources, increased ability to focus on core business, more flexibility for business innovation, and improved communication with all stakeholders and constituents (Hofmann, 2010; Saeed et al., 2012; Salleh et al., 2012). Given our multi-distributed university setting, we needed to focus on each of these elements to provide a robust ePortfolio system that would work within a variety of instructional modalities. In addition, the selection committee wanted to emphasize categories such as user-friendliness, functionality, reporting capabilities, and vendor support and training when evaluating each ePortfolio vendor. At the same time, the committee needed to ensure that faculty-training issues, appropriate buy-in for the program (see Day and Dellinger & Hanger, this collection), and integration with the learning management system were addressed in drafting the evaluation criteria for selecting an ePortfolio vendor.

Software Vendor Selection

From the IT perspective, software selection begins with the identification of user and system requirements by documenting the functionality of existing systems. With this analysis, the process of business reengineering (which is a catalyst for redesign and improved productivity) can begin (Motiwalla & Thompson, 2012). After studying the existing processes for building digital portfolios and re-designing these processes to create a more efficient approach for students to create their own ePortfolios, we were able to document crucial requirements for determining which ePortfolio system to select. Identifying the requirements provided us with a baseline for understanding how data would flow among cross-functional areas of our university. Understanding the functional requirements of our ePortfolio model allowed the selection committee to best determine which vendors and the products they offered would suit our needs.

After analyzing the current ePortfolio process embedded in the curriculum, we developed a workflow diagram to demonstrate the process of creating and maintaining digital portfolios, then we aligned and mapped the contents of the course- and program-level learning outcomes. The alignment and mapping step allowed us to visualize the impact the ePortfolio would have on the curriculum. In turn, the visualization better prepared us to talk about our ePortfolio model to external vendors.

In our first communication with third-party vendors, we sought information about their organizational maturity and positioning in the market. The initial solicitation, or request for information (RFI), went out to 27 vendors. We created the vendor list through an exploratory internet search and by seeking input from the Association for Authentic, Experiential, and Evidence-Based Learning (AAEEBL) and the Electronic Portfolio Action and Communication (EPAC) Community of Practice. We wanted to understand how each vendor described its situation both from a financial health perspective and its position within the digital community. Twenty vendors responded to the initial RFI (see Appendix A for the technical component of the RFI). After receiving these twenty responses, we began the selection process.

The selection committee conducted a full search for a third-party ePortfolio vendor and sent a request for proposals (RFP) to the 20 vendors who responded to the RFI. We discovered that in order to evaluate the various proposals from these vendors, we needed to add a matrix for comparison of specific requirements. Additionally, we started scanning for "best practices" matching our requirements list. During the selection of the ePortfolio platform, we felt it was imperative to take into account the reputation and integrity of the companies under consideration. By investigating vendors' histories and backgrounds—such as how long each organization had been in business, customer reviews, customer renewal rates, financials, number of customers, and pricing models—the selection committee could determine critical success factors and potential risks associated with the vendor selection.

After a series of committee meetings and deliberations, we narrowed the list of 20 potential vendors to 12. The selection committee requested sample digital portfolios from these vendors as part of the request for proposals after cross-checking all RFPs against our list of requirements for any "knock-out" items or major areas of concern. The committee eliminated vendors that did not meet non-negotiable requirements, such as security. Through this extensive elimination process, we narrowed the field of possible vendors to five and requested a live web-based demonstration. The live demonstration served two purposes: first, it allowed us to interact with the platform and learn about its features, and second, it allowed us to experience a training session orchestrated by the vendor. One of our long-term requirements included vendor training for all ERAU stakeholders.

Additionally, each vendor provided three customer references. The committee then requested a letter of reference directly from each of these customers (see Appendix B for the questions sent to customer references); we received all but two reference letters back. As well, we eliminated one vendor from the competitive process due to their poor communication responsiveness and the company's general poor attitude toward our requests; this vendor was hard to work with during the selection process, and we did not want to enter into a contract with a difficult company.

Scorecard Criteria

The selection committee met weekly over a period of three months to discuss the stakeholders' wants and needs. We used a Delphi technique (a systematic approach which relies on a panel of experts) to both brainstorm and prioritize our criteria. Several main factors within the vendor selection process included:

- Accessibility to ePortfolios after graduation
- Use of ePortfolios for assessment purposes
- Portability of ePortfolios to external locations for storage
- Security roles and sharing options
- Outcomes assessment features and alignment to course and program outcomes
- *Rubric* development and design capabilities
- Integration with existing university systems
- Training

These user-defined functional requirements are further defined within Appendix C, The ePortfolio System Product Evaluation Scorecard.

The selection committee used the scorecard criteria to conduct the final evaluations. The chief information officer (CIO) tallied the scores to provide a final comparison of the top vendors recommended for advancement. At this point in the process, the committee members were given user accounts to fully explore each product. After analyzing collected data from the scorecard, meeting several times to deliberate, and communicating with major stakeholders, we used the priority criteria to compare the final two vendors (Figure 2.1).

The selection committee met to make a final decision based on the analysis of data collected (live demo recordings, responses to RFPs, etc.) and input from committee members, academic programs, support units, the Information Technology security team, and Institutional Effectiveness subject matter experts. Based on the results, the selection committee made a recommendation to all stakeholders and handed the project over to the university contracting office to negotiate a contract with the vendor, including a proposed implementation plan and timeline.

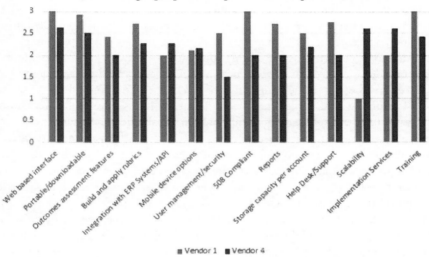

Figure 2.1. ERAU ePortfolio system evaluation results—final round.

Recommendations

First and foremost, we recommend that institutions who undertake a similar process ensure that all stakeholders understand the difference between actual needs and quasi-needs. Ryan Watkins, Maurya West Meiers, and Yusra Visser (2012) define needs as "the differences between your current achievements and your desired accomplishments" (p. 20). Roger Kaufman and Ingrid Guerra-Lopez (2013) would call the differences in "what is needed" and "what is desired" a gap to close. It is important to make this distinction because if you do not clearly define the ends and the means, you could end up with a mismatched platform.

When the requirements list is loaded down with too many "wants," the project's complexity may be falsely inflated and then deemed unaffordable.

We also recommend inviting students to be part of the selection process. When putting together our selection committee, we did not solicit enough input from our student population. Our committee included a staff member who was also pursuing her undergraduate degree, and we relied on her for both perspectives, neglecting to understand the type(s) of training venues from which our student population would best benefit. The committee focused on the result, and we did not put enough thought into the training component at start-up. Providing a menu of options for instruction on the software would have ensured a smoother transition between adoption and implementation and perhaps even thwarted the knee-jerk reaction to change.

Finally, we caution readers not to underestimate resistance to change. Despite the energy behind the project, the strength in curriculum enhancements, and the wow-factor of the platform, the implementation of the new ePortfolio platform proved difficult and frustrating at ERAU. For example, while our Center for Teaching and Learning Excellence (CTLE) offered a series of webinars (e.g., An "Introduction to ePortfolios," "Building Integration Assignments," "Assessment") and sponsored a contest for the best personal ePortfolio and the best assignment for the ePortfolio, the participation in these events proved poor at best.

At the annual faculty meeting, the student ePortfolios were on display, along with testimonials from the students about their heightened learning experience. The few faculty using ePortfolios demonstrated their rich assessment data and spoke about the curriculum improvements that had resulted. Even with these evidence-based conclusions, however, the adoption rate remained minimal.

Looking back, investing in additional ePortfolio champions could have made our launch more successful (see Day, this collection). Such investment could be in opportunities for conference attendance. For example, the Association of American Colleges and Universities has an annual ePortfolio Forum; The Association for Authentic, Experiential, and Evidence-Based Learning (AAEEBL) hosts both an annual conference and regional conferences; and The Online Consortium hosts several conferences focusing in on digital learning. By adding additional ePortfolio champions into the faculty fold, full-scale adoption might have been more successful.

The documented successes of the ePortfolio selection committee were replicated when selecting an institutional-wide assessment platform. The ERAU Assessment Committee used the process described in this chapter to create a scorecard and evaluate third-party vendors. They benefited from our lessons learned and completed the selection process in half the time it took our committee to select an ePortfolio vendor.

In sum, our take-aways as a committee and as an institution do not vary widely from those of other institutions represented in this collection with regard to faculty buy-in and resistance to change. As well, training issues we encountered during the implementation phase might have been avoided by affording ERAU students a voice equal to that of the other stakeholders during the initial planning stage. If we would have piloted the use of ePortfolios to a few select courses, we could have identified the problem areas and minimized student frustration. Equally, we could have incentivized student champions to adopt the new technology; a small group of eager students could have jump-started the initiative organically. However, our otherwise close attention to needs assessment at the beginning of the software selection process, coupled with the discernment between what we needed and what we wanted in our final requirements list, proved invaluable in the evaluation and ultimate selection of the perfect ePortfolio platform for Embry-Riddle Aeronautical University.

References

Barrett, H. C. (1998). Strategic questions: What to consider when planning for electronic portfolios. *Learning & Leading with Technology, 26*(2), 6–13.

Barrett, H. (2001). Electronic portfolios = multimedia development + portfolio development: The electronic portfolio development process. In B. L. Cambridge, S. Kahn, D. P. Tompkins & K. B. Yancey (Eds), *Electronic portfolios: Emerging practices in student, faculty, and institutional learning* (pp. 110–116). American Association for Higher Education.

Barrett, H. (2007). Researching electronic portfolios and learner engagement: The REFLECT initiative. *Journal of Adolescent & Adult Literacy, 50*(6), 436–449.

Barrett, H. & Knezek, D. (2003). E-portfolios: Issues in assessment, accountability and preservice teacher preparation. https://www.electronicportfolios.com/portfolios/AERA2003.pdf.

Cambridge, B. L., Kahn, S., Tompkins, D. P. & Yancey, K. B. (2001). *Electronic portfolios: Emerging practices in student, faculty, and institutional learning.* American Association for Higher Education.

Chatham-Carpenter, A., Seawel, L. & Raschig, J. (2009/10). Avoiding the pitfalls: Current practices and recommendations for ePortfolios in higher education. *Journal of Educational Technology Systems, 38*(4), 437–456.

Butler, P., Anderson, B., Brown, M., Simpson, M., Higgins, A., Northover, M. & Wyles, R. (2006). *A review of the literature on portfolios and electronic portfolios* [PDF]. https://www.researchgate.net/publication/239603203_A_Review_Of_The_Literature_On_Portfolios_And_Electronic_Portfolios.

Campbell, D. M., Cignetti, E. B., Melenyzer, B. J., Nettles, D. H. & Wyman, R. M. (2001). *How to develop a professional portfolio: A manual for teachers.* Allyn and Bacon.

Dreisiebner, G., Riebenbauer, E. & Stock, M. (2017). Using eportfolios to encourage reflection and competency development. *The Journal of Research in Business Education, 58*(1), 31.

Ehley, L. (2006). *Digital portfolios: A study of undergraduate student and faculty use and perceptions of Alverno College' Diagnostic Digital Portfolio.* [Doctoral dissertation, Cardinal Stritch University]. ProQuest Dissertations & Theses Global (Publication No. 3216273).

Herner-Patnode, L. M. & Lee, H. J. (2009). A capstone experience for preservice teachers: Building a web-based portfolio. *Educational Technology & Society*, *12*(2), 101–110.

Hofmann, P. (2010). Cloud computing: the limits of public clouds for business applications. *IEEE Internet Computing*, *14*(6), 90–93.

Jun, M. K., Anthony, R., Achrazoglou, J. & Coghill-Behrends, W. (2007). Using eportfolio for the assessment and professional development of newly hired teachers. *TechTrends*, *51*(4), 45–50.

Kaufman, R. & Guerra-López, I. (2013). *Needs assessment for organizational success.* American Society for Training & Development.

McKenna, G., Baxter, G. & Hainey, T. (2017). E-portfolios and personal development: A higher educational perspective. *Journal of Applied Research in Higher Education*, *9*(1), 147–171.

McNeill, M., Parker, A. & Cram, A. (2014). Trialing e-portfolios for university learning: The devil in the detail. In M. Gosper & D. Ifenthaler (Eds.), *Curriculum models for the 21st century* (pp. 351–367). Springer.

Mehlenbacher, B. & Kelly, A. R. (2015, March 2–4). Assessing student learning: Research-based rubrics and evaluation instruments for measuring technology-augmented learning [Presentation]. Proceedings of INTED2015 Conference, Madrid, Spain. https://library.iated.org/view/MEHLENBACHER2015ASS.

Mills, J. M. (2013). *What are the issues involved in using e-portfolios as a pedagogical tool?* [Unpublished doctoral dissertation]. University of Bedfordshire.

Motiwalla, L. & Thompson, J. (2012). *Enterprise systems for management* (2nd ed.). Pearson.

Reynolds, C. & Pirie, M. S. (2016). Creating an eportfolio culture on campus through platform selection and implementation. *Peer Review*, *18*(3), 21.

Saeed, I., Juell-Skielse, G. & Uppstrom, E. (2012). Cloud enterprise resource planning adoption: Motives and barriers. In C. Moller & S. Chaudhry (Eds.), *Advances in enterprise information systems II* (pp. 99–122). CRC Press/Balkema.

Salleh, S. M., Teoh, S. Y. & Chan, C. (2012, July). Cloud enterprise systems: A review of literature and its adoption [Presentation]. Proceedings of the 16th Pacific Asia Conference on Information Systems (PACIS 2012), Vietnam, Paper 76. https://aisel.aisnet.org/pacis2012/76/.

Schuessler, J. N. (2010). *Self-assessment as learning: Finding the motivations and barriers for adopting the learning-oriented instructional design of student self-assessment* [Unpublished doctoral dissertation]. Capella University.

Slade, C., Murfin, K. & Trahar, P. (2017). A strategic approach to institution-wide implementation of ePortfolios. In J. Rowley (Ed.), *ePortfolios in Australian universities* (pp. 173–189). Springer Singapore.

Tsai, H., Lowell, K., Liu, P., MacDonald, L. & Lohr, L. (2004). Part two: Graduate student perspectives on the development of electronic portfolios. *TechTrends*, *48*(3), 56–60.

Yusuf, J. & Tuisawau, P. (2011). Student attitudes towards the use of e-portfolios: Experiences from the University of the South Pacific. *Malaysian Journal of Educational Technology, 11*(4), 31–41.

Watkins, R., Meiers, M. W. & Visser, Y. L. (2012). *A guide to assessing needs: Essential tools for collecting information, making decisions, and achieving development results*. World Bank.

Wetzel, K. & Strudler, N. (2008). Costs and benefits of electronic portfolios in teacher education, *Journal of Computing in Teacher Education, 22*(3), 99–108.

Wilhelm, L., Puckett, K., Beisser, S., Wishart, W. & al, e. (2006). Lessons learned from the implementation of electronic portfolios at three universities. *TechTrends, 50*(4), 62–71.

Yusuf, J. & Tuisawau, P. (2011). *Student attitudes towards the use of ePortfolios: Experiences from the University of the South Pacific*. [Conference presentation]. ePortfolios Australia Conference 2011. Perth, Australia.

Appendix A. Request for Information Form

To whom it may concern:[1]

Embry-Riddle Aeronautical University is seeking a partnership with an electronic portfolio vendor to support two residential campuses and one worldwide campus with a student population of over 25,000. Our first step is an official Request For Information (RFI).

To be considered, please respond to this RFI by 1 December.

Years in business	
Years offering ePortfolio	
Parent Company	
Number of customers	
Number of educational customers	
Customer renewal rate	
Financials	
Public or Private	
Number of employees dedicated to portfolio product	
Student license pricing model	
Institutional pricing model	
Post graduate/transfer student pricing model	
Implementation Services	
Understanding of accrediting bodies	

---

1.   This is representative of the original RFI's data request. The actual RFI contained seven pages of legal declarations.

Web based interface for portfolio creation	
Long term web access of portfolios for assessment or student use	
Searchable by key words/subjects	
Portable/downloadable	
Supported file formats	
Security and sharing options	
Drag and drop	
Outcomes assessment features	
Schema for aligning program objectives to learning outcomes to artifacts	
Private comments	
Build and apply rubrics	
Integration with existing university Systems/Learning Management Systems/Single sign-on	
Training	
Privacy policy	
LDAP Compliant	
Mobile device options	
User management/security	
508 Compliant	
Web Services Framework	
Multi-language capable	
Reports	
Measure learner growth	
Storage capacity per account	
Hosting	
Scalability	
Help Desk/Support (including online)	
Proprietary products	

Appendix B. Letter of Reference

To whom it may concern:

Embry-Riddle Aeronautical university is seeking a partnership with an electronic portfolio vendor. /// **Vendor's name here** /// suggested we contact you about a reference letter. We are interested in hearing your opinion on the following questions:

- How long have you been using the /// Vendor's name here /// solution?
- Why did you choose /// Vendor's name here /// as your vendor?
- What products and services do you use?
- How long did the implementation take?
- How responsive was /// Vendor's name here /// to your needs?
- How does the system perform for you?
- What impresses you most about the system?
- What are the system limitations?
- Did /// Vendor's name here /// provide you or your team training? If so, was the training adequate?
- How knowledgeable was the support staff?
- What surprises did you encounter during this process?
- What advice do you have as we move forward with our project?
- Would you recommend /// Vendor's name here /// as a vendor?

Appendix C. ePortfolio System Product Evaluation Scorecard

Final ePortfolio System Product Evaluation			
	Assign Y for Yes and N for No	Assign scores for each feature (1 = poor, 2 = basic, 3 = excellent)	
	Feature Available (Yes or No)	Score	Notes
Vendor Name:			
Participant Name (optional):			
Features/ Functionality			
Web based interface for portfolio creation			
Long term web access of portolios for assessment or student use			
Searchable by key words/subjects			
Portable/ downloadable			
Supported file formats			

Features/ Functionality—*continued*			
	Feature Available (Yes or No)	Score	Notes
Security and sharing options			
Drag and drop			
Outcomes assessment features			
Schema for aligning program objectives to learning outcomes to artifacts			
Private comments			
Build and apply rubrics			
Integration with ERP Systems/Blackboard and API			
LDAP Compliant			
Mobile device options			
User management/ security			
508 Compliant			
Web Services Framework			
Multi-language capable			
Reports			
Measure learner growth			
Storage capacity per account			
Additional Information			
Hosting			
Help Desk/Support (including online)			
Scalability			
Implementation Services			

Additional Information—*continued*			
	Feature Available (Yes or No)	Score	Notes
Minimum Hardware/Software Requirements			
Training			
Proprietary products			
Understanding of accrediting bodies			
Privacy policy			
Total Score		0	
Comments			

Part 2. Institutional Implementation

Chapter 3. Zero to Sixty: Utilizing a First-Year Seminar to Scale a System-wide ePortfolio Initiative

Daniel Terry
QUEENS UNIVERSITY OF CHARLOTTE

David Whillock
TEXAS CHRISTIAN UNIVERSITY

A challenge to building habits of life-long learning has always been the inability of students to integrate knowledge over the span of their four-plus years of higher education. In many cases, students take courses for their majors, minors, and core requirements without considering the connection between them. While they write papers, participate in projects, and create documents, rarely is there a central place for students to archive *artifacts* of those learning experiences for the purposes of review, *reflection*, and representation to others.

The provost and vice chancellor for academic affairs at our university wanted to address these issues in a proactive way to promote integrative thinking between curricular and co-curricular learning experiences. The vision for this initiative included creating a large-scale, institution-wide ePortfolio program as quickly as we reasonably could. Questions that needed immediate answers included: How can we scale this initiative quickly, going from "zero to sixty" as efficiently as possible? Where does one start with a project that is as inclusive and widespread as this one, considering the decentralized nature of a university? And what effective practices exist to introduce students to the what, why, and how of building an ePortfolio while supporting them in this process?

This chapter explores how one institution addressed these questions via a unique first-year seminar course where building an ePortfolio is nested within larger conversations about the nature of college learning. In the seminar, first-year students are introduced to fundamental aspects of the university experience, including such topics as the nature and purpose(s) of higher education, critical thinking, studying for and reflecting upon course material and learning experiences, academic and personal integrity, and setting learning goals, among other pertinent topics. Building a personal learning ePortfolio is the thread running through these conversations, during which the ePortfolio is framed for students as a tool to make the content and meaning of their learning experiences visible to themselves and others. In the pages that follow, we describe the process by which we decided to launch a system-wide ePortfolio program and the course we created as a means to launch it—a first-year seminar called Introduction to University Life.

DOI: https://doi.org/10.37514/PRA-B.2020.1084.2.03

Too often the structure of higher education encourages students to fragment their learning experiences. With core requirements, majors, and minors, students rarely have the opportunity or support to integrate their learning experiences in a holistic way. Indeed, core requirements become a checklist to "get through" before the students focus on the "real reason" they came to college: to learn skill sets to broaden their career opportunities. Seldom are they asked to critically reflect on their experiences in a holistic way or to integrate their learning as they progress through their academic lives. Another aspect of student life that continues to be ancillary to the learning experience is the co-curricular opportunities that occupy more hours than in-class seat time. Profound learning happens there, too. The college educational experience often occurs in academic silos that encourage students to focus narrowly on their major requirements. The isolation created by silos impacts students' ability to think and work productively. Drawing on the framework of Maslow's hierarchy, Gary Schulman, Milton Cox, and Laurie Richlin (2004) suggest that silos create a bubble where self-esteem and self-actualization are not met, thereby constraining the imagination, socialization, and awareness needed for supporting the potential for full development. Siloed learning environments do not promote integrative thinking—this can be as true among faculty as it is among our students. The provost at our institution felt that an ePortfolio would be a perfect tool to integrate and make visible the learning that occurs for students across the breadth of college experiences.

A steering committee representing both Academic Affairs and Student Affairs was established to develop a year-long pilot program. We spent many hours discussing not only how to structure and implement the ePortfolio program on campus, but also how to centralize the importance of mentoring students in the process of developing their ePortfolios. Mentoring quickly became a deeply held value of the committee. We were in agreement that we did not want to simply give the student an ePortfolio account without providing a context that included a means of feedback and support early on. Our desired outcome was pretty straightforward: to discourage fragmented learning and support *integrative learning* across a student's experiences at the institution (see Polly et al., this collection). The road map to achieve this goal, however, was anything but straightforward.

A primary objective of our initial discussions was to consider student learning outcomes in the use of ePortfolios. In the process of discussion and research, we encountered "habits of mind" used by St. Olaf College (Minnesota) that resonated with us:

- Reflective thinking: ability and habit of looking back at previous learning and setting those experiences in a new context by subsequent learning
- Thinking in community: ability and habit of seeking connections between one's learning and the learning of others who have shared interests
- Thinking globally: ability and habit of seeking connections between one's

learning in college and subjects, debate, and discussions in the wider world (Lorenzo & Ittelson, 2005, p. 5)

As well, our thinking about student learning outcomes was shaped by the Association of American Colleges and Universities' (AAC&U) "Integrative Learning Value Rubric" (Rhodes, 2010). Taking these existing approaches into account, in addition to our commitment to foster integrative thinking, we settled on the following mission to drive our work: "to create a community of reflective, integrative, and intentional learners who take responsibility for their education by assessing their experiences and making their work visible through the use of ePortfolios." Vis-à-vis student learning, we articulated the following desired outcomes:

- students will reflect upon learning process and outcomes
- students will integrate insights across general and specialized studies and co-curricular experiences
- students will organize, interpret, and represent learning experiences
- students will connect their learning experiences to personal values, a sense of meaning and purpose, and future goals

One of our first decisions was to find a name for our ePortfolio initiative that reflected the culture and uniqueness of our institution. We chose "FrogFolio" after our athletic mascot, the Horned Frogs. With the new name in place, we began to spread the word about FrogFolio and brought Digication, our vendor, to campus for a workshop with stakeholders on how to use the software. We decided to pilot our FrogFolio initiative focusing on both academic and non-academic programs within the university. We included a diverse group of approximately 200 students in the pilot: 70 third- and fourth-year honors students in our colloquia courses, 50 first-year students in our Chancellor's Scholars cohort, 40 first-year students in our Connections leadership development program, and 20 undergraduate student athletes. As noted, an essential part of the discussion was how to utilize faculty and staff to mentor students in the process of creating and building an ePortfolio (FrogFolio). We held train-the-trainer workshops on the use of Frog-Folio for would-be mentors, at which time we educated them on ePortfolio philosophy and software navigation (see Balthazor et al., this collection). We created a simple template ePortfolio adopted by all students in the pilot that allowed them to *showcase* curricular and co-curricular artifacts.

We learned some important lessons from our pilot program:

- students created more thoughtful, reflective ePortfolios in the content courses than they did in institutional programs
- to successfully mentor a class of 20 students we needed two course instructors
- we would have to create a course to teach and mentor students on how to use FrogFolio as well as how to integrate course content

- we would need to create a structure to support students as they consider how to build their FrogFolio to demonstrate reflection and integrative thinking through their selection of and reflection on learning artifacts (see Garriott, this collection)

With the support of the provost, we hired a director of ePortfolio to oversee the implementation of FrogFolio in our institutional culture. The provost's charge to institutionalize ePortfolios spanned the seven colleges of our university—a daunting task. With our charge in hand, we had to consider an all-too-common question: what is the best use of our resources to make the greatest impact considering the parameters within which we work? We decided to put our energy into reaching as many first-year students as we reasonably could as they entered the "front door" of the university. We were not going to ignore the current, upper-division students, but we were not going to focus on them either. Instead, we chose to focus on new students as they came into our academic community. Once we were clear on this focus, we had to decide the means by which we were going to introduce students to the what, why, and how of an ePortfolio. As noted previously, our pilot program taught us that students who received their ePortfolio in a course that included instruction and guidance on how to use it created a more robust ePortfolio in terms of learning artifacts and depth of reflection on their learning experiences.

Our challenge, then, was how to introduce as many first-year students as we reasonably could to ePortfolios, and to do this in the context of a course. We chose to focus on students in their first semester in order to build habits of reflection from their earliest days as students. Unfortunately, our institution does not have a traditional first-year seminar or other similar course that is common to all (or most) first-year students. Our sense was that if we had such a course, we could embed the portfolio into that course and reach students via one method. This approach stands in contrast to a more scatter-shot method of using multiple entry points for ePortfolio delivery. In the absence of a common course for first-year students, we set out to create one. With the support of the provost, the director of ePortfolio began to put together a one-credit hour course that not only could serve as an entry point for receiving and building an ePortfolio, but that also could contextualize the portfolio within a much larger conversation about what it means to be a thoughtful, intentional learner in an academic community. The remainder of this article is the story of this course.

The Birth of Introduction to University Life

You may wonder why we did not simply use an existing course or courses—perhaps a large "gateway" course—as a course-based delivery system for getting ePortfolios into the hands of large numbers of students. The truth is, we did embed the ePortfolio within a large existing course (Oral Communication) in addition to creating the course that we are describing in this chapter. But our results were not what we had hoped. In time, we found that embedding the ePortfolio within the large oral communication course did not serve either the ePortfolio initiative or the communications course since the ePortfolio felt like a contrived "add-on" to the course content. Our concern, therefore, was that introducing students to the ePortfolio via the oral communications course would taint student perception of the ePortfolio's usefulness to such an extent that they would not continue using it after completing the course (see Dellinger & Hanger, this collection).

Data from student feedback confirmed our sense when we learned from student surveys of both the first-year seminar course and the oral communications course that those who took the first-year seminar were 20% more likely to answer in the affirmative when asked whether they planned to continue using their ePortfolio throughout their student career. In hindsight, this result was not surprising. As you will see in the remainder of this chapter, the first-year seminar course provided the context for an intentional and coherent introduction of the ePortfolio to students, such that more than 95% of the students who took the course indicated their intent to continue using the ePortfolio throughout college.

It is worth noting that every institution is different. What works at College A may well have little chance of success at University B, and vice versa. A multiple entry-point approach to delivering ePortfolios to students may well work at institutions different from ours. That is entirely possible, given good leadership and coordination. Our fear was—and remains—that too many entry points creates a "quality control" issue to the extent that a thoughtful introduction to ePortfolio work for students becomes harder to maintain across multiple channels, potentially breeding incoherence. We put a great amount of thought and intention behind how we were going to introduce students to the ePortfolio. In the eyes of some on campus, we were perhaps thoughtful to the point of controlling. Admittedly, we were concerned—based on conversations with other institutions with ePortfolio initiatives—that if we did not have an intentional "front door" process, then the initiative would have an initial spark but no staying power.

As noted earlier, our primary institutional motivation for adopting the ePortfolio was for the purpose of promoting reflection and integrative learning among students. We were convinced that while our students were having meaningful learning experiences at the curricular and co-curricular levels, they were, in a sense, left to their own devices when it came to making important connections between and among those experiences. At its core, our adoption of ePortfolios was an attempt to operationalize our commitment to help students collect and reflect upon their learning experiences, and then creatively represent those experiences to others in such a way that (1) the students were more deeply immersed in the meaning of their learning and (2) others were more aware of the identity, knowledge, and skills of the student as a result of seeing the student's portfolio.

The name of our first-year seminar is Introduction to University Life. The course is an elective, one-credit-hour course that is offered on a pass/no credit basis. In our most recent offering of Introduction to University Life, approximately one-quarter of our entering class of students registered for the course. We put the idea of college learning at the heart of the course, which is designed to engage students in an exploration of what it means to flourish as a learner in an academic community. In addition, the students receive a tool—the ePortfolio—to assist them in telling the story of their learning in that community.

When students create an ePortfolio in the first-year seminar course, we start them with a particular template—a personal ePortfolio that is designed to cover the scope of their learning experiences as college students over the next several semesters, of which Introduction to University Life is but one aspect. In other words, the ePortfolio that students receive in the course is not course-specific. It is, in a sense, the architecture for students to begin reflecting and archiving artifacts across learning experiences. Students may well end up with multiple ePortfolios before their time is complete at our institution, but our purpose in this course is to start students with a personal learning ePortfolio that has both depth and breadth. We have chosen a broad, common template that applies to all students as the starting place in this course. The template "maps" the structure of a student's learning experiences, no matter their eventual major or discipline of study.

A unique aspect of Introduction to University Life is how we seek to combine or blend some traditional elements of a first-year seminar course with an intentional introduction to *portfolio thinking* and learning. Making the case that these two elements can or even should be blended has, at times, been a challenge. Students tend to latch onto the idea of building an ePortfolio to the exclusion of much of the course content and some faculty and staff wonder whether we have just "smashed" (their word) two disparate course ideas together into a single course. As a result, we strive to carefully craft how we talk about this course. We bridge first-year seminar elements with ePortfolio creation by emphasizing learning. Below you will find the course description for Introduction to University Life as it appears in the student syllabus. The description demonstrates how we frame and contextualize the ePortfolio within a broad conversation about learning and higher education:

> This one-hour course for first-semester students explores the university as a learning community and the student as a learner within it. Within this course, students are introduced to fundamental questions and issues of the university experience—the nature and purpose(s) of higher education, critical thinking, how to study for and reflect upon course material and experiences, the importance of academic and personal integrity, setting learning goals, self-management, persistence & follow-through, learning alongside a diverse array of people and perspectives, and the meaning and importance of learning that is reflective, life-long, and life-wide. A primary feature of the course is the creation of a FrogFolio, a dynamic digital platform where students reflect upon, organize, archive, and display their

significant learning experiences, both inside and outside the classroom. FrogFolio captures the breadth and depth of student learning as it occurs in the academic community. (Terry, 2016)

This course description makes clear that our first-year seminar is much more than an "ePortfolio course." We do not need an entire course—even at the one credit hour level—to thoughtfully introduce ePortfolio work to students. The intent was to create a course about learning in an academic community within which we intentionally tucked the ePortfolio as an extension of the learning conversation. Our position is that the ePortfolio is best understood in the context of the learning experience, as opposed to one more social media platform or a gimmick or a useful means to getting a foot in the door for a potential job. Introducing the ePortfolio within a course about learning in college allowed us to do something that was important to us—namely, to introduce a large number of students to the purpose and uses of the ePortfolio in a coherent way with consistent messaging. To help students better understand the ePortfolio and our view of its importance, one of us (Terry) wrote an essay about the portfolio that addresses both theoretical and practical concerns. The essay, called "Making Student Learning Visible" (See the Appendix at https://wac.colostate.edu/books/practice/portfolios/) is written as a guide to students and seeks to introduce them to the what, why, and how of ePortfolios as we ask students to use them. This essay is an assigned reading for all sections of the course during the third week of the semester.

True to the mission of our ePortfolio initiative, the essay frames the portfolio as a learning tool with showcase qualities. We impress upon students that the ePortfolio they create in the course is more than simply a "warehouse" of artifacts from their student experiences. It is a tool that allows them to reflect on important learning experiences, explore what those experiences mean in the context of their education, and make connections between those experiences and the TCU mission. As well, we note that the ePortfolio is a place to display specific skills and competencies related to a student's emerging professional identity (see Polly et al., this collection). In the essay, we emphasize to students that they are in the driver's seat when it comes to their ePortfolios. As the creators and authors, they determine what artifacts and learning experiences to include in their ePortfolios. In this way, they assume ownership and take responsibility for their "learning career" (Terry, 2014). We take this approach because when students take responsibility for what to include and how to represent their learning experiences in an ePortfolio, they are engaging in metacognitive thinking.

The Design & Structure of the ePortfolio in Introduction to University Life

The depth-and-breadth templated ePortfolio that students adopt within Introduction to University Life contains six sections. Because students in all disciplines, majors, and colleges take the course, the template is structured to apply to any first-year student that might enroll. The sections are as follows:

Home/ About Me	Personal Learning Goals	My Learning Experiences	TCU Learning Goals	Résumé	Attributions

Concerning the Home/About Me page, we coach students to craft an engaging introduction—major field of study, hometown, interests, passions, and commitments. As well, we engage them in a conversation about audience so that they will understand that peers, faculty and staff, and, eventually, prospective employers and/or graduate schools may see this ePortfolio as well. We strive to instill the idea that it is important to communicate a sense of professionalism, while also providing an informative introduction to their identity as a student. While a professional photo is not entirely necessary, we tell them if they choose to include a photo, it is important that they choose one that communicates the type of image they want to portray to others in the TCU community.

We strive for integration in the course by linking the course-content discussions we have with our first-semester students to the work they are doing in their ePortfolios. As an example, we take students through an intentional goal-setting exercise in class two weeks prior to the due date for the Personal Learning Goals section. Students work with instructors and one another to identify and articulate goals for their first year of college (and beyond). We take them through a frequently-used process of making sure that their goals are *SMART*—Specific, Measurable, Attainable, Realistic, and Time-bound (Rubin, 2002) (see Day, this collection). Students have two weeks to work on creating meaningful goals before we ask them to represent those goals in the appropriate section of the ePortfolio. Of course, goals change, shift, and (in some cases) go away over time, but we believe it is important to have students do this kind of reflection in their portfolios and update their goals along the way. The ePortfolio is a "living document" and as such is never really finished, even though we make certain sections of the portfolio due at certain times of the semester.

Each section of our first-year seminar course is team-taught by a faculty member and staff member. We chose to teach the course this way because it allowed us to mentor the students more intentionally in each section of the course. Co-instructors split the number of mentoring meetings in half, which allowed each student in the course to meet face-to-face with a mentor (one of their instructors) two times during the semester outside of class time. The purpose of the mentoring sessions was to check in with each student about their transition to college, but to do so by using the ePortfolio as the means by which to talk to the student about their learning experiences in college. By the time of their first mentor meeting, students complete two sections of their portfolio—the Home/About Me and Personal Learning Goals. Together, the student and mentor review the ePortfolio and talk about the student's reflections as presented in these two sections. In this way, the ePortfolio functions as an occasion for conversation guided by the student's learning thus far in college.

By the time of their second mentor meeting later in the semester, each student completes a section of the ePortfolio that we call My Learning Experiences. This section of the portfolio is the most robust section in the template we give first-year students. It contains two pages: Courses and Co-Curricular Experiences. Within Courses, students create a page for each of their academic courses. Through class discussion and prompts embedded in the template, we coach students through writing a brief overview of each class, selecting learning artifacts from the class, reflecting on their meaning, and then representing those artifacts on the page. If a student is in a course with few artifacts (for instance, exams are the only means of evaluation), then we encourage the student to simply reflect on the impact of the course. For Co-Curricular Experiences, we encourage students to creatively tell the story of their involvement in groups, events, organizations, etc., that have shaped them and contributed to their learning in college.

Some of the best reflections in the ePortfolio emerge in the My Learning Experiences section. We try our best—both through prompts embedded in the template itself and through mentoring and class discussions—to elicit thoughtful reflection on the part of students concerning not simply what they are learning, but what it means to them as a learner and as an emerging professional in the world (see Sanborn & Ramirez, this collection). To this end, we coach students to contextualize the learning artifacts they choose to share in their ePortfolios. In the "Making Student Learning Visible" essay that students read for class, we invite them to provide a "context statement" for the artifacts they choose wherein they briefly describe each artifact and why they have chosen to share it with their audience. This practice fosters reflection, and reflection deepens learning. The My Learning Experiences section of the ePortfolio, once it is completed, follows the structure of the following example:

Courses: Fall 2015

Introduction to University Life

Basic Speech Communication

English Course A-B-C

Religion Course D-E-F

Economics Course X-Y-Z

Co-Curricular Experiences

Student Government

Chancellor's Leadership Program

Volunteer Experience at Community Agency 101

We introduce the ePortfolio during the third week of the semester. The first two weeks are reserved for introductions, housekeeping, and important conversations about the meaning and purpose of college. Upon arriving for class in the third week, students are expected to have read the "Making Student Learning Visible" essay described earlier in this chapter (See the Appendix at https://wac .colostate.edu/books/practice/portfolios/)

Instructors and students take about half of the class to discuss the essay, during which time the instructors reiterate key points about the philosophy, purpose, and benefits of building an ePortfolio. Students then spend the remainder of class logging into their new ePortfolio account and following along with a video tutorial that explains how the ePortfolio software functions. The tutorial explains navigational features as well as sections of the template ePortfolio that students adopt. The video tutorial is a 20-minute instructional video created by the ePortfolio team on our campus, which is comprised of the director, a graduate assistant, and a team of student coaches we call "eTerns" (see Garriott, this collection).

A member of the team is present in each section of the course during the third week to troubleshoot issues, answer questions, offer tips, and generally coach students through the early stages of ePortfolio creation. eTerns lead most of these "workshops." At times, the eTern will pause the video tutorial to answer questions or clarify points before re-starting the video. We find that the presence of the eTern in class on this day lends credibility to the overall project, which helps with student buy-in. Additionally, our eTerns have a high level of expertise when it comes to how and why to build a robust, attractive ePortfolio. More often than not, eTerns are students that we have recruited based on the quality of their own ePortfolio work. When we have an opening on our team of six, we reach out to students on the merits of their work and recruit them to coach other students for several hours per week, with compensation. In almost every case, their level of expertise is significantly greater than either of the course instructors and their presence takes the pressure off the instructors to know the answers to the inevitable questions about software and utility that arise during the on-boarding process (see Garriott, this collection).

Our student eTerns are available throughout the semester and frequently return to classes later in the semester to answer lingering questions and to coach our most ambitious students through some of the more technical aspects of ePortfolio design. In addition to returning to classes as needed throughout the semester, our eTerns are available for consultation with other students in our FrogFolio Lab (see Garriott, this collection). The lab is located in a prominent location adjacent to our library and is open Monday–Thursday in the afternoon. We make students aware of the lab via the course syllabus, and throughout the semester instructors reinforce information about this resource during class. The eTerns and the FrogFolio Lab operate under the supervision of the ePortfolio director and a graduate assistant.

An additional level of support for students in the course comes in the form of online support resources developed with significant input from the eTerns. Many of our resources are found within a "FrogFolio about FrogFolios" that can be easily found on the landing page of our ePortfolio system. We also link to the "FrogFolio about FrogFolios" from our website (https://tcu.digication.com/metafrog/About_Me/published). This *metafolio* of resources features videos, tips, walk-throughs, prompts, and suggestions concerning the what, why, and how of ePortfolios at our institution. In some cases, we link to external resources that we have found helpful, but most often the resources found in the metafolio have been created in-house by our team to apply directly to ePortfolio use on campus. That said, the "FrogFolio about FrogFolios" is publicly accessible and, to our surprise, is frequently used by people beyond our institution. We believe that a strength of our metafolio is the array of student-friendly resources offered—best practices, design and layout tips, short how-to videos, prompts about reflective thinking and artifact selection, digital résumé tips, links to exemplary portfolios of other students, and many other resources. The students in the first-year seminar course are made aware of this resource and it receives several thousand "hits" per semester.

One of the ways we ensure that students receive a thorough immersion in the theory and mechanics of ePortfolio use is to weave portfolio creation into the fabric of the course over the length of the semester (see Castaño & Novo, this collection). As noted, we introduce the ePortfolio via a required reading, followed by an on-boarding workshop with one of our eTerns present. Thereafter, students work on different sections of their ePortfolios—beginning with their homepages—throughout the semester. The three primary sections that students spend time creating, as noted earlier, are Home/About Me, Personal Learning Goals, and My Learning Experiences. Students also complete the Résumé and Attributions[1] section during the semester. The TCU Learning Goals section requires a level of integration and thinking that is best reserved for students later in their academic careers, as it asks students to reflect on artifacts that "map" to cognitive and ethical outcomes for the university. We use this section to talk to students in the seminar about "higher learning," but do not expect them to begin working with this section in their first semester.

Each section of the ePortfolio—minus TCU Learning Goals—is due at different points throughout the semester, each approximately three weeks apart. This timeline allows students to focus on different (and increasingly challenging) parts of the ePortfolio throughout the semester. Spacing due dates throughout the semester helps ensure that students work on their ePortfolios over time, as opposed to hastily throwing things together right at the end of the semester. We are less concerned that students come up with a stellar final product by the time of each due date than we are with ensuring that students are working thoughtfully and consistently throughout the semester. Having benchmarks throughout the semester for ePortfolio submissions tends to yield stronger final products.

---

1.   In the *Attributions* section, students cite and give credit for images or sources used in the creation of their ePortfolio.

As noted earlier, more than 95% of students enrolled in this course indicated that they were either Likely or Very Likely to continue using their ePortfolios throughout their academic careers. Student evaluations of the course consistently rank above 4.0 (on a 5.0 scale) on almost every student perception question measured by our institution's course evaluation system. Students opt in to this course based on its merits alone. It is not a required course, although an increasing number of our colleges strongly encourage their students to enroll in the course so that their students will have a solid ePortfolio background before entering their major courses (see Day, this collection).

As we write this chapter, the provost at our institution has reiterated his strong support for growing the number of course sections offered in subsequent semesters. Our next short-term goal is for approximately one-half of our incoming students to take Introduction to University Life whereby they would be given the opportunity to receive mentoring as they create an ePortfolio in the manner we have described in this chapter. While there are certainly other ways for a student to receive an ePortfolio in their first year on our campus, we consistently find that among the roughly 40% of our undergraduate student population now working with ePortfolios, the vast majority of the students doing exceptionally creative and thoughtful portfolio work took Introduction to University Life in their first semester. We are convinced that this is the case because of the intentional way we weave portfolio thinking and portfolio best practices throughout the fabric of this semester-long course.

References

Lorenzo, G. & Ittelson, J. (2005). Demonstrating and assessing student learning with E-Portfolios. In D. Oblinger (Ed.), *EDUCAUSE learning initiative*. ELI Paper 3.

Rhodes, T. (Ed.) (2010). *Assessing outcomes and improving achievement: Tips and tools for using rubrics.* Association of American Colleges & Universities.

Rubin, R.S. (2002). Will the real SMART goals please stand up? *The Industrial-Organizational Psychologist, 39*(4), 26–27.

Schulman, G. M., Cox, M. D. & Richlin, L. (2004). Institutional considerations in developing a faculty learning community program. In M.D. Cox & L. Richlin (Eds.), *Building faculty learning communities* (pp. 41–50). New Directions for Teaching and Learning: No. 97, Jossey-Bass.

Terry, D. (2014). Making student learning visible: A guide for students and those who mentor them. [Unpublished white paper]. Texas Christian University.

Terry, D. (2016). UNPR 10211: Introduction to university life. [Unpublished syllabus]. Texas Christian University.

Resources Mentioned in This Chapter

The Metafolio: FrogFolio about FrogFolios. https://tcu.digication.com/metafrog/About_Me/published.

Chapter 4. Meeting the Challenges of ePortfolio Implementation at Four-year Institutions: Software, Support, and Collaboration

Mary Ann Dellinger
Laurin Hanger
VIRGINIA MILITARY INSTITUTE

Well, sometimes the magic works. Sometimes, it doesn't.

—*Old Lodge Skins, Little Big Man* (Penn, 1970)

The implementation of an institutional-wide ePortfolio model at a four-year institution can present a series of challenges that community colleges and large universities do not customarily face. These issues range from providing sufficient, meaningful support—technical, pedagogical, and philosophical—to ensuring ownership among all stakeholders. Furthermore, well-staffed, interdisciplinary learning/teaching centers are not always a given on undergraduate campuses, while smaller student populations often result in a limited instructional technology (IT) staff serving multiple departments and/or purposes at the same time. Thus, the workload required for launching an institutional ePortfolio program lands squarely on the shoulders of teaching/research faculty.

We do not mean to suggest that these unique challenges exempt four-year colleges from the same problems discussed in other chapters of this book or vice-versa: software choice, faculty buy-in, mobility, and intra-/extramural access, to name a few. Resolution of the same questions on our campuses, however, necessitates a different approach, one that not only considers the availability and nature of human and financial resources, but also respects equity among disciplinary programs within the context of undergraduate education.

This chapter focuses on "what we know" (now) from the proverbial hits and misses in the attempt to implement an institutional ePortfolio at the Virginia Military Institute (VMI). Looking back on a very effective *backend/frontend* collaboration and a less-than-successful interdisciplinary ePortfolio program, we identify specific strategies for the 5Ws and the H[1] of starting small and fomenting a collective vision.

---

1. The 5Ws and the H: What, Who, Where, When, Why, and How

DOI: https://doi.org/10.37514/PRA-B.2020.1084.2.04

Priorities and Expenses on Four-Year Campuses

Prompted by the demand for support programs on the one hand and accreditor oversight on the other, priorities in undergraduate education have shifted dramatically since the final decade of our last century. As a result, new spending categories have emerged while traditional classifications have fused or entirely collapsed. Concepts traditionally associated with K–12 education such as reading/math remediation, developmental education, and counseling now vie for space, faculty, staff, and funding against traditional academic programs.

In its 2016 publication, "Trends in College Spending: 2003–2013," the American Institutes for Research (AIR) report an ongoing trend in non-instructional student services spending at four-year colleges, marked by an 11.1% increase at public institutions and a 21.8% increase at private colleges (Desrochers & Hurlbut, 2016). By comparison, academic support spending increased by 8% and 5% respectively during the same time period, with instructional expenses accounting for 3% of the budget at public institutions and 5% on private campuses (Desrochers & Hurlbut, 2016). Department of Education (DOE) statistics per full-time-equivalent (FTE) student in their category "student services, academic support, and institutional support" at public four-year colleges between 2010–2011 and 2015, for the most part, support the AIR findings.[2]

Reading, Writing, and Math remediation costs and other types of developmental education have increased exponentially since the beginning of this decade. Data collected by The Hechlinger Report, published in 2017, showed that 96% of the 911 reporting colleges enrolled students in remediation courses during the 2014–2015 academic year at a cost of $7 billion a year to colleges, students, families, and taxpayers (Butrymowicz, 2017). Other researchers and think tanks estimated that one of every four college students was enrolled in a remedial program during the 2015–2016 academic year at a cost of between $1.3B and $1.5B (Jimenez et al., 2016), with the middle class footing most of the bill (Education Reform Now, 2016).

As the demand for developmental education has increased, so has the number of students seeking psychological and counseling services provided on campus (Reilly, 2018). The American College Health Association reported that in the same time period (2015–2016) 40% of 63,000 college students surveyed had suffered depression that affected their ability to perform, while another 61% reported feeling "overwhelming anxiety" (Reilly, 2018). Forty-eight percent of four-year colleges provided psychiatric services (Kwai, 2016).

At the heart of these remedial and counselling expenditures lie both attrition and completion rates. Four-year degrees have taken college students increasingly more time to complete since 2010, climbing to an alarming 62% of students who

---

2.   At the time of writing, the most recent statistics available correspond to the 2015–2016 academic year.

spend six years earning their degree at four-year institutions, according to the Department of Education (National Center for Education Statistics, 2018). However, retention rates reached an all-time high of 81% in the 2015–2016 academic year, suggesting the worthiness of investment in student/academic support services and its correlation to the six-year completion rates (National Center for Education Statistics, 2018).

With the declining interest in a liberal arts education and the very real struggle to endure, especially in non-urban settings, four-year colleges find themselves in a precarious financial position. Raising tuition costs to maintain support services is rarely wise, and state governments can prohibit public institutions from raising tuition. Private institutions have fared worse. According to US News & World Report (2018), 28% of some 500 small private colleges studied over the last 50 years, mostly liberal arts institutions, have either shut down, merged, or redefined their mission statements.

Ironically, students enrolled in remedial programs or receiving mental health services more likely than not would find refuge and purpose through the developmental ePortfolio process, in addition to witnessing their own academic and emotional growth—albeit perhaps in different ways than their classmates. But given, on the one hand, the financial stress of providing non-academic services and the ensuing snowball effect on tenure lines, hiring, funding, and teaching assignments on the other, it is understandable that the implementation of a campus-wide ePortfolio program may not head the list of priorities among the principal stakeholders at four-year institutions.

Background: The VMI ePortfolio Project (2009–2014)

Fortunately, VMI does not typically face the financial and existential challenges of other four-year institutions; alumni contribute generously to their alma mater. Our learning center, for example, exists thanks to one alumnus' earmarked donation. Two very important alumni groups, in addition to the VMI Foundation, have funded countless research, experiential, and study abroad programs for both cadets and faculty. The 2008 recession, however, hit us hard, despite the ongoing gifts from alumni.

Coinciding with the economic downturn, the VMI ePortfolio Project was initiated in the fall of the 2008–2009 academic year as part of the Institute's "Quality Enhancement Plan" (QEP) for reaccreditation through the Southern Association of Colleges and Schools (SACS). Consistent with the military environment that defines VMI, the decision for the ePortfolio Project was made at the top of the academic chain of command and passed down to the faculty, along with the mandate that all departments would participate in the program through their curricula.

The ePortfolio Project remained housed in the ethernet for the duration of its life (Spring 2009–Spring 2014), even though the dean assigned the oversight of the project to specific senior faculty. On their advice, Edward M. White's (2005) "Phase 2" writing (print) portfolio scoring model for *assessment* was adopted, as it had proved efficient in the rating of traditional paper portfolios.

All instructors teaching ePortfolio-embedded courses received an invitation to participate in the two-day scoring session. In accordance with the White (2005) model, institutional ePortfolio scorers rated only a hard copy of the required reflective essay with no access to cadets' ePortfolio *artifacts*. Organization of the assessment venue, from ordering paper clips to collating data, was the responsibility of an appointed "Director, VMI ePortfolio Project." The director received a course release as compensation for assessment duties and year-long responsibilities related to faculty and cadet training as well as pedagogical and technological troubleshooting. Two tenured professors served consecutively in this role, but not autonomously.

For the first three years of the program, a plugin to our learning management system (LMS), Angel®, served as the sole ePortfolio platform. An IT Help Desk specialist and the ePortfolio Project director worked closely to separate pedagogy from technology and developed a system for addressing the inevitable issues that stakeholders had (see Appendix for "ePortfolio Troubleshooting Flowchart"). Cadets and faculty responded positively, and our system proved quite successful, as we could resolve issues quickly and with relative ease.

The advantage of the LMS plugin centered on user-friendliness for faculty and cadets. It required only the most basic computing skills, while not unnecessarily complicating the collection and coding of data for assessment. An ePortfolio icon on cadets' LMS home page provided direct access to the ePortfolio *workspace*, organized as per the following six tabs:

My Info	Artifacts	History	Blogs	Objectives	Publications

In the "My Info" section, cadets entered their VMI timeline and major and details of other formal educational experiences in the "My Education History" ("History" tab). Learners could import work directly from the LMS to their ePortfolio artifact repository ("Artifacts" tab) as well as upload any other evidence they deemed relevant to their academic and personal development. Individual instructors could assign the "Blogs" section for logging and reflecting on learning experiences. As well, instructors had the option of posting the course objectives and/or the institute-designated learning outcomes for ePortfolio courses in the "Objectives" section. Cadets could then link their evidence to the corresponding learning outcome.

The "Publications" section of the program proved especially clunky and inconsistent with the long-term goals of the VMI ePortfolio. Cadets had to publish a different ePortfolio for each course; hyperlinks connecting publications often failed and detracted from the already limited cohesiveness and aesthetics. Similarly, the program offered no design options, merely the organization of artifacts and choice of font. Every publication shared a uniform white background.

In a very short time, the limited affordances provided by the LMS plugin proved frustrating, especially to tech-savvy cadets and faculty. In addition, with access restricted to the VMI intranet, cadets could not continue developing their ePortfolios after graduation. The assessment components of the plug-in, although uncomplicated, weakened the pedagogical benefits of the ePortfolio for learners and faculty, alike. Assessment was driving the technology and in turn, the technology was driving the pedagogy when it should be the other way around (see Summers et al. and Day, this collection).

Therefore, on the recommendation of a new ePortfolio director, a Word-Press platform hosted by EduBlogs, now CampusPress, became the sole program permitted for the VMI ePortfolio. Tied less to assessment and more to reflective learning, this platform offered some of the benefits of the LMS plug-in, with LDAP-integration and the protection of student data, but also allowed for a more creative *showcase* for *multi-modal* assignments, *reflection* in blogs and pages, and considerations for building a career profile for use after graduation. EduBlogs also provided backend support, thus relieving an already overstretched IT staff and taking the burden of technology-related issues off the shoulders of the ePortfolio director, allowing him to concentrate his efforts on training.

Much like the Western hero, the VMI ePortfolio Project, as a mandate to departments and faculty, disappeared slowly over the horizon (but sadly no one yelled out, "Come back . . . come back"). The Institute has continued to renew the EduBlog/CampusPress license for the WordPress ePortfolio, which at this writing is housed in the VMI Writing Center and used almost exclusively by the Department of English, Rhetoric, and Humanistic Studies (ERH). Interest from co-curricular programs such as Career Services, the academic support center, and ROTC has waned along with that of the majority of teacher/scholars and cadet stakeholders.

The 5Ws and the H

What? What is an electronic portfolio? What is it not?

A decade ago, electronic portfolios did not have the visibility they have across U.S. campuses today, so many of the questions with which we dealt at VMI would now qualify as moot. Nonetheless, and at the risk of eliciting a studentesque "duh" from our readers, we must emphasize that the beginning point for all stakeholders is to understand the purpose of the institutional ePortfolio (see Richardson et al., this collection). Failing to ensure that everyone begins with a common understanding of purpose, audience, and agency during the planning stage will mean unnecessary frustration in the long run; stakeholders' understanding of the "big ideas" and baseline components of an ePortfolio is non-negotiable. That said, planning committees may increase their chances for an auspicious roll-out by starting from what an ePortfolio *is not*.

Confusion about new ways of presenting information is not unique to our age, but merely the most recent iteration of misunderstandings that have occurred throughout human history, as we have defined and redefined communication and literacy across the millennia. In Ancient Greece, Socrates mistrusted the newly created alphabet, "believ[ing] that the seeming permanence of the printed word would delude [the young] into thinking they had accessed the heart of knowledge, rather than simply decoded it" (Wolf, 2007). Consider as well, the epistemology of film-making from the Lumière brothers' inventions—the movie camera and projector—in 1895 and cinematography as we know it today, or the establishment of film studies as its own discipline, separate from literature.

From the very beginning of the VMI ePortfolio Project, we struggled with stakeholders' confusion about "electronic ink"—an electronic, verbatim version of an original printed text—vs. "digital text," which exploits hypermedia to produce a multi-layered, multimodal version of the text (Escandell Montiel, 2014). Much of the misunderstanding was rooted in the required reflective essay, scored with no consideration of ePortfolio artifacts and evaluated in hard copy only, which in turn generated a litany of faculty concerns regarding ePortfolio ownership, *curation*, and extradepartmental directives.

Who? Who Gives the Orders and Who Marches? Or Do We March Together?

Without faculty buy-in, there can be no faculty engagement, no matter how authoritative the mandate (see Richardson et al. and Summers et al., this collection). The top-down decision to initiate an institutional ePortfolio program at VMI compromised faculty commitment from the very beginning, and the same indifference to faculty input ultimately led to its failure. At our college, faculty received no invitation to join the conversation about implementation of an institutional ePortfolio and, thus, had no opportunity to seek compromises or to discuss the non-negotiables. We posit that a broader discussion about the steps required for implementation would have gained greater faculty support early in the process (Mullaney, 2018).

Cadets quickly formed their own definition of the reflective essay, which varied little from that of their instructors. With the reflective essay as the focus of ePortfolios, and that essay being based on the same prescribed, uniform prompt across all disciplines, we deprived cadets of cultivating curation skills, career connections (see Polly et al. and Coleman et al., this collection), *folio thinking* (see Sanborn & Ramirez and Day, this collection) and, worst of all, agency. Although cadets chose artifacts from their course ePortfolio to provide evidence in their essays, they had no guarantee that their audience for those artifacts would extend beyond the course instructor. Furthermore, in spite of both ePortfolio directors' investment of their own free time, including Saturdays, for workshops with new cadets to work on a broader, longitudinal ePortfolio to document their cadetship, the lack of incentive, on the one hand, and want of encouragement outside the workshops, on the other, resulted in only one professional, longitudinal ePortfolio in the six years of the project.

Hypotheticals do not change previous mistakes, but the "should-haves" and "could-haves" can serve to inform subsequent initiatives as well as peer institutions in the planning stages of ePortfolio implementation. We cannot overstate the importance of involving as many stakeholders as possible in the planning, assessment, and ongoing revision of any ePortfolio model or program (see Polly et al. and Coleman et al., this collection). Students, IT staff, co-curricular program representatives, librarians, and institutional assessment officers as well as cross-generational faculty members across all disciplines must have a voice and play an active role in any ePortfolio initiative if it is to be successful (see Richardson et al., this collection). As outlined by William Mullaney (2018), support or backing—buy-in if you will—depends on: 1) conversation—"lots of it"; 2) openness to compromise; and 3) consensus on non-negotiables. Finally, we urge the recruitment of ePortfolio enthusiasts and curious stakeholders for the ePortfolio committee; attempts at converting non-believers only lead to frustration and burnout. An inclusive, engaged ePortfolio exploratory and ongoing steering committee stands as the first and, if it must, the only non-negotiable.

Why? Why Are We Doing This?

Like mortar on bricks, a collective vision—the *why* of an institutional ePortfolio program—not only safeguards stability, but also creates a cohesive whole without compromising the strength of the individual parts. Different perspectives, all of which are rooted in the particular expertise of stakeholder groups, inform and nurture the collective vision. Spending time, energy, and money on putting out small fires constantly ignited and reignited by confusion is a waste of resources that would better serve the initiative through other ePortfolio-related events.

By different perspectives and areas of expertise, we are referring to the concomitant relationship between disciplinary or departmental-specific goals, computer competency, and the institutional ePortfolio in terms of purpose and scope (see Terry & Whillock and Day, this collection). When we reflect on the VMI ePortfolio Project, we can easily identify two groups whose input would have given shape to a collective vision in the very beginning: the IT staff and the cadets. The cost and 2008 economic climate aside, IT staff in conjunction with the Academic Technology Committee or individual faculty members committed to the project, along with a cross-section of cadets, would have laid a much firmer foundation on which to build both our why and our ePortfolio program.

The Institute contracted the Angel plug-in around Thanksgiving and implementation began in January. On the backend, IT assumed there would be no difference in licensing between the Angel LMS and the plug-in, and that the Angel ePortfolio platform would provide sufficient storage and ample file-size limits. Faculty and cadets also expected generous file-size and storage limits on a platform that would foment creative thinking and discourage uniformity.

The reality proved quite different. VMI purchased a block of licenses for the LMS which covered all cadets, faculty, and staff; however, the ePortfolio licenses were sold separately. Since an ePortfolio license was now needed for every LMS user, the Institute needed to contract X-number of licenses, one for each cadet, faculty member, and staff member who would be using the ePortfolio. As the ePortfolio users changed, the licenses were updated manually to free them up for other users. Limited storage and file size obligated ePortfolio creators to link artifacts rather than embed them within the ePortfolio, which, in turn, quelled originality. The rigid layout and extramural inaccessibility countered our assertions about the potential of an interdisciplinary ePortfolio program. Groups and individuals looked at the ePortfolio in different ways (mostly as a chore), and coped by devising their own definition of artifacts (e.g., a collection of scholarly articles) and publication, which included links from the assignment drop box on Angel to the ePortfolio plug-in or a one-time-only upload of artifacts at the end of the semester. Some professors required cadets to print all their artifacts along with their essay for grading.

We had no collective vision or shared mission beyond compliance with the mandate, which forcibly made the ePortfolio the dreaded "add-on" very quickly. Even the more flexible WordPress platform failed to turn back the tide of frustration; it was simply too late: coping mechanisms had become habits through which instructors rejected or redefined the ePortfolio's purpose and significance for the learner.

To those in the planning stages, we reiterate the urgency of starting small, but with a broad, diverse spectrum of experience and expertise, and a positive disposition towards collaboration. The fusion of different perspectives and aptitudes can only enrich the collective vision and illuminate the process (see Richardson et al. and Summers et al., this collection).

Where? Where Is the ePortfolio Housed?

An important consideration for the ePortfolio committee members at four-year institutions is where to house the ePortfolio, both for financial reasons and proprietary attitudes of faculty, more often than not in conflict with each other. Housing in a department implies ownership but, more importantly, it creates the perception/misperception that specific disciplinary conventions define ePortfolio pedagogy, which in turn serves the host department with no benefit to the rest.

In our case, the barebones definition we presented to faculty—a collection of a student's artifacts with reflections on learning—generated skepticism and increased resistance. The name, after all, suggests that an ePortfolio is a digital repository in which students collect their work and reflections. Understandably, some faculty members felt that the VMI network should house individual cadet folders to serve as electronic portfolios. Others suggested using a dedicated drop box or message board within the LMS or third-tier webpages for each cadet on the VMI website to save the investment of both time and funds. Still others asked why social media, in particular Facebook, would not prove more economical and user-friendly.

The question for exploratory committees becomes: if not in a department, where? Small colleges cannot afford the budget or the personnel for the creation of an in-house ePortfolio platform (see Day and Terry & Whillock, this collection) and/or the IT staff is limited to assisting with the technology and cybersecurity, not instruction or assessment beyond LMS administration. The missions of learning centers, while not necessarily in conflict with those of ePortfolio programs, establish separate priorities and designated performance expectations.

Housing also applies to the adopted software; in fact, the software may in itself resolve the ownership issue and subdue doubts about a hidden agenda. Back-end support offered by ePortfolio vendors combined with the ubiquitous cloud storage available these days nullifies many of the issues we had a decade ago. Ideally, the ePortfolio home pertains to a neutral academic space shared by all departments and programs, but that is a cost-prohibitive solution these days for four-year colleges, as we have previously discussed. An instructional technology specialist, on campuses lucky enough to have one, removes the burden on faculty and IT alike and mitigates the (mis)perceptions of propriety.

It is likely that the determination of the ePortfolio's cloud or department home may bring with it the first opportunity for negotiation among the stakeholder representatives (see Terry & Whillock, this collection); perhaps not. Nevertheless, the collective vision together with the well-defined shared mission we discussed previously should certainly facilitate the discussion.

When? When Will We Know We've Reached the Endgame?

If our reader is to take just one thing away from this chapter—in addition to the non-negotiable ePortfolio committee—it should be the need to identify the endgame and the milestones to getting there. One of our colleagues, now retired, used to cite what he called "the good ideas fairy." The good ideas fairy, he maintained, came around at night, sprinkling good ideas across campus and academic divisions. The worthiness of the ideas themselves notwithstanding, it seemed to him that good ideas outnumbered the long-term, fruitful initiatives.

As the British Army's 7Ps bluntly state, "proper planning and preparation prevents piss-poor performance" ("7 Ps," 2019), and proper planning and preparation include a timeline from planning to endgame, all of which can count on administrative support.

How? How Can We Implement an Interdisciplinary ePortfolio?

Grant Wiggins and Jay McTighe's (2007) *backward design* framework has radically changed the way we plan instruction and assess learning for those teaching faculty and programs who have embraced it. We suggest backward design can serve as purposefully in the conception and development of an institutional ePortfolio program. In fact, it is only logical, as most instructors will, at the very least, have heard the term. Colleges with a teacher education program have the advantage of faculty members with a command of the "Understanding by Design" (UbD) model.

Backward design consists of three phases: 1) identifying desired results; 2) determining acceptable evidence; and 3) planning learning experiences and instruction (as cited in Bowen, 2017). UbD assessment and learning activities align with the tenets of *Constructivist* methodology, valuing *authenticity*, evidence of learning, and heuristics. Using the template that can be downloaded from Jay McTighe's website, backward design of an ePortfolio program may look like Figure 4.1:

Stage 1—Desired Results

ESTABLISHED GOALS

Provide a platform for students to demonstrate learning, make connections, and reflect on academic and co-curricular experiences

Widen the lens through which faculty view both their discipline and individual students

Support interdisciplinarity and qualitative assessment.

Transfer

The ePortfolio will allow students to independently use their learning to . . .

- make connections between academic, extracurricular, and life experiences
- demonstrate digital literacy
- define their digital identity as a student, pre-professional, and citizen

Meaning

UNDERSTANDINGS (aka "big ideas")	ESSENTIAL QUESTIONS
Students will understand that . . .	• What? So what? Now what? (Balthazor et al)
• learning is not linear	• How can I evidence learning?
• evidence of learning is not limited to exams, essays, and reports	• In what ways can I show career-readiness?
• "we do not learn from experience, we learn from reflecting on experience" (John Dewey)	

Acquisition	
Students will know . . .	*Students will be skilled at . . .*
• how to exploit the affordances of technology for multiple purposes • ways of thinking critically in the process of creation, curation, and selection/substitution	• demonstrating understanding in multiple ways • providing and accepting suggestions and friendly criticism from peers • using social media in new ways and in the projection of a digital self

Stage 2—Evidence and Assessment	
Evaluative Criteria	**Assessment Evidence**
Rubrics Assessment venues Qualifications of evaluators	**PERFORMANCE TASK(S):** • multimodal publications • curation • peer review • conferencing • service learning experience(s)
	OTHER EVIDENCE: • reflective pieces • artifact captioning • hyperlinks

Stage 3—Learning Plan
Summary of Key Learning Events and Instruction • Appointment of an ePortfolio Exploratory Committee • Identifying stakeholder needs

Figure 4.1. Backward design template for an institutional ePortfolio program.

Adamantly opposed to prescriptiveness as ePortfolio practitioners, we are not putting forth this design as a blueprint for any institution. Its purpose is merely to show an efficient way for four-year colleges to address the 5Ws and the H we have outlined in this chapter. We hold that "ePortfolio" defines an ethos, which extends far beyond "an/the ePortfolio" in any form. Different methodologies merge in proved techniques because good teaching is just good teaching, regardless of learning styles and exceptionality. ePortfolio is no exception.

Conclusion

Hindsight is 20/20, and as we look back on our attempts to establish a meaningful and thriving institutional ePortfolio program, we can easily identify the "should-haves" and "would-haves" of our didn't-do list, all of which, in reality, hindered the program from the start. Even with the top-down directive, appointment of an exploratory or steering committee comprised of cross-generational, cross-disciplinary, tech savvy teaching/research and academic support faculty, along with cadets, representatives from IT, and staff from the library might have assuaged the tension and frustration.

We understand that in today's environment, the omnipresence of ePortfolios in higher education, together with the number of software programs on the market, have short-circuited a great number of the issues we faced a decade ago and have discussed in this chapter. But in other cases, the same types of challenges exist, prompted by the budgetary exigencies of student services, academic and non-academic support, together with the costs of sustainability and ultimately survival for many four-year colleges.

The financing of a sustainable, compelling institutional undergraduate ePortfolio represents one of many considerations that colleges should include in the backward design of a viable program. "Understandings" and "essential questions" defined by the principal stakeholders, even in the case of mandated goals or standards, will facilitate the discussion during the exploration phase. Defining what students will know about the ePortfolio (declarative knowledge) and what they will be able to do with their ePortfolio ensures the minimal required standardization, but also allows students to exploit the affordances of ePortfolio publication interdisciplinarity without violating disciplinary boundaries.

In sum, the endless possibilities of ePortfolios leave the door open to creativity in all aspects of exploration, adaptation, implementation, assessment, and revision, even funding. Starting small with an open door and representation of all stakeholder groups facilitates implementation and ensures a plan for dealing with the inevitable challenges to sustainability.

References

Bowen, R. S. (2017). Understanding by design. Vanderbilt University Center for Teaching. https://cft.vanderbilt.edu/understanding-by-design/.

Butrymowicz, S. (2017). *Most colleges enroll many students who aren't prepared for higher education.* The Hechinger Report. https://hechingerreport.org/colleges-enroll-students-arent-prepared-higher-education/.

Desrochers, D. M. & Hurlburt, S. (2016). Trends in college spending: 2003–2013 where does the money come from? Where does it go? What does it buy? American Institutes for Research. https://www.air.org/resource/trends-college-spending-2003-2013-where-does-money-come-where-does-it-go-what-does-it-buy.

Education Reform Now (2016). Americans spending at least $1.5 billion in college remediation course: Middle class pays the most. https://edreformnow.org/accountability/release-americans-spending-at-least-1-5-billion-in-college-remediation-courses-middle-class-pays-the-most/.

Escandell Montiel, D. (2014). *Escrituras para el siglo XXI. Literatura y blogosfera.* Iberoamericana-Vervuert.

Eynon, B., Gambino, L. M. (2017). *High-Impact ePortfolio practice: A catalyst for student, faculty and institutional learning.* Stylus; AAC&U.

Hechlinger Report. (2018, May 17). Making the case for liberal arts. *U.S. News and World Report.* https://www.usnews.com/news/education-news/articles/2018 -05-17/liberal-arts-programs-struggle-to-make-a-case-for-themselves.

Jimenez, L., Sargrad, S., Morales, J. & Thompson, M. (2016, September 28).The cost of catching up. Center for American Progress. https://www.americanprogress .org/issues/education-k-12/reports/2016/09/28/144000/remedial-education/.

Kwai, I. (2016, October). The most popular office on campus. The Atlantic. https:// www.theatlantic.com/education/archive/2016/10/the-most-popular-office-on -campus/504701/.

Mullaney, W. P. (2018, March 7). What we talk about when we talk about "Faculty buy in." Academic Briefing. https://www.academicbriefing.com/leadership /skills-and-development/talk-talk-facuity-buy/.

National Center for Education Statistics (2018). Undergraduate retention and gradu-atiob rates. U.S. Department of Education. https://nces.ed.gov/programs/coe /indicator_ctr.asp.

Penn, Arthur (Director). (1970). *Little Big Man* [Film]. Cinema Center Films and Stockridge-Hiller Productions.

Reilly, K. (2018). Record numbers of college students are seeking treatment for depression and anxiety—But. schools can't keep up. Time. https://time.com /5190291/anxiety-depression-college-university-students/.

7 Ps (military adage). (2019, August 14). Wikia. https://military.wikia.org/wiki/7_Ps _(military_adage).

White, E. M. (2005). The scoring of writing portfolios: Phase 2. *College Composition and Communication, 56*(4), 581–600.

Wiggins, G. P. & McTighe, J. (2007). Schooling by design: Mission, action, and achievement. Association for Supervision and Curriculum Development.

Wolf, M. (2007, September 6). Socrates' nightmare. New York Times. http://www .nytimes.com/2007/09/06/opinion/06iht-edwolf.4.7405396.html.

Appendix. Troubleshooting the VMI ePortfolio

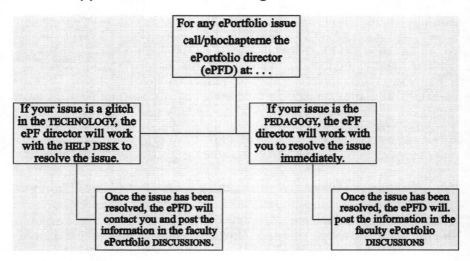

Chapter 5. Expanding Pedagogies: The Productive Tensions of ePortfolio Pedagogies and Peer Consultant Specialists in the Twenty-first Century Writing Center

Deidre Anne Evans Garriott
UNIVERSITY OF SOUTH CAROLINA

In the summer of 2014, when I arrived to begin my first tenure-track appointment at the Virginia Military Institute (VMI), which included a position as the coordinator of the writing center, I learned I would also coordinate the college's ePortfolio initiative. Therefore, in addition to revitalizing a writing center in disrepute, I would also need to learn about and integrate ePortfolio pedagogy, *assessment*, and best practices into the writing center. Although my academic background is in rhetoric and composition and I had prior experience with assessment, I had not used or learned about ePortfolios during my graduate coursework. It is an understatement, then, to say that this new addition to my job induced anxiety. And I dealt with that anxiety in the way most academics do: through research.

While research on ePortfolios as assessment tools is plentiful, I did not find much that discussed the intersection of ePortfolios and writing center pedagogies. Debates surrounded assessment, effectiveness, and digital literacy, but I needed insight into ePortfolios as a part of writing-across-the-curriculum (WAC) pedagogies; equally importantly, I struggled with considering how to marry this writing center's pedagogy of non-directive, non-evaluative consultations with what first appeared to be a medium in which students and faculty would require directive help. By "directive help," I mean that students and faculty needed help not just with the concept of ePortfolios but also with how to use the WordPress interface, which cannot be taught through traditional writing center pedagogies and must be taught through directive tutoring, which I distinguish from consulting, which I suggest is non-directive in practice.[1]

---

1. In directive tutoring, tutors direct students through the session; in other words, tutors tell students what to do. In non-directive tutoring, or consultations, tutors engage in various methods, including the Socratic, to help students learn how to improve their own work. In writing centers, non-directive tutoring may look like consultants providing reader-response reactions (e.g., "As a reader, I interpret this passage as . . .") or asking questions. They may also teach and model rhetorical strategies for students to practice in a session. The purpose of non-directive tutoring is to emphasize learning rather than prescriptive answers.

DOI: https://doi.org/10.37514/PRA-B.2020.1084.2.05

More specifically, the overwhelming majority of the student and faculty populations had little to no experience with WordPress web platforms, despite excellent efforts in the past by several previous ePortfolio directors to create buy-in and provide basic literacy of the platform. Therefore, whatever staff I would hire would seemingly violate the VMI Writing Center's pedagogy (which previous administrators had established as non-directive before I had arrived) by directly telling clients where to go and what to click on the dashboard. VMI's stringent, single-sanction honor code informs this non-directive approach as well. Cadets agree to live and submit work as outlined in the honor code and a policy called "work for grade." The honor code states that cadets will not tolerate lying, cheating, or stealing, while "work for grade" policies provided by the institute, departments, and instructors outline approved avenues for student support. Editing and proofreading are not permitted avenues. In writing center practices, editing and proofreading are considered directive practices. Telling students what to write or writing content for them is both directive and forbidden for students to seek out. Therefore, the VMI Writing Center does not provide such services; however, integrating ePortfolio instruction into the writing center complicated the center's alignment of the honor code and work for grade policies and the center's own pedagogy, because consultants would need to engage in directive tutoring when telling cadets how to use the interface.

In this chapter, I discuss the successes and failures of coordinating a team of peer consultants to facilitate the expansion of ePortfolios at a small liberal arts college. I will argue that peer consultants can be effective ePortfolio ambassadors to faculty and students and, with the appropriate continuing training and engagement, effective consultants of digital portfolios in writing centers. Moreover, integrating ePortfolios expands a writing center's scope as a student resource into the digital realm, which, for centers still focused on traditional, print-based papers, can help introduce tutors, students, and faculty to digital pedagogies and environments. Additionally, I assert that integrating ePortfolio pedagogies and outcomes into writing centers creates opportunities for writing center administrators (WCAs) and consultants to confront and challenge the tensions between directive and non-directive pedagogies and discover ways of wedding the two practices.

Peer Consultants, ePortfolios, and Disrupting Writing Center Pedagogies

Peer consultants hold a contested place at VMI, although less so within the broader field of writing center scholarship and pedagogy. The college's mission celebrates providing opportunities for leadership for their students, or cadets. In its preparation to build cadets into "citizen soldiers," VMI purports that its aim "is to produce men and women educated for civilian life and also prepared to serve their country in the Armed Forces. . . . All cadets participate in service opportunities at some point during their cadetship. Classroom experiences and hands-on participation in community projects give cadets an awareness of the importance of service to others" (Civic Engagement, 2018). Faculty and cadets were skeptical, however, of the integration of cadet consultants into the VMI Writing Center, despite their academic background acquired through completion of a three-credit "Teaching Writing" course and ongoing pedagogical training while working in the writing center. Because of the faculty's general resistance to ePortfolios and peer consultants, I expected increased skepticism directed toward a team of cadet consultants who specialized in WordPress ePortfolios.

Peer consultants, however, are a staple of writing centers.[2] The International Writing Centers Association annual convention and its regionalized publication, *Southern Discourse*, elevate undergraduate tutors and their labor in writing centers. In "Training and Using Peer Tutors" (1978), Paula Beck, Thom Hawkins, and Marcia Silver, with contributions by Kenneth Bruffee, Judy Fishman, and Judith Matsunobu, call integrating peer consultants in writing centers "the promising 'new' way of applying the principles of collaborative learning" into traditional learning environments (p. 432). Ongoing research into peer tutors both validates the importance of peer consultants' presence in writing centers and extends this research into questions of peer authority in writing centers and the academy.[3]

In the VMI Writing Center under my leadership, peer consultants epitomized the learner-teacher identity that writing centers often develop among their staffs. First, it is important to note that writing center scholars Steven J. Corbett (2005), Peter Carino (2003), Patricia Rizzolo (1982), Teagan Decker (2005), and Melissa Ianetta and Laura Fitzgerald (2012), among others, have acknowledged the uncomfortable paradox of peer tutors, noting that while writing centers seek to destabilize hierarchies, consultants still often rely on traditional models of authority to bolster their own ethos in writing centers and to build trust during consultations. Moreover, several scholars have critiqued nondirective tutoring as a myth of writing center dogma, especially in peer consultations. In "Power and Authority in Peer Tutoring" (2003), Carino parses the slipperiness of nondirective

---

2. In this chapter, I will use "consultant(s)" rather the "tutor(s)" to refer to non-administrative writing center employees. I use this term because it is consistent with the workplace titles used in the writing center I coordinated. Moreover, because consultants' work extends beyond tutoring of prescriptive rules of grammar and mechanics and because consultants do not own a students' work and are not "correctors," the word "consultant" better implicates the study and practice of writing center laborers. When I use the words "tutor" or "tutoring," or its variants, I suggest the directive pedagogical models in which the tutor directs the tutee through prescriptive processes.

3. For additional reading about peer authority in writing centers, see Steven J. Corbett's (2005) chapter "Bringing the Noise: Peer Power and Authority" in *On Location: Theory and Practice in Classroom-Based Writing Tutoring* edited by Candice Spigelman and Laurie Grobman and Peter Carino's (2003) chapter "Power and Authority in Peer Tutoring" in Michael A. Pemberton and Joyce Kinkead's collection, *Center will Hold*. I draw from both of these chapters throughout my argument here.

peer tutoring, suggesting that nondirective tutoring practices—or at least claims of practicing them—mystify and obscure the intersections of authority, ownership, and hierarchies that exist in writing center work.[4]

On the surface, such a discussion may seem irrelevant to integrating ePortfolios into writing centers, but to me, it is a central issue. The writing center I coordinated at VMI adheres closely to the nondirective, nonevaluative pedagogies consistent with many small liberal arts colleges (SLAC) writing centers. It is so central to the center's core mission and unit description that many departmental faculty and students assume—and not without reason—that the VMI Writing Center does not provide assistance with lower-order concerns, such as grammar and mechanics. ePortfolios discomfit this position and the idea of "peerness" for a variety of reasons.

Part of this discomfiting that I note comes from how peer consultants will have to direct clients' navigation of the mechanics of setting up ePortfolios. Because setting up an ePortfolio requires a rote set of steps, tutors will have to use directive strategies with clients. Whether setting up an ePortfolio on a blog-based platform, such as WordPress, or on a learning management system (LMS), such as Canvas' internal ePortfolios, students and faculty creating their portfolios need to learn the correct ways to set up menus, posts, and pages, as well as attach media, among other actions. Such knowledge, in this case, requires directive and evaluative consultations in which the consultant (a peer, in the VMI Writing Center's case) tells other cadets what they need to do to begin to customize their ePortfolios. Because there are specific "clicks" that content-creators must make to build their portfolios, the consultant will tell the clients where to point and click—directive instruction at its finest.

I struggled with this conflict as a professional trained in non-directive pedagogies and as a writing center administrator (WCA) training her own staff in these pedagogical principles. I wondered how I could help the peer consultants balance clients' needs while staying true to our pedagogy and the spirit of the VMI Honor Code. Through multiple conversations with the ePortfolio team and by receiving my own consultations from cadets to teach me how to use Word-Press and build my own ePortfolio, I realized the answer was complex, yet obvious. First, the ePortfolio team I would cultivate would have to be directive in their consultations, at least when clients came with technical questions. Cadets need to know what to click to enable them to write a post. They need to know what to click to publish a post after they have written it. If they want a post to

---

4. For more critiques of peer consultants and nondirective pedagogies, read Shamoon and Burns' "A Critique of Pure Tutoring" (1995), Carino's "Power and Authority in Peer Tutoring" (2003), which provides an excellent literature review of the issue up to the early twenty-first century, Corbett's chapter "Bringing the Noise: Peer Power and Authority" in *On Location* (2005), and Lori Salem's "Decisions . . . Decisions: Who Chooses to Use the Writing Center?" (2016).

include media, they need to know how to add the media (much like one adds an attachment to an email). They need to know how to organize the posts and pages they have created into a menu. They need to know how to add media, especially Word documents and PDFs, to a post or page. They need to know what to do to edit a post. These are not questions that can be answered through the Socratic method or conversations about global concerns; they must be answered through a combination of telling and showing and learned through repetition. Thus, I had to loosen the restriction against directive tutoring.

The second part of the answer complicated the approach above by reintroducing traditional writing center pedagogies. Teaching web and ePortfolio design weds point-and-click tutorials and learning about global concerns, some of which we may rarely discuss in traditional, paper-based writing center consultations, such as navigation, layout, content arrangement, and visual rhetorics. We might talk about copyright with content borrowed from stock images, videos, gifs, and other digital files, adding more nuance to conversations about intellectual property and plagiarism. Hyperlinking and other tasks provide opportunities to make concepts such as Kenneth Burke's (1973) parlor[5] more concrete and prescient to twenty-first century audiences. As consultants work with cadets developing web sites and web content vis-a-vis ePortfolios, they may extend consultations into conversations about public content and digital identities. Consequently, as students approach graduation, they likely have developed opportunities for joint conversations with their faculty, career services, and writing centers about adapting their portfolios for the job market (see Polly et al., this collection).

Thus, ePortfolios can, under the right conditions and with the right training, offer new opportunities for writing centers. In addition to the opportunities I outlined earlier, I also assert that ePortfolios expand writing center pedagogy through training. When ePortfolios and, by extension, basic web design are integrated into writing centers' purview, WCAs have new avenues to discuss the relationships and differences between tutoring and consulting. In my experience, comparing approaches between tutoring students on learning how to use an interface with consulting on the global concerns of web design have helped peer consultants, in particular, understand the difference between tutoring and consulting and how to navigate between the two. Perhaps most importantly, the WCA will contribute to consultants' learning—and perhaps the WCA's as well—by adding digital literacies to their toolbox.

---

5. In *The Philosophy of Literary Form: Studies in Symbolic Action* (1973), Kenneth Burke introduces what scholars now call "the Burkean parlor." Through the metaphor of the parlor, Burke illustrates scholarship as an ongoing conversation that began before a student enters and will continue after the student leaves. The parlor helps students understand the importance of listening (or researching) to other voices and strategize ways to enter the conversation.

I want to pause here to remind readers that WCAs should not and cannot assume that twenty-first century consultants—whether they are younger Millennials or Generation Z—are fluent in digital literacies. The VMI Writing Center, for example, employs a staff across four generations—Baby Boomers, Generation X, Millennials, and Gen Z. Not surprisingly, the staff demonstrate varied digital literacies. One Gen X-er is skilled with digital tools, from Photoshop to web design. Several, though not all, of the Millennial peer consultants use social media platforms, especially Instagram, Snapchat, and Twitter, as well as word processing interfaces such as Microsoft Word; however, in my experience at this particular institution, students admit that they know to use these platforms only in basic ways. When I teach them applications that I consider "old" (i.e., something I learned as a college student myself in the early 2000s), they express surprise and, in a first-year writing class, students suggested that the college offer a for-credit course to teach them how to use common programs such as Word and Excel, as well as Google docs and Google drive.

I am illustrating here gaps that the WCA may need to fill through consultant training. Because WCAs should not assume that their peer consultants are literate in ePortfolio platforms and should acknowledge that they may be only superficially familiar with other software, WCAs should plan to provide introductory and ongoing training in the software and platforms students will use as they create and maintain their ePortfolios. In my case, I, too, had to learn along with the peer consultants and, sometimes, from them. For me, this was an exciting opportunity to demonstrate learning as a continuing and collaborative process. By sitting and learning among them, the WCA takes on "peerness" with the tutors; when two of the first members of the ePortfolio Cadet Team taught me how to build my own ePortfolio, they continued to destabilize the teacher-student relationship by tutoring me in the points-and-clicks I needed to complete the process and offering their advice for my content. Rather than create an uncomfortable situation between administrator-faculty and the student, this process allows the student to cultivate teaching skills and learn how to perceive their "clients" as people not in need of remediation but education. The educator learns to sit as a student, to ask questions, and to reengage with a role they may have long abandoned. Such events provide opportunities for reflection on the concept of "peerness," the WCA/consultant relationship, and peer authority in the writing center.

In "Bringing the Noise: Peer Power and Authority" in *On Location: Theory and Practice in Classroom-Based Writing Tutoring* (2005), Stephen J. Corbett reflects on his own participation in student peer groups as a tutoring administrator and first-year writing teacher. Corbett draws from Teagan Decker's concept of "meta-tutoring" to explain the results of his peer-teacher activity and its results. In "Diplomatic Relations: Peer Tutors in the Writing Classroom," Decker (2005) explains that even when instructors seek to help students learn how to give advice in peer-review situations, students often do not achieve the metadiscourse and actions needed to provide helpful advice. However, when peer writing consultants participate in these groups, students learn how to become tutors through "meta-tutoring" (p. 27). Corbett notes that by working in the classroom or within peer groups (which may include the teacher/administrator), peer consultants learn how to become better tutors through the modeling that happens in the group (see Terry & Whillock, this collection). Thus, Corbett notes, "[peer consultants] model for students and teachers how to talk about what they're learning" (2005, p. 109). I take Corbett's and Decker's observations further, suggesting that by working together with the WCA in peer groups where the consultants and WCAs learn together and explain ePortfolios to each other, both WCAs and peer consultants become better teachers.

Thus far, the only faculty-peer consultant relationship I have discussed is the one between the WCA and peer consultants. Yet it is likely that teaching faculty, too, will draw on ePortfolio peer consultants as resources, should they adopt ePortfolios into their curricula. For example, faculty did invite ePortfolio peer consultants to lead workshops during course meetings. Some faculty came to the writing center or invited an ePortfolio Cadet Team member to their offices to help them learn how to create and maintain their own portfolios. These opportunities to work with faculty, whether collaborating to design workshops or helping faculty feel more comfortable integrating portfolios into their own professional lives, redefine "peerness," as students transition into collaborators and developers.

Although I see the ePortfolio work providing opportunities for professional development and new opportunities to understand what "peer consultant" means, it would be unwise not to consider the ways that students and peer consultants will still be constrained by the realities of working in traditional higher educational environments. First, I feel it necessary to point out that while ideally students should have freedom and agency to design their ePortfolios in ways that represent the identities they want to project and that foster occasions for authentic reflection about learning (see Terry & Whillock and Coleman et al., this collection), students will still contend with faculty *rubrics* for their portfolios. By rubrics, here, I refer to the various requirements that instructors, departments, and other stakeholders may place on how students use their ePortfolios. For example, as of this writing, the VMI English department requires students to curate an "English Major Showcase" in compliance with various rules for collecting their work. Students must keep an archive of work from classes in their major (which, in this case, include art, art history, philosophy, as well as traditional literature, creative writing, and rhetoric courses encountered in most English departments). In their last year, students move work from their archives to their showcase. Additionally, the department requires students to add certain common documents to their ePortfolio, such as the reflective essay they write in response to their capstone project.

Additionally, in my experience,[6] instructors—especially those who are less familiar with web design and current practices to create content navigation—often dictate how students should set up class portfolios. This tendency is even more evident for instructors who do not understand that a student may use their single ePortfolio platform to house multiple course portfolios; these instructors therefore write rubrics that govern how students design their entire portfolio, which often will lead to students creating an ePortfolio dedicated to one class only. Thus, while there may be no one "right way" to organize a website, students may have to adapt their plans to fit instructors' expectations for their portfolios. In these cases, peer consultants will likely help students negotiate digital assignments in much the same way they help students navigate their goals with instructors' expectations in traditional written assignments.

Despite such challenges when negotiating relationships with peer clients, WCAs, and faculty, peer consultants who specialize in ePortfolios in writing centers have unique opportunities to build confidence and model academic conversations for their peers. Corbett (2005) argues as much when he discusses Kenneth Bruffee's scholarship on collaboration and peer tutoring. Corbett posits that students who negotiate directive and nondirective approaches to consultations with students, faculty, and administrators are a different breed: "But it takes a directive, confident tutor to be able to share valuable information with students and teachers. A tutor satisfied with playing a strictly minimalist role may learn a lot but lose out on important opportunities to teach" (2005, p. 110). Corbett concludes that confidence and teaching include, but are not limited to, directive informational transactions. I concur with Corbett that these traits benefit all the constituents involved in the educational relationship, and I go further to suggest that ePortfolios provide a rich avenue wherein students can more easily navigate the tensions between directive and nondirective practices, develop confidence, and complicate—in positive ways—the relationships among students, faculty, and administrators.

Peer Tutors as ePortfolio Ambassadors

Writing center scholarship has increasingly advocated for empowering peer tutors by extending to them authority and collegial status both in their centers[7] and in higher education. Molly Wingate reminds us in "Writing Centers as Sites of Academic Cultures" (2001) that "a writing center is full of talented, bright, and academically serious people" and that, because of the qualities that writing center employees bring to the university, they enrich "the academic culture of

---

6.   Which is, admittedly, limited and influenced by my time as a WCA at a military-styled college.

7.   I would suggest here that peer consultants, especially at SLACs, are already afforded such collegiality and status in their centers, in the most general terms.

our schools by getting more people engaged in the academic enterprise of critical thinking and writing" (p. 8). This is especially true of peer tutors, who bring to their centers and classrooms models of students enacting academic cultures for their peers to study.

Modeling, as I have discussed earlier, is critical work of peer consultants. Corbett (2005) explains, "When tutors enter classrooms, they can bring profound knowledge of how to maneuver within disciplinary discourses" (p. 110). By extension, when peer consultants come to classrooms to teach ePortfolios to their peers, they can speak from experience about the challenges of building ePortfolios to please multiple audiences and fulfill various strictures (see Terry & Whillock, this collection).

Beyond these benefits, peer consultants can help create buy-in (see Richardson et al. and Summers et al., this collection), much in the same way they do in their traditional roles in writing centers. This is especially true, I would argue, at SLACs. In their article "SEUFOLIOS: A Tool for Using ePortfolios as Both Departmental Assessment and Multimodal Pedagogy" (2016), Ryan S. Hoover and Mary Rist remind readers that students adopt ePortfolios more readily when they recognize the usefulness of technology. Administrators' and instructors' insistence that ePortfolios are useful rarely persuades students that they are, indeed, relevant and valuable to them.

This is where peer intervention—or ambassadorship—proves useful. Peer consultants who have bought into ePortfolios and are excited by them can help generate interest among their peers. Peer consultants interrupt the administrator- and instructor-centric approaches to talking about and marketing ePortfolios to students. Perhaps most importantly to students, peer advocacy distances ePortfolios from many administrators' end goal—assessment. Moreover, peer ambassadorship centers the student as part of the process rather than the instructor, administrator, or abstract goals.

Ideally, through this student-centered process of ePortfolio creation, students will develop a sense of ownership over their ePortfolios. At St. Edward's University, Hoover and Rist (2016) report that their student population feels that sense of ownership over their WordPress ePortfolios, despite the fact that the university has shifted interest to LinkedIn profiles. Again, this is why I made students, rather than me, the faces of ePortfolio at VMI. Cadets own very little at VMI and have even fewer opportunities for individualism and self-expression. ePortfolios provide cadets with opportunities to develop public personas apart from their cadetship and think of themselves as part of larger communities. While VMI is a unique educational environment that encourages homogeneity, many colleges and universities would benefit from providing opportunities for students to develop and control ePortfolios in which they develop individual expression outside of classroom expectations. As noted previously, researchers at St. Edwards, a college VMI's population would call "ordinary" and that does not have an orientation towards homogeneity, have identified benefits from students' sense of ownership over their ePortfolios. Differentiating themselves from other students likely creates parallels with social media, where users may often customize their accounts, and could serve them well on the job market when they need to set themselves apart from other candidates.

Additionally, peer leadership, such as the ePortfolio Cadet Team in VMI's Writing Center, can complement an institution's commitment to peer leadership. Despite the uncertainty about adding peer consultants to the VMI Writing Center's staff, such positions are essential to student development as leaders and teachers. Moreover, peer-driven ePortfolio resources (see Appendixes) allow students to think about their own positionality as learners, not just students, and as teachers within a community of learners. In their ambassadorships of ePortfolios, they share the teaching stage with instructors, lead new trends in using the media, and help the WCA keep abreast of student perceptions of ePortfolios. Ambassadors, of course, unite two communities through their work.

Approaches: Successes, Challenges, Failures, and Suggestions

Building a community of ePortfolio student consultants and seeking to bridge multiple communities is challenging work, and it certainly comes with its stories of successes and failures. I have shared at length my advocacy for employing students as ePortfolio consultants and the benefits I saw emerging from their work. But it is important to discuss practical matters, including the challenges, failures, and successes the team and I experienced, and the new approaches I identified for future cadet teams.

Successes: Resource Creation and Curation

Because of my inexperience with WordPress and ePortfolios, I needed people in the Writing Center to offer support; additionally, those people needed to help me learn WordPress design while I *curated* and shared ePortfolio research with them. Moreover, the support people needed to be familiar with VMI's distrust of online platforms. Based on these factors, I decided to recruit an "ePortfolio Cadet Team" to the Writing Center staff. They would not consult on written documents because they did not have the course work to qualify for a writing consultant position, but they would help their peers design ePortfolios in response to instructors' assignments.

The team, especially in its first two years, was particularly successful in creating new and updating existing tutorials, adding to the wealth of multimedia resources that the previous ePortfolio Director, Howard B. Sanborn, had created. The first two cohorts of the team, each led by an "ePortfolio Cadet Team Manager," bonded together as they wrote and curated a variety of resources for student audiences. The cadets learned to write instruction sets, include illustrations vis-a-vis screenshots, and anticipate audience questions. These two cohorts were particularly invested in the ePortfolio project; it was used for X-designated "civ-ilizations and cultures courses" (see Sanborn & Ramirez, this collection), which cadets took across the curriculum, and they had mastered the prescribed reflec-tive essay required at the end of all such courses at VMI. Many of these ePortfolio peer consultants demonstrated independent curiosity about digital humanities. Two cadets in particular, both English majors, used some of their personal time and scheduled shifts to learn coding independently to enhance their ePortfolios. One of these cadets has even secured a career in the digital humanities.

This success crystallizes the importance of curiosity and initiative as ideal qualities for strong ePortfolio peer consultants. These students were enthusiastic about spearheading a new initiative and being the first of a new cohort of consul-tants in a reinvigorated writing center. These students also had previous experi-ence with the WordPress platform and were eager to teach each other what they learned as they developed their resources and researched the FAQs for the plat-form. These cadets had also taken Digital Rhetorics or other courses that included theories and practices with respect to the digital humanities. This means that they had already studied theories, trends, and practices that would serve them in the writing center, similar to the three-credit writing pedagogy course the peer writ-ing consultants take before applying for their positions. These students brought their prior experiences and education to bear on resource creation.

The English department also included this cohort in discussions about assess-ment; thus, even when the peer consultants disagreed with the way the English department wanted to proceed with using ePortfolios (and disagree they did), they understood firsthand the rationale behind the tasks they were assigned and had opportunities to ask questions of the departmental assessment committee about resources rather than have those questions and answers mediated through the WCA. These students thus felt included in decision-making (see Richardson et al., this collection), even when the committee decided to take directions other than the ones the peer consultants recommended, and they understood their role in producing resources for both cadet and faculty audiences.

Failure: Training

While the initial two cohorts had great success, which I mostly credit to their own initiative and experiences, I learned more from them than I wager they learned from me. Over the years, new members joined the team. Many of these students were more interested in working in the writing center in general than expand-ing the existing ePortfolio resources or singling themselves out as ePortfolio peer consultants. I want to point out here that I do not blame this attitude on the cadets. I believe I generated this attitude when I sought to recruit more broadly and intended training sessions to make up for gaps in background knowledge. The problem, here, rested on the absence of curiosity and interest in ePortfolios and/or web design.

With the third cohort, I scheduled regular meetings for training and discussion. I oriented training from a purely instructor-centered and academic approach because this team was less familiar with ePortfolios and I was interested in introducing them to pedagogy. These cadets were supposed to read scholarship I had gleaned from writing center publications to introduce the tensions between directive and nondirective practices I had anticipated and addressed with previous cohorts, and to provide research about ePortfolios and assessment, as well as the digital humanities. Regrettably, I often had to cancel the biweekly, evening meetings because the cadets had competing obligations that interfered with our training sessions. When we did meet, the peer consultants were focused on my agenda for meetings rather than their own questions and experiences. Additionally, these students were not using ePortfolios in any of their own courses; thus, their investment in ePortfolios was lower than the first cohort that had designed ePortfolios in many of their own previous courses. The academic curriculum I designed for training thus focused the cadets on scholarship over their own experiences and questions. While I would, in the future, continue to introduce ePortfolio peer consultants to writing center work with traditional readings, such as Stephen North's seminal work, "The Idea of a Writing Center" (1984), and consultant training texts, I would also make student concerns and expertise central. Furthermore, I would try to motivate curiosity and interest among the team. Because I directed the meetings, I did not carve out opportunities for cadets to contribute their insights or to explore ePortfolios beyond the topics of pedagogy and assessment.

In hindsight, I realized that the third cohort of cadets also did not recognize what they were contributing to the writing center and institution, both in terms of progressing ePortfolios and providing academic support. The first two cohorts had already written the most-consulted resources, so the third cohort did not have an obvious gap in resources to fill and to occupy their time. Additionally, in training, I too had difficulty explaining what they were adding to our existing archive of resources and what they were contributing that was new and original, especially in light of the decline of interest in ePortfolios outside of the English major and a few select instructors in other departments. The department's assessment committee had also stopped inviting the ePortfolio peer consultants to assessment meetings; therefore, I would report back to them decisions made about them and their work by the committee. These cadets consequently had minimal agency as decision makers and contributors to the ePortfolio initiative, the department, and writing center work. Without concrete goals for development and engagement in institutional conversations, the students were aimless. I blame my leadership for this.

Suggestions

First and foremost, I want to advocate for stronger digital pedagogical training for peer consultants specializing in ePortfolios. I advocated unsuccessfully that the VMI Writing Program should require students interested in working as ePortfolio consultants to take the 200-level Digital Rhetorics course, so that cadets hired in the writing center would have backgrounds both in using digital media to create content and in responding to peers in partnerships or groups. In my mind, this is the minimum requirement for students interested in working as ePortfolio consultants in writing centers.

The importance of course work cannot be understated because it provides essential pedagogical and experiential foundations for future peer consultants. Drawing from Joanna Goode (2010) and Lindsey Jesnek (2012), Joy Bancroft (2016) reminds readers that with the myth of the problematically-termed "digital native" debunked, higher education instructors cannot and should not assume that students in their courses have encountered explicit and directive instruction on using the technologies that they will be required to use, and they are not likely to encounter such education in a higher education classroom.

Prospective peer consultants should be introduced to learning and composing in digital environments. I suggest, too, that the WCA should be the instructor-of-record for any gateway course for peer ePortfolio consultants, and the instructor should require the creation of an ePortfolio as part of course requirements and integrate outcomes and aims connected to ePortfolio assessment in their syllabus. ePortfolio integration in a course on digital composition should include transparent discussions about pedagogy. In addition to developing basic design and writing skills, the course assignments should engage students in research about digital environments.

In addition to coursework as a prerequisite, I would suggest that WCAs require that students submit their own ePortfolios and reflections of them as part of the application process. Thus, the WCA and whatever consultants confer with them to make hiring decisions would have evidence of proficiency. Such a requirement would encourage student applicants who are interested in digital humanities and student resource work. I would couple this submission requirement with mock tutorials, which I would suggest for all recruiting interviews. Rather than "screening out" potential consultants, this process would allow the WCA to identify applicants' strengths and areas for development in order to build a community in which staff members complement each other and help each other grow as professionals.

To foster curiosity, the WCA should ask prospective peer ePortfolio consultants to consider how their research from their previous coursework and experiences might contribute to the writing center's body of knowledge about ePortfolios, digital topics relevant to undergraduate students, and to their own professional development. Thus, the WCA could help the prospective consultant align the job not just with consulting but with professional development and continuing education. The WCA should work with new ePortfolio consultants to identify unique areas of ePortfolio or digital learning for the consultant to research as a focus of their professional development while also including the consultant as a facilitator in the staff's training.

Secondly, I suggest that WCAs strongly encourage ePortfolio peer consultants to take writing pedagogy courses. To me, such coursework is critical because at VMI the cadets who had not taken the writing pedagogy course could not consult on written work, such as reflective pieces. They were not allowed to offer consultations on actual content, that is, because if they had not taken the course, they were not allowed to offer responses to other students' writing. Therefore, cadets' work with their peers' ePortfolios was limited to directive sessions on using the platform and dialectic conversations about the global concerns of web design. In other words, they were limited to directive tutoring about using the interface and could not extend their conversations to address the ePortfolio written content.

Training must include presentation and large-group workshop training. VMI prides itself on its one-credit public speaking course (also offered through the English department) as a core requirement for all cadets; however, we should not assume that peer consultants are ready for classroom visits even if they are the brightest students or the sharpest peer reviewers in our courses. These training sessions should draw from the meta-tutoring and collaborative peer response group models Decker (2005) and Corbett (2005) discuss in their respective chapters in *On Location*. Training that draws from ePortfolio, digital literacy, writing center, and WAC pedagogies cultivates opportunities for consultants to encounter an array of pedagogical possibilities and develop an innovative approach to consulting that is more flexible than traditional writing center pedagogies. Consultants should also receive training in effective public speaking and presentations. Then, with the WCA, they can facilitate script writing and presentation materials while developing their individual teaching identities. The writing center, then, becomes the metaphorical and intellectual

> bridge as a location inhabited by bodies and minds [, which] better describes new media writing where the reader/participant does not approach the text from without, but from the center, from within. The bridge as a dwelling, however, further describes the reader/participant's ability to pause and reflect and to claim that location as a place of social connection and pleasure. (Davidson, 2018, pp. 76–77)

Through training and research, the WCA can help the consultants build and inhabit this bridge and invite the campus community to visit this dwelling place.

Moreover, writing centers need technology to make them flexible spaces for ePortfolio consultations. In addition to computers with fast network and Wi-Fi speeds, the computers must come equipped with software necessary for photo, video, and podcast editing and production, as well as graphic design software. All of the software I mention is necessary for basic and advanced content development, and learning to use and teach these programs will enhance the consultants' digital literacies and pedagogical offerings as consultants. Facilities at VMI included two studios in the library that had been locked and inaccessible to cadets for some time and an additional lab in the computer information sciences department, but both spaces are located in buildings separate from the writing center. Students could check out hardware and use software for projects, but the lab had to be scheduled for appointment times and accessed with a faculty keycard. Cadets who wanted to include multimedia work had to go to multiple departments before they could come to the Writing Center for support, which is why I suggest that WCAs have a small collection of hardware and software in the writing center space to support students.

Conclusion

Peer consultants are clearly valuable members of writing center communities. Integrating ePortfolio peer consultants, who specialize in helping peers and faculty with building and maintaining ePortfolios, adds layers of nuance and complexity to writing center practice. As ambassadors for ePortfolios and the face of writing centers' digital opportunities, peer consultants can chart new territory by creating new collaborations and professionalizing themselves as novice teachers. ePortfolios as medium and text challenge existing pedagogies and practices and challenge writing center administrators to reassess the interplay between directive and nondirective pedagogies. Adding ePortfolio peer consultants to this mix carves out new possibilities for writing center work, professional development, student leadership, and campus outreach. Unsettling the writing center produces new avenues for training, pedagogies, and student ownership of campus resources and their work.

At VMI, ePortfolios have not been widely accepted or adopted across the curriculum, for a variety of reasons I will not explore here. My colleagues editing and contributing to this book, particularly Dr. Dellinger and Dr. Sanborn, have adopted varied and engaging uses for ePortfolios in their courses, and the English, Rhetoric, and Humanistic Studies department, the department with which I was affiliated, is moving forward with Canvas LMS-based ePortfolios for their mandatory "English Major Showcase" ePortfolios. The peer consultants who specialize in ePortfolios have uncertain roles in the VMI Writing Center, but I am hopeful that they will continue to exist as a team in some form after the department transitions from WordPress to Canvas ePortfolios. Regardless of their future at VMI, they have certainly disrupted pedagogy in the writing center in the very best ways by challenging outdated pedagogies and highlighting areas for potential growth and development for the space.

References

Bancroft, J. (2016). Multiliteracy centers spanning the digital divide: Providing a full spectrum of support. *Computers and Composition, 41*, 46–55.

Beck, P., Hawkins, T., Silver, M., Bruffee, K. A., Fishman, J. & Matsunobu, T. J. (1978). Training and using peer tutors. *College English, 40*(4), 432–449.

Burke, K. (1973). *The philosophy of literary form: Studies in symbolic action*. University of California Press.

Carino, P. (2003). Power and authority in peer tutoring. In B.A. Pemberton & M. A. Kinkead (Eds.), *The center will hold* (pp. 96–113). Utah State University Press.

Civic Engagement (2018). Virginia Military Institute. https://www.vmi.edu/cadet-life/civic-engagement/.

Corbett, S. J. (2005). Bringing the noise: Peer power and authority. In C. Spigelman & L. Grobman (Eds.), *On location: Theory and practice in classroom-based writing tutoring* (pp. 101–111). Utah State University Press.

Davidson, C. (2018). Reconstructing ethos as dwelling place: On the bridge of twenty-first century writing practices (ePortfolios and blogfolios). In R. Rice & K. St. Amant (Eds.), *Thinking globally, composing locally: Rethinking online writing in the age of the global internet* (pp. 72–92). Utah State University Press.

Decker, T. (2005). Diplomatic relations: Peer tutors in the writing classroom. In C. Spigelman & L. Grobman (Eds.), *On location: Theory and practice in classroom-based writing tutoring* (pp. 17–30). Utah State University Press.

Goode, J. (2010). Mind the gap: The digital dimension of college access. *The Journal of Higher Education, 81*(5), 583–618.

Hoover, R. S. & Rist, M. (2016). SEUFOLIOS: A tool for using ePortfolios as both departmental assessment and multimodal pedagogy. In W. Sharer, T. A. Morse, M. F. Eble & W. P. Banks (Eds.), *Reclaiming accountability: Improving writing programs through accreditation and large-scale assessments* (pp. 187–210). Utah State University Press.

Ianetta, M. & Fitzgerald, L. (2012). Peer tutors and the conversation of writing center studies. *The Writing Center Journal, 32*(1), 9–13.

Jesnek, L. M. (2012). Empowering the non-traditional college student and bridging the digital divide. *Contemporary Issues in Education Research (CIER), 5*(1), 1–8.

North, S. M. (1984). The idea of a writing center. *College English, 46*(5), 433–446.

Rizzolo, P. (1982). A successful writing program: Peer tutors make good teachers. *Improving College and University Teaching, 30*(3), 115–119.

Salem, L. (2016). Decisions . . . decisions: Who chooses to use the writing center? *The Writing Center Journal, 35*(2), 147–171.

Shamoon, L. K. & Burns, D. H. (1995). A critique of pure tutoring. *The Writing Center Journal, 15*(2), 134–151.

Wingate, M. (2001). Writing centers as sites of academic culture. *The Writing Center Journal, 21*(2) 2, 7–20.

Appendix A. Creating a Menu

Creating A Menu

Creating a menu helps you organize your blog, and it helps others navigate your blog. Menus will look different from each other and have different locations on the blog depending on the theme that you use. Some themes may allow you to use multiple menus on the same page. Try to keep your menus organized and easy to read. You can attach pages, categories, and links (including links to posts!) to a menu.

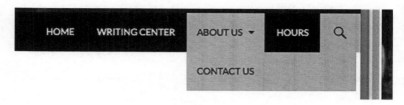

A Sample Menu

Getting to your Menu Workspace

1. Go to your **Dashboard**.
2. Hover over **Appearance.** Then click on **Menus.**
3. This is your menu workspace. From here you can enter a name for your menu (which is important if you maintain multiple menus), add content to your menu, and reorganize your menu.

Getting to the Menu Workspace

Adding a Page or a Category to Your Menu

1. Click either **Page** or **Category**, depending on what you want to add.
2. You will see a bank with all of your pages and categories. If you many, you may need to click **Search** and find the page or category by name.
3. Click the box next to the page/category you want to add.
4. Click Add to Menu.
5. Your menu item will now be in the menu workspace on the right.

Most Used | View All | Search

☐ Class and Homework Writings
☐ English Major Showcase
☑ ePortfolio Responses
☐ In Class Writings/Homework Writings
☐ Rhetorical Traditions
☐ Senior Capstone
☐ SP-204X

elect All   Add To Menu

Adding a Page or Category

Adding a Link (internal or external) to Your Menu

On your menu, you can link to an outside source, like another blog you are running. You can also link to a place within your own site, like the home page or a specific post.

1. To add a link to your menu, click **Links.**
2. In the text box labeled **URL,** enter the url of the website to which you're linking.
3. In the text box labeled **Link Text,** type what you want the link to appear as (ex. Home)
4. Click Add to Menu.
5. Your menu item will now be in the menu workspace.

Organizing Your Menu

Once you upload your menu items, it is very simple to organize them.

1. Just drag menu items around in the workspace to change the way that they are ordered.
2. To create a sub-heading on a menu item, just drag the item to the right beneath another menu item (see **Contact Us**) in the figure below.
3. To choose where your menu will be seen, check a box in theme locations. In many cases, the default menu location should be **Primary Menu**. If you are having problems getting your menu to work, this is usually what the problem is.

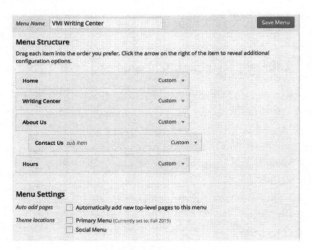

Organizing Your Menu

Appendix B. Inserting Media

Inserting media into your site positively reflects on you and makes the site more distinctive.

One way to insert media is by inserting pictures. Remember: ePortfolio is a social medium. You need to remember to use appropriate and professional Internet etiquette. In other words, only post appropriate pictures.

Inserting / uploading a picture into your post:

1. Sign into ePortfolio using your VMI Post View I.D.
2. On the left-hand menu, click "Dashboard."
3. From the Dashboard, scroll your mouse over to the top menu where it says "+NEW."
4. After hovering your mouse over "+NEW," a dropdown menu will appear. On that menu, you will see an option for "Post." Click "Post."
5. Now you will be in the new post page. On the menu above the text, box click on the "Add Media" button.
6. You should see two tabs: "Upload Images" and "Media Library." Click on "Upload Images." From here you can upload any image that you have saved onto your computer or other media (flash drive, Google drive, etc.).
7. After you have uploaded the image, click "Insert into Post" at the bottom right portion of the screen. Doing this will bring you back to the post page where your image should appear.
8. Make sure to click "Publish" or "Update."

By uploading images onto your post, you make your site better by engaging more with your view-ing audience on a personal level. Your profile stand out from the rest.

Appendix C. Using Comments

For your class, you may want to look at your peer's work and give them feedback on it through the comment system. This guide will teach you how to use the ePortfolio comments.

Posting a Comment

1. Navigate to either a page or a post on your peer's blog. (ex: sites.vmi.edu/smithjw12)
2. Select a post to which you want to respond. There should be a comment box near or underneath the post.
3. Fill in the comment box (location will vary depending on theme) and click post.
4. During this time you may be given the option to subscribe to the post which means you will receive e-mail notifications when others make posts after your.

Managing/Deleting Received Comments

Your peers can also make comments on your posts and pages. As the moderator of your blog, you can control what your peers can post. If you want to delete a comment from your post, you can do it from the page or post itself just by finding their post and clicking delete.

If you want to manage or approve comments on your blog you can do it through the comment manager:

1. Hover your mouse over "My Sites" and hover over the blog you wish to manage comments for.
2. Click "Manage Comments."
3. From here you can look at all the comments that on your posts and pages and approve/disapprove them, delete them, reply, or edit comments that you have already published.

Changing Comment Settings

While managing your ePortfolio site, you may decide that you want to change settings for comments made on your posts. However, we suggest that you use default settings.

1. Go to your dashboard and over your mouse over "Settings."
2. Click "Discussion."
3. You will now be able to view various privacy options for your comments on your blog.

Help

If you continue to experience any problems with making and managing your comments on posts and pages, please schedule an appointment with the Writing Center ePortfolio Team at https://vmi.mywconline.com/.

Appendix D. Exporting Your Blog After You Graduate

While at VMI, your blog exists on VMI's network where people need to have VMI network cre-dentials (username and password) to access your blog.

Upon graduating or leaving VMI, you may want to keep your blog as a net-working tool to show-case your past work, remember what you have done, or continue developing the work that you started at VMI.

To keep your blog when you leave VMI, you may create a new Wordpress blog, export your exist-ing VMI blog, and import the data from the VMI blog onto the new Wordpress blog you've creat-ed.

Creating a New Blog

Creating a new blog is easy and allows you a variety of options to customize your online identity and accessibility (e.g., privacy settings). Creating a new blog will separate you from the VMI sys-tem:

1. Go to https://wordpress.com
2. Enter your username/desired url into the text box and click "Create Website"
3. Fill out all of your personal information to make an account
4. Since you are no longer on VMI's system, you will no longer have all of the same accessibility options, memory, and functionality you had before and may choose to pay for a subscription.

Exporting Your Blog Information

You will now need to log into your VMI blog to export all of the information from it:

1. Hover your mouse over "My Sites."
2. Hover your mouse over the blog you wish to export information from.
3. Click "Dashboard"
4. Hover your mouse over the "Tools" icon
5. Click "Export"
6. From here, you can choose what you want to export and what you do not. You may decide you want everything, but you may run into the problem that you do not have enough memory to carry everything over onto your new blog. You will be given the opportunity to keep certain posts/categories and to choose certain types of content from a certain date range. (ex. Your first class year)

Chapter 6. Developing Learning-Centered Approaches across the Discipline: Implementing Curated ePortfolios in Information Technology and International Studies

Kathryn Coleman
University of Melbourne

Sophie McKenzie
Deakin University

Cai Wilkinson
Deakin University

Higher education has seen significant changes in the focus of digital learning, teaching, and *assessment* in the last decade. The shift has moved to focus on assessment *as* learning, rather than *of* learning, and to a more evidence-based understanding of assessment. In response to this shift, Deakin University recently engaged in a university-wide process of course/program[1] enhancement to offer anywhere, anytime learning to its learners. Deakin University's teaching and learning strategic goal presented in LIVE the future[2] (Oliver, 2015) tackled "course enhancement" by implementing an underpinning curriculum model and assurance of learning through aligned learning outcomes and *evidence-based assessment*. Course enhancement was a faculty-wide program of evaluation, graduate attribute alignment, innovative digital learning design, and academic development. Under the leadership of Professor Beverley Oliver, Deputy Vice-Chancellor (Education), and the Deakin Learning Futures team, this high-quality course enhancement was an innovative and groundbreaking university-wide approach to learning design, student experience, and higher education teaching. It allowed for a broad and wide-reaching program of deep professional learning for faculty to co-design and co-develop future focused, *authentic*, and digital learning, teaching and assessment programs. Commencing in late 2012, it was an initiative of Deakin's LIVE the Future: Agenda 2020 and led by a set of overarching and

---

1. In the Australian context, a course is a program of study leading to a degree and is made up of a number of units (courses), normally 24 in a three-year undergraduate degree.
2. LIVE is an acronym for Deakin's curriculum framework.

DOI: https://doi.org/10.37514/PRA-B.2020.1084.2.06

guiding principles. Course enhancement was "designed to ensure that courses are enhanced to enable graduates to be highly employable through unit and course experiences that are personal, relevant and engaging wherever learning takes place—on campus, in the cloud, in industry settings" (Course Enhancement Guidelines, 2015). LIVE the future stands for:

- *Learning*: Offer brilliant education where you are and where you want to go.
- *Ideas*: Make a difference through world-class innovation and research.
- *Value*: Strengthen our communities, enable our partners and enhance our enterprise.
- *Experience*: Delight our students, our alumni, our staff and our friends. (2016)

Course enhancement included *scaffolding* to facilitate the university's strategic goals. That same scaffolding also supported learners' efforts to show how their portfolios evidenced skills, experience, and knowledge that aligned to employer requirements.

The course enhancement process focused on key employability skills, or graduate learning outcomes, and how best to integrate these within courses and degree programs as learning outcomes (O'Brien & Oliver, 2013). Graduate learning outcomes are designed to align across knowledge, skills, and experiences that have been applied and demonstrated through assessment across a course or program and show what has been achieved to a range of audiences—including the learner. With a shift in both the language of assessment and an understanding of how learners demonstrate their learning, ideas, knowledge, experiences, and skills within programs for themselves and potential employers, ePortfolios emerged as a pedagogical tool for learning and assessment (see Sanborn & Ramírez, this collection). The construction and *curation* of learning evidence helps a student develop and sustain an authentic professional identity. This digital learning environment, along with opportunities for cloud learning[3] at Deakin University, provided us the space to design and develop ePortfolios for learning and assessment that presented a student's collected knowledge focused within a framework for employability (see Polly et al., this collection). The selection of the platforms allowed not only for the aggregation of *artifacts* in a wide range of formats, but also for the embedding of ongoing *reflection* through curation based on self-review, peer review, and peer assessment. This selection of platforms was an important factor to enable the sharing of the ePortfolio via social networks that related to the needs of the discipline in authentic contexts.

Deakin is a multi-campus university in Melbourne, Australia and uses the Desire2Learn Brightspace platform and embedded ePortfolio. The template of

---

3.   Cloud learning denotes an opportunity to teach, learn, and assess digitally, using digital pedagogies.

the Learning Management Space (LMS) is customized to suit the needs of the Deakin teaching and learning community and is called CloudDeakin. A small number of programs at Deakin have been using ePortfolios, for a range of purposes, more typically at the class and/or course level for small learning experiences. Through the course enhancement process, a growing number of programs have begun to adopt ePortfolios across their curriculum for evidencing learning to a range of stakeholders. This evidence of learning approach demonstrates the value of the ePortfolio as a pedagogical tool to support institutional change for learning-centered approaches.

The chapter explores our learning connections as a professional network of educators and researchers during the course enhancement process and presents how two pilot subjects at Deakin University embedded ePortfolio in two different disciplinary contexts: Information Technology and International Studies. These two ePortfolio pilots have since been integrated in the curriculum to assure learning outcomes in evidenced-based assessment, while facilitating career development learning and preparing learners for a rapidly changing future in the new knowledge economy.

Course/Program Enhancement at Deakin

Course enhancement opened a range of opportunities to approach curriculum design and development through a renewal of perspectives on learning, teaching, and assessment in all courses/programs at Deakin. It also enabled a multidisciplinary and transdisciplinary collaboration to learning design and a thorough critique of program learning outcomes using a *design-thinking* methodology. The focus on the program-wide approach invited all academics to plan, co-design, and implement an evidenced-based approach collaboratively rather than as individuals. This evidenced-based collective approach to program design, as a course team, presented particular opportunities to review how students demonstrate learning outcomes holistically through assessment across a program rather than focusing on a single unit or subject. Additionally, teaching teams invited a critical gaze on the quality and capacity of assessment design to provide evidence of program learning outcomes as the first point of reference for curriculum review. Importantly, teaching teams in higher education settings vary considerably in collaborative experiences of program renewal (Benjamin, 2000; Pegg, 2014; Savage & Pollard, 2014), and this may have some bearing on the extent of engagement with ePortfolios from a program perspective.

The course enhancement process included developing program coherence through course scoping and course (re)design. Course scoping consisted of the program being reviewed through a number of lenses, including an external review, learning analytics, and course and unit student and staff evaluations. Program needs were identified (school, faculty, professional accrediting bodies). These highlighted needs were then mapped for further exploration in the curriculum design (i.e., Australian Qualifications Framework[4] requirements, research needs, etc.) through the development of co-designed new program learning outcomes in alignment with the Deakin graduate learning outcomes. Finally, the program learning outcomes were aligned to discipline-specific professional standards (if any) and discipline threshold learning outcomes in order to create and define a set of minimum standards to evidence learning.

This collaborative exploration of new course design further extended the LIVE the Future: Agenda 2020[5] by structuring teaching and learning across all programs to align with the eight graduate learning outcomes. LIVE the Future: Agenda 2020, launched July 2012, encapsulates Deakin University's plan to bring the opportunities of the digital age into the real world of Learning, Ideas, Value, and Experience (LIVE). The course design included both cloud and located learning, teaching, and assessment with the learning design focusing on the alignment of assessment in each unit with learning outcomes, as well as resourcing the units and courses. Consequently, learning, teaching, and assessment center on the course rather than a collection of units or subjects.

ePortfolio at Deakin

Since 2014, Deakin's commitment to *portfolio thinking* and *integrative learning* has been shown by the continual uptake of ePortfolio into programs. Deakin's ongoing cultural change through learning and teaching and its focus on evidence in assessment for learning have provided impetus for faculty to further explore ePortfolio pedagogies. This shift in thinking at Deakin has allowed opportunities for exploration into the very nature of digital learning evidence for our students. To help support our understanding of ePortfolios in higher education, we consulted a range of practice-based research and evidence-based research on ePortfolios for learning and assessment to inform the learning design (Allen et al., 2012; Batson, 2013, 2014, 2015; Eynon et al., 2014; Hallam et al., 2008; Rhodes et al., 2014). In addition, we consulted research on ePortfolios for integrated learning (Huber & Hutchings, 2004; Peet et al., 2011), career development learning (Coleman et al., 2012), and graduate employability (McKenzie et al., 2014) to support the development of Deakin's ePortfolio pedagogy in these programs. Deakin University's commitment to both evidence-based portfolio pedagogy and assessment *as* learning has continued, with digital credentials making a significant impact on evidenced portfolios and digital *learning pathways* (Deakin Hallmarks, 2016; Gibson et al., 2016).

Deakin University is working within a *standards-based assessment* framework (Boud & Falchikov, 2006) and Constructively Aligned Learning Outcomes curricula (Biggs & Tang, 2011) to better ensure validity and reliability in

---

4.   A national system of qualifications encompassing all post-compulsory education.
5.   Deakin University's teaching and learning strategic plan.

assessment. Higher education institutions in Australia are accountable to the Higher Education Standards Framework (HESF) (2014), the Australian Qualification Framework (AQF), and the Tertiary Education Quality and Standards Agency (TEQSA), Australia's independent national regulator of the higher education sector. Standards-based assessment informs students of the criteria and performance standards used to judge their work. Standards-based assessment enables students to compare their learning evidence based on their achievement of the learning outcomes, which are designed to support the HESF and TEQSA criteria. Through alignment of learning outcomes and standards via engaging assessment, the course enhancement process at Deakin enabled a university-wide approach to develop clear and explicit processes for assessment as learning that support student experience in the cloud and on-location.

In this process, we reframed assessment as an opportunity for students to create evidence of their achievement of the Deakin graduate learning outcomes (see Figure 6.1) and demonstrate skills, experiences, and knowledge differently. As a result, all students are now encouraged to curate their learning evidence in an ePortfolio, whether it be an ePortfolio in CloudDeakin, a personal digital space, or a personally reflective professional social media ePortfolio created using Weebly, Wix, or LinkedIn.

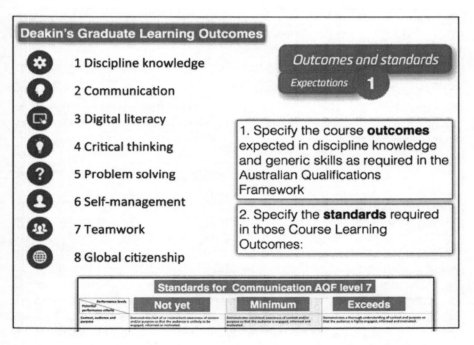

Figure 6.1. Deakin University's graduate learning outcomes framework.

Deakin's curriculum framework has four key aspects. Programs at Deakin are designed for:

- *Expectations*: outcomes and standards clearly signal expectations aligned with the Australian Qualifications Framework.
- *Evidence*: assessment tasks enable compelling evidence of outcomes and standards, focusing on graduate employability.
- *Experience*: inspiring educators offer personal, interactive, and engaging learning experiences and resources in cloud and located learning.
- *Enhancement*: emphasis is on the systematic evidence-based enhancement of courses.

Figure 6.1 demonstrates our key graduate learning outcomes (Oliver, 2014) and the ways in which these outcomes are constructed to reflect the high standards put forward in the Australian Qualifications Framework. ePortfolios are a major contributor to Deakin's ability to demonstrate student achievement of these outcomes.

Research Questions

As a part of the course enhancement process, the following research questions guided the qualitative, case study-driven research presented in this chapter:

- What does an ePortfolio for learning, assessment, and careers look like at Deakin?
- What is the value of an ePortfolio in our context for evidencing graduate learning outcomes? (see Figure 6.2)

Our case study into ePortfolio practice focused on students' ePortfolios in the Bachelor of Information Technology (BIT) and the Bachelor of International Studies (BIS).

Research Inquiry

To ensure the research critically engaged with what we knew about ePortfolios for learning, assessment, and careers, our approach considered *metacognition* (Wozniak & Zagal, 2013), personalized learning (Batson, 2015), and self-regulated learning (Pintrich et al., 2000) that were deemed necessary components of our program. To identify the value of ePortfolios at Deakin, we developed our own experiential and problem-based learning opportunity through a focus in the BIT and BIS programs. With support from the university via the course enhancement process, we co-designed and developed ePortfolios for learning, assessment, and careers through an iterative design process. The Stanford School *design thinking* methodology, as well as the stages set out by Morris and Warman (2015), best supported the learning design process, as well as the approach of this study. Design thinking has worked well in Deakin's interdisciplinary and cross-disciplinary approach to ePortfolio learning design and was key to the shared successes described in the case studies. We followed this five-step process to support our research:

1. *Empathize*: Through discussion, reflection, observation, and investigation of the terrain of ePortfolios in higher education, our research was based in the fields of ePortfolios for career development and employability, personalized learning, and evidenced-based learning through assessment.
2. *Define*: Through examination of a range of views and perspectives (POV) as a multidisciplinary team, we developed the learning design requirements to support a range of learners and learning needs.
3. *Ideate*: An iterative phase for learning design and research asks that all stakeholders bring their ideas to the table to be sorted through and reflected upon to collectively decide on the perceived needs for learning. In this instance, the collaborative ideation phase led to an iterative design and development of a range of prototype templates for the Bachelor of IT
4. *Prototype*: In a design-thinking process (Naiman, 2016), the prototyping requires an iterative implementation followed by a redesign to take into account evaluation and new ideation based on evidence from learning analytics (see Castaño & Nova, this collection). In this instance, it led to a new research question and focus on developing clearer pathways for ePortfolios as we reviewed the student feedback (from an ethics-approved research project) based on value to learning.
5. *Test*: Through our graduates, we examined what ePortfolios would look like collaboratively as a course in the BIS and BIT. This feedback and evaluation of the test led the team back to ideation and prototyping a new program design.

Figure 6.2. Deakin's underpinning curriculum model.

Our cyclic and design-thinking approach to curriculum development was supported by shared reflective practice that opened up new opportunities for learning design and a re-visioning of the research inquiry to suit individual and collaborative reflections. To address the research questions, we focused on a number of areas. First, we explored the language of ePortfolios from local, national, and international perspectives to look for overlaps, connections, contextual differences, and synergies. Secondly, we examined the different contexts and purposes of an ePortfolio (process, product, showcase, career/cv, assessment, learning, and journal). Thirdly, we focused on the varied pedagogy and technology needs in a range of sites. Over time it became apparent how discipline-specific (local) issues impacted not only the ways in which both faculty and students adopt ePortfolio, but also how they utilize ePortfolio for evidencing claims to learning.

To develop the local, national, and international language of ePortfolio, we made significant changes to learning design and assessment. These changes ensured appropriate and effective evidence mapping of student skills to learning outcomes could be reported in ePortfolios. Not only did students need to embrace the discipline-specific/local language of ePortfolio, they also needed to consider how to successfully reflect and build skills from a global perspective as graduates. The teaching and research team involved in this study agreed upon the importance of reflection towards successful ePortfolio creation (in any context); however, development of reflection within each discipline was a variable. Each discipline grappled with what reflection is, the action of curation as reflection, the reflection of intent, and whether reflection is an artifact (a piece of evidence) or something else altogether.

The following case studies highlight and explore examples from the BIT and BIS programs and demonstrate the local language of ePortfolio.

Case Study 1: Bachelor of Information Technology (BIT)

The BIT is a technically-oriented computing discipline with specialized majors such as Games Design and Development and Security, which are offered both online and on campus. At Deakin University, we introduced an ePortfolio in the BIT in 2012. At this time, the School of Information Technology regarded development of a professional portfolio (physical or electronic) as a useful tool to enhance students' career preparation, thus a campus-wide initiative to introduce ePortfolios began. Endeavors to support students in ePortfolio creation continue; however, it was from the early investigations into ePortfolio (in 2012) that the true nature and use of an ePortfolio in IT became apparent. The following case study summarizes the experiences of a student from IT in creating an ePortfolio and how it can be used as a careers and assessment activity.

Games Design and Development (GDD) is one particular IT discipline that requires curation and dissemination of an ePortfolio. As a competitive employment, the GDD environment requires that educational providers strongly support students' efforts to collate and present their skills and abilities in ePortfolios. Therefore, Deakin supports students to ensure career readiness and high levels of self-efficacy so they can negotiate the employment market. We rolled out an ePortfolio assessment model in the GDD classes at Deakin in 2012, with one class (called "Audio and Visual Game Elements") in particular focusing on the skills required for successful ePortfolio construction. Instructors required students to construct an ePortfolio based on the audio and visual game components developed during the teaching period. Progressive and final folio submissions as well as an oral presentation to demonstrate the ePortfolio work constituted the ePortfolio assessment model. The assessment epitomized a student-centered approach via progressive submission of ePortfolio assets with formative feedback and guidance provided throughout the teaching period. Progressive ePortfolio construction enabled a reciprocal, one-on-one feedback and discussion activity that prompted students to critically engage with gaps in their ePortfolios to improve future submissions. Figure 6.3 is an example of a final ePortfolio submission from the student in the class Audio and Visual Game Elements.

A critical part of the ePortfolio construction process in Audio and Visual Game Elements was the ability to reflect upon progress and act upon reflection to improve outcomes. Reflection allows students to refine their ePortfolio focus and requisite skills to achieve their goals. To assist the students in the class Audio and Visual Game Elements with the process of reflection, institutional stakeholders developed a set of resources in partnership with the student cohort.

Figure 6.3. A student ePortfolio example from Games Design and Development (published with permission).

The change to ePortfolio pedagogy as achieved in Audio and Visual Games Elements was new for many IT students, yet they highly appreciated how the ePortfolio provided individualized learning experiences. For example, one student commented in their end of class review: "I really liked the way the work was planned out, showing weekly progress was possibly the best way of me keeping up to date and getting the best out of my portfolio." In addition to such student comments, the grades show that student outcomes from the course since refinement have been higher, with High Distinction (HD) and Distinction (D) grades rising from 13% and 20% in 2011 to 20% and 28% respectively in 2012. The outcomes from using ePortfolios for assessment in Audio and Visual Game Elements proved positive. Students valued the institutional commitment to ePortfolio creation, as it facilitated their personalized learning and supported them in the development of relevant skills. In addition, the revised approach to assessment in Audio and Visual Game Elements reflected the requirements of the GDD industry (as confirmed by the School of IT industry advisory board), as it equipped students with a platform to demonstrate their skills beyond the final class grade. Furthermore, the approach allowed for greater alignment to unit (class) and program learning outcomes.

Other ePortfolio explorations have occurred in the School of IT in an effort to assist students in developing skills for successful curation. However, this research has uncovered issues in the ways in which ePortfolio pedagogy should be employed for students in IT, as they find the concept of creating an ePortfolio for their future career as secondary to achieving good grades. The value of ePortfolio as a tool to assist future employability is lost without clear articulation of assessment and activities that focus on ePortfolio construction (see Dellinger & Hanger, this collection). It is difficult to teach students the value of curating, reflecting, discussing, and reporting on learning through ePortfolios. Developing motivation in ePortfolio pedagogy is not limited to students; instructors, too, are often unaware of the extent to which using an ePortfolio requires significant modifications to their pedagogy. Thus the use of ePortfolios in the School of IT largely remains a class-based approach, pushed forward by faculty who embrace the value of students curating personal learning outcomes. Future activities in the School of IT to change practice and embrace ePortfolio pedagogy across the program include implementation of extensive online resources that assist students to develop their own ePortfolio for employability.

Case Study 2: Bachelor of International Studies (BIS)

The Bachelor of International Studies (BIS) is an interdisciplinary humanities degree program with a compulsory international experience requirement and an explicit commitment to facilitating the development of skills and capabilities required for working in international environments.[6] Launched in 2009, it has since gone through three iterations to reach its current structure.

---

6. The BIS degree structure is built around six core courses, an eight-credit major sequence (selected from a choice of nine), and at least two credits of international experience.

Implementation of an ePortfolio in the BIS had been attempted prior to Deakin's course enhancement process via one of the core units, but was not successful. Nonetheless, interactions with students undertaking internships along with discussions with student representatives on the program Advisory Board indicated that there was a clear need to help students articulate and evidence the skills they were gaining over the course of the program. Almost all of them described their international experiences as "the best thing I've done in my studies" but even in the case of strong students, few were able to explicitly articulate how these experiences linked to their classroom studies and overall development.

Through the Course Enhancement process, the use of an ePortfolio became evident as a way for students to reflect on their learning both from their international experiences and the duration of the whole program, thus enabling them to better articulate the knowledge and skills they had developed.

In order to better understand what a BIS Graduate ePortfolio would look like, two students were recruited to build a graduate ePortfolio and provide feedback on their experience. Both students were completing the final 23 units of their program and undertook the project as a credit-bearing internship. While it was initially tempting for the supervisors to try and give prescriptive instructions about technological and content requirements, the students instead received a brief that set parameters for the ePortfolio, but left them to work out the details themselves. The students were asked to:

- Develop and compile an ePortfolio on a platform of their choice using audio-visual elements.
- Report Bachelor of International Studies Program Learning Outcomes and Deakin Graduate Learning Outcomes via a development report.
- Reflect on their learning experience with support from evidence.
- Commit approximately 150 hours (equivalent to 20 working days) to ePortfolio development (writing, making notes on what worked/didn't work, what questions arose while they were working on the project), plus approximately 150 hours consulting with their supervisor, conducting research, and completing assessment tasks.

The two ePortfolios produced for the BIS were very different. One was outward-looking and focused on showcasing the author to an external audience such as potential employers, while the other was more inward-looking and explicitly reflective, centering on how each Deakin Graduate Learning Outcome could be evidenced.

Encouragingly, both students felt that the process of creating an ePortfolio proved beneficial for them. As they commented:

> Over the past three months I have researched, analysed and self-reflected upon many different aspects of my degree and

delved into the world of ePortfolios and their benefits to one's education. The use of ePortfolios is a beneficial tool for educational purposes in order to self-reflect upon many different aspects of your degree and academic achievements. It allows you to creatively present how those achievements have influenced you as a graduate and a professional. . . . Reflecting upon all the incidents when I have achieved these Outcomes [sic] has been one of the most influential academic, professional and personal achievement of mine, as previously stated, creating a [sic] ePortfolio of this magnitude allows me to take enormous pride in my achievements and academic pursuits over the past three years. (Emily)

An ePortfolio is particularly useful as a tool for reflection on learning. It creates an environment where a student remains engaged with a body of work during an entire program of study rather than consigning first year work to a box in the back of a cupboard, for example. (Matthew)

While only a very small-scale project, these conclusions confirmed that the process of creating an ePortfolio has significant potential for scaffolding students' understanding and articulation of the meta-narrative of their learning pathways by encouraging them to shift their focus from individual units towards making connections between units and experiences both inside and outside the classroom and institution (see Terry & Whillock, this collection).

However, the students' reports on their experiences of creating ePortfolios in response to the brief provided confirmed that they had encountered similar issues in developing their ePortfolios. Four issues in particular stood out, as outlined below, along with our interpretation of their importance: 1) What was the point of doing this?, 2) Issues with digital platform and format, 3) Understanding evidence, 4) Community of ePortfolio.

What's the Point of Doing This?

Especially early on, even though they understood the brief and output, it was evident that the students struggled to link the process of ePortfolio creation and curation to the development of metacognitive skills and the capacity for reflective narration. Rather, they identified how the process could assist them with demonstrating specific skills or learning outcomes such as digital literacy or global citizenship, or could help them use the final ePortfolio in a particular way, such as a *showcase* for potential employers. Helping them see the "bigger picture" of their program involved reframing the students' experience of being university students as one of telling a retrospective story about their personal and professional growth over several years, as a teaching assistant's email (sent February 18, 2015) to Emily illustrates: ". . . a ePortfolio at its most basic is a *multimodal* narrative. A story retold and constructed by you in a curated space" (Teaching Assistance comment, 2015).

Over the duration of the experiments in BIS, the narrative potential of ePortfolios became far more evident to both students. However, it is not a process that can be left to chance and points to the fact that ePortfolio thinking needs to be explicitly presented and discussed with students when they begin creating their ePortfolio. Having an explicit discussion with students about the process and purpose of creating ePortfolios is especially important as it often contrasts starkly with students' preexisting understandings of learning as being primarily time limited (that is, occurring only over the duration of a specific unit) and measured by outcomes. Shifting to emphasize process and the culmination of knowledge and experience involves "unlearning" in a similar way to that required by problem-based learning (Wilkinson, 2013). Scaffolding this process effectively is crucial as one is in effect removing the old scaffolding (dependent students for whom learning is equated with success in assessment), leaving students feeling unsupported, which is likely to reduce their capacity to transition to viewing themselves as independent and lifelong learners, at least in the shorter term.

This metaphor has become an important theme in our practice particularly in the BIS. In *The Postmodern Condition: A Report on Knowledge*, Jean-François Lyotard (1979) refers to narrative knowledge and the role of storytelling as narrative. Translated to the BIS, students need to be able to explain what they have studied. As an interdisciplinary program, students select one major from a choice of nine (International Relations; Politics and Policy Studies; Middle East Studies; Anthropology; Language and Culture Studies; Arabic; Indonesian; Chinese; or Spanish), choose up to 10 electives, and are required to have at least one international experience. Beyond the six core courses, the program is highly personalized. While in many ways choice of subjects to study is a positive element, graduates must be able to narrate their course selections and how their program developed. Employers need to understand the student's journey within the BIS, as each journey is not standardized as with other degree programs. Lyotard's (1979) concept is taken a step further in that the BIS aims to facilitate the creation of reflective storytellers who can explain not only what they did, but also why they made a particular choice, what they gained from that decision, and the applicability of their learning to other contexts. While ideally this construction of narrative knowledge would be an ongoing process over the program of a student's studies, in practice Søren Kierkegaard's maxim that life must be lived forward but can only be understood backwards more closely reflects the experience of most students. As such, we wanted to explore how ePortfolios could be used to support the sense-making and narrative processes for BIS students at the end of their programs by providing an opportunity to look back at their studies and achievements and understand how they all link together.

Platforms and Format

While platform selection must be informed by the pedagogy, disciplinary context, and the audience who will engage with the ePortfolio as a product (see Richardson et al., this collection), the choice of platform is also important for student ownership and personalization. *Authenticity* is key component of ePortfolio pedagogy, and one that is often overlooked in assessment and learning design. We concluded that open digital platforms more often permit external engagement and provide authenticity and usefulness to the ePortfolio by giving students "real world" experience. In contrast, we viewed the internal Deakin ePortfolio as clunky and limited in terms of audience and learning community.

At the same time, not all students will be familiar with suitable platforms from the outset, so if instructors permit student choice, they must factor in time for students to explore and experiment with different platforms. Moreover, the use of open platforms increases the importance of discussing aspects of digital literacy such as copyright and protecting intellectual property rights, as well as reputational management (see Garriott, this collection). While initially this may seem like an additional burden, integration of such discussions links well to ePortfolio thinking and promotes reflection, while providing a way to scaffold the ePortfolio creation process in the early stages.

What Evidence Is There?

Asking even the most engaged students to recall everything that they did over a three- to five-year period is a tall order. The task becomes doubly challenging when students are expected to evidence program and graduate learning outcomes that are constantly changing, even over the duration of a standard three-year program. Retrofitting learning outcomes is not desirable and risks reducing student buy-in and confidence. Developing an ePortfolio can facilitate student thinking about how to evidence each Deakin Graduate Learning Outcome effectively by giving them an initial opportunity to conduct a "stock take" of potential artifacts and sources of evidence. The need for students to link curricular and extracurricular activities in their ePortfolio evidence came to light as a second issue that demanded our attention. For example, despite being an on-campus student, Emily's evidencing of how she met the Teamwork Deakin Graduate Learning Outcome drew not only on her engagement in courses and successful completion of group assessment tasks, but also volunteering experiences that she had undertaken independently. In addition to describing the evidence, she reflected on the progress that she had made over the duration of her studies, commenting that "Understanding how I can contribute to a team environment is something I value greatly and have developed further over the past three years and strive to further develop throughout my Honours year" (Emily http://emilyebbott.wixsite.com /deakineportfolio2015/collaborative).

Matthew's discussion of Global Citizenship, the final of the eight Deakin Graduate Learning Outcomes and paramount for the BIS, took the combining of curricular and extracurricular a step further. Using the ePortfolio to produce a new artifact and reflection in one (see Figure 6.4), he demonstrated his understanding of global citizenship through a photo essay that illustrated how residents of a New York neighborhood "enact their local and global citizenship just by their very existence within this geographical space." (Matthew, Figure 6.4)

The photo below depicts a storefront window advertising services to immigrants mainly from the Bengali community who need connections to their country of origin. The services advertised include airline tickets, international money transfers, and mobile phones and their associated services. These are valuable services for immigrants who have yet to establish themselves in their new country of residence and may not have traditional bank accounts or personal infrastructure.

Posters advertising services to local residents, especially immigrants wanting to remain connected to their country of origin.
Photo: Matthew Hall

Figure 6.4. Excerpt from Matthew's photo essay about global citizenship
(https://matthewhallportfolio.wordpress.com/global-citizenship/)

In addition to highlighting the need to bridge the curricular/extra-curricular divide, constructing an ePortfolio demonstrated the importance of seeing the program as a whole story with multiple interwoven, connected threads and moments. It began to break down the distinction between learning undertaken in a formal learning environment (whether in a classroom or online), and learning in other settings via participation in different activities and communities: an important "aha moment" in reframing students' perceptions of the value and benefit of their university experiences. Finally, it confirmed the idea that reflection can serve as an artifact in its own right and hence a potential solution to any lack of evidence that has the additional benefit of demonstrating reflection as an iterative and ongoing practice.

Community, Collaboration and Evolution

The temptation is to see ePortfolios as highly individual and as individualized projects that primarily showcase the student or graduate. However, with the shift to focus on process and promotion of a new model of learning, the importance of collaboration and opportunities for discussion became very evident. Both students noted the challenge of feeling isolated, although Emily's perception was perhaps more acute due to having completed the majority of her program on campus and starting work on her ePortfolio while still travelling in Europe.

> During the beginning of the project I felt slightly separated from both my supervisor and my fellow student [Matthew]. This was rectified once I began to share ideas and worries with my fellow student. Once I returned home I spoke to my supervisor and the level of information was greatly appreciated because there is only so much one can convey via email through no fault of either party. More integration and possible Skype sessions would have been beneficial although due to time difference made it quite difficult. (Emily)

We set up a Facebook group at the start of the project, which served as an effective forum for discussion and sharing of ideas. As a platform that all participants in the project already used, students avoided having to log into Deakin's Learning Management System. Matthew clearly explained the importance of the Facebook group in the concluding recommendations of his project report:

> Students in many units are encouraged to use discussion groups on the Deakin cloud system to interact with cohort (sic), either informally or with particular relevance to unit topics. In some cases, this interaction is compulsory and forms part of assessment. In my experience, unless interaction in discussion forums are compulsory, use of that platform is non-existent. Using the

Deakin experience as a guide, this "closed room" approach was counter-productive. The best communication tool is one that students already use—platforms like Facebook or Twitter. In units that adopted these platforms there was more engagement, communication and—importantly—sharing of ideas. Enabled by active social networks, communication bloomed. Content from an e-portfolio can be shared via these platforms (Facebook, Twitter), again expanding the opportunity for student communication, feedback, and reflection. This could be of particular use to off-campus students as experiential evidence suggests in-house platforms do not encourage wide nor regular participation. (Matthew)

Matthew's and Emily's greater awareness of the collaborative nature of learning that developed while creating their ePortfolios also led to a different understanding of outcomes, with a move away from the idea of learning as finite and merely about finding the "right" answer and towards embracing contingent and iterative knowledge production. Matthew illustrated this point with reference to a comment to students by David Carr that an online course he was teaching for the first time would be "exciting and sometimes very confusing" (Carr, 2014, Addendum, para. 1), reflecting that:

Part of Carr's point in this comment is that the digitalization of media and communication is inescapable, offers great opportunities, and is evolving. In an environment that therefore is evolving, perfection is difficult to achieve and trial, error, and failure can be considered an important part of a learning process. What is considered right today can be wrong tomorrow or, at least, improved upon later. While Carr was referencing—perhaps even warning students about—his approach to teaching, the same philosophy can and should apply to learning. An e-portfolio which documents a student's evolution is the perfect tool, much like an analog scrapbook, to accompany that transition. It will not always be perfect—the finished article—but, like the student, it will or at least should evolve. (Matthew).

This final reflection got to key aims of introducing ePortfolios to the Bachelor of International Studies: to increase students' awareness of the contingency of knowledge and to promote an understanding of learning as an ongoing, dynamic, and interactive process, rather than being finite and static. In the process, both Emily and Matthew came to see the primary value of the ePortfolio as the process, rather than the product—a shift in thinking that reflects the importance of portfolio thinking and the willingness to challenge students' perceptions of the ePortfolio, which are often overly focused on how they can utilize the finished version.

Discussion

Our case study has explored the complex ways in which ePortfolios can be used in a particular discipline, focusing on their particular contextual, purpose-driven learning design, and issues of audiences when curating. Embedded in a specific disciplinary focus, each case study demonstrates a certain "lens of learning" through particular language and cultural semantics. Similarly, the ways in which the instructor(s) articulate and explicitly demonstrate the aims of an ePortfolio and its outcomes to students highlight the significance of ePortfolio pedagogy. Both the learner's identity development and their growing knowledge of the content become evident in their integration of multimodal media selections as well as the curatorial decisions they make in constructing a presentation for a particular audience. The interaction of artifacts and evidence as a curated page creates a narrative that represents the learner in the discipline/profession and reflects the learner's representation of self. The viewer of the ePortfolio not only sees the transformative evidence curated by the learner but also how the learner has designed their learning journey. Again, these outcomes depend on the purpose and audience of the ePortfolio and differ from discipline to discipline. Overall outcomes from the case study include:

- Reflection: The nature of reflection in each discipline differs. The examples allowed exploration of exactly what constitutes reflection within each discipline, as well as mechanisms for how students build and articulate reflection. This "skill" takes time to build, yet reflection represents an important layer in the assessment process. The way we view reflection either as a lower-case r or an upper-case R has many disciplinary-specific contextual differences that influence the language and style. When we teach reflection and/or Reflection, we are also using different disciplinary models and need to be aware of this difference by making it explicit in our teaching and research outcomes. We found that students could identify the relationship between the evidence and reflective pieces through constructed reflections on evidence or "in action" (Schön, 1983, ix) through the curatorial decisions they made as they designed the pages or presentations.

- Evidence: We view evidence through a range of perspectives that depend on a number of contexts, from evidence of learning, evidence of a skill, experience, or as a whole program. We understand evidence to have many meanings and connotations when we talk about ePortfolios, for example: a curated ePortfolio of evidence; an ePortfolio that contains artifacts as evidence; a curated ePortfolio that uses evidence to support claims through reflection.

- Materiality: An artist or designer discusses material practice and materiality to present his/her intent through the media. This perspective has implications for the way we use it in ePortfolios; we could be referring to the multimodal media explored throughout the ePortfolio composition, the actual composition as a whole, or the way materials are used to lead the viewer from one artifact to another and the impact or impression of that artifact. For instance, how the I-Am statement language in the BIS is used by the artist or designer impacts the way an audience views a photograph to the way they read the page structure. The materiality can shape our lenses as viewers and lead the reader through the constructed narrative.

- Standards: We view standards in each of our educational contexts, nationally and internationally, through a range of perspectives. We use standards to define achievement and evidence of learning outcomes, have our own standards as teachers and educators, and have standards that we must adhere to in our institutions. One set of standards becomes confused with others when we talk about them in relation to ePortfolios.

Conclusion

The course enhancement process at Deakin has enabled us to explore the value of ePortfolios and present the ways in which we use ePortfolio for learning, assessment, and careers. It also opened our practice to seeing the role that explicit standards had in the learning design of a course. Other educators considering ePortfolio pedagogy across programs must carefully consider discipline-specific issues particularly when determining the nature of reflection, evidence, materiality, and standards. Context issues impact the way in which students curate their ePortfolios. The implementation of technical proficiency for both staff and students takes time as do developing appropriate pedagogical understandings of the tools and the ability to critically reflect and select work for assessment. Overall, as educative spaces, ePortfolios enable both a self-directed and personalized approach to learning that promotes lifelong and life-wide capabilities for reflection and collection of work samples for a range of audiences. ePortfolios also offer the opportunity to present competing or evolving standards enabling both students and educators to negotiate their relevance while validating the course outcomes. As learners develop the appropriate skills to self-regulate their learning and become responsible for their learning outside of the formal learning environment, ePortfolios offer a space to engage both individually and collaboratively for a purpose that is both personalized and assessable. Educators seeking to develop personalized learning spaces or authentic learning environments in their assessment will find that ePortfolios can enable this transition.

References

Allen, B., Caple, H., Coleman, K. & Nguyen, T. (2012, November 26). *Creativity in practice: Social media in higher education* [Conference paper]. Ascilite 2012 Future Challenges, Sustainable Futures. Wellington, New Zealand.

Batson, T. (2013, January 16). The taming of the MOOC—With ePortfolio evidence, Campus Technology Digital Magazine. https://web.archive.org/web/2013 0318015052/http://campustechnology.com/articles/2013/01/16/the-taming-of-the -mooc.aspx.

Batson, T. (2014, April 23). Telling your story: Making sense of diverse learning experiences: Feature article in conversation with Mary Grush. Campus Technology Digital Magazine. https://campustechnology.com/Articles/2014/04/23/The -Narrative-Telling-Your-Story.aspx.

Batson, T. (2015, April 19). Ontology of "ePortfolio" platform? Batson Blog. Association for Authentic, Experiential and Evidence-Based Learning. https://web .archive.org/web/20160406004742/http://www.aaeebl.org/blogpost/1008436 /213232/Ontology-of-ePortfolio.

Benjamin, J. (2000). The scholarship of teaching in teams: What does it look like in practice? *Higher Education Research and Development, 19*, 191–204.

Biggs, J. & Tang, C. (2011). *Teaching for quality learning at university* (4th ed). McGraw-Hill; Open University Press.

Boud, D. & Falchikov, N. (2006). Aligning assessment with long term learning. *Assessment and Evaluation in Higher Education, 31*, 399–413.

Carr, D. (2014, August 4). Press play: Making and distributing content in the present future we are living through. Medium, 4 August. https://medium.com/press-play /press-play-4b26bed77b7d#.aelsku8l8.

Coleman, K., Cox, J., Das, M., Flood, A., Polly, P., Thai, T. & Yang, J. L. (2012). Eportfolios in the sciences: The role of reflection as students build professional skills and career readiness. In M. Brown, M. Hartwell & T. Stewart (Eds.), Proceedings of Ascilite Wellington 2012: Future challenges, sustainable futures (pp. 219–222). Australian Society for Computers in Learning in Tertiary Education.

Deakin University. (2016) Deakin Hallmarks. http://www.deakin.edu.au/about -deakin/teaching-and-learning/deakin-hallmarks.

Deakin University. (2015). Course Enhancement Guidelines 2015. https://www .deakin.edu.au/__data/assets/pdf_file/0003/321744/Deakin-Course-enhancement -guidelines-2015.pdf.

Eynon, B. & Gambino, L. (2015). *The high impact ePortfolio practice: A catalyst for student, faculty and institutional learning*. Stylus.

Eynon, B., Gambino, L. M. & Török, J. (2014). What difference can ePortfolio make? A field report from the Connect to Learning project. *International Journal of ePortfolio, 4*, 95–114.

Gibson, D., Coleman, K. & Irving, L. (2016). Learning journeys in higher education: Designing digital pathways for learning, motivation and assessment. In D. Ifenthaler, N. Bellin-Mularski & D. K. Mahin (Eds.), *Foundation of digital badges and micro-credentials: Demonstrating and recognizing knowledge and competencies* (pp. 115–138). Springer.

Hallam, G., Harper, W., Mccowan, C., Hauville, K., Mcallister, L. & Creagh, T. (2009). *ePortfolio use by university students in Australia: Informing excellence in policy and practice* (Altc Project Final Report). Queensland University of Technology.

Huber, M. T. & Hutchings, P. (2004). *Integrative learning: Mapping the terrain: The academy in transition.* Association of American Colleges and Universities.

Lyotard, J. (1984). *The postmodern condition: A report on knowledge* (G. Bennington & B. Massumi, Trans.). University of Minnesota Press. (Original work published 1979).

McKenzie, S. (2014). Incorporating career ePortfolios as a course wide learner tool. *Proceedings Of The EPortfolio Australian Workshop.* EPortfolios Australia.

McKenzie, S., Palmer, S., Coldwell-Neilson, J. & Coleman, K. (2014, December 8–10). *Understanding career aspirations of information technology students at Deakin University: A pilot study* [Conference presentation]. IEEE International Conference on Teaching, Assessment, and Learning for Engineering 2014. Wellington, New Zealand.

Morris, H. E. & Warman, G. (2015). Using design thinking in higher education. *Educause Review*, 12 Jan. 2015. https://er.educause.edu/articles/2015/1/using -design-thinking-in-higher-education.

Naiman, L. (2016). *Creativity at work: Design thinking as a strategy for innovation.* http://oro.open.ac.uk/39207/1/curriculum_reform_final_19th_Dec.pdf.

Oliver, B. (2013). Assuring graduate capabilities: Evidencing levels of achievement for graduate employability. https://ltr.edu.au/resources/Oliver_Report_2015.pdf.

Oliver, B. (2014). Deakin University: Agenda 2020 curriculum framework. https:// www.deakin.edu.au/__data/assets/pdf_file/0013/300091/AGENDA-2020-curri culum-framework-DEC-2014.pdf.

Oliver, B. (2015). Deakin curriculum framework, LIVE the future: Agenda 2020, http://www.deakin.edu.au/learning/deakin-curriculum-framework.

Pegg, A. (2014). We think that's the future: Curriculum reform initiatives in higher education, Higher Education Academy. https://s3.eu-west-2.amazonaws.com /assets.creode.advancehe-document-manager/documents/hea/private/curricu lum_reform_final_19th_dec_1_1568037077.pdf.

Pintrich, P. R., Walters, C. & Baxter, G. P. (2000). Assessing metacognition and self-regulated learning. In G. Schraw & J. C. Impara (Eds.), Issues in the measurement of metacognition (pp. 43–97). Buros Institute of Mental Measurement.

Polly, P., Thai, T., Flood, A., Coleman, K., Das, M., Yang, J. L. & Cox, J. (2013, December 3). *Enhancement of scientific research and communication skills using assessment and ePortfolio in a third year pathology course* [Conference presentation]. 30th Ascilite Conference. Sydney, Australia.

Peet, M., Lonn, S., Gurin, P., Boyer, K. P., Matney, M., Marra, T., Himbeault Taylor, S. & Daley, A. (2011). Fostering integrative knowledge through ePortfolios. *International Journal of ePortfolio, 1*(1), 11–31.

Rhodes, T., Chen, H. L., Watson, C. E. & Garrison, W. (2014). Editorial: A call for more rigorous ePortfolio research. *International Journal of ePortfolio, 4*(1), 1–5.

Savage, J. & Pollard, V. (2014). Engaging academics in collegial online professional development during a course renewal process: Intent and reflection. In A. Kwan, E. Wong, T. Kwong, P. Lau & A. Goody (Eds.), *Research and development in higher education: Higher education in a globalized world.* (Vol. 37). (pp 274–283). Higher Education Research and Development Society of Australasia.

Schön, D. (1983). *The reflective practitioner: How professionals think in action.* Temple Smith.

Wilkinson, C. (2013). More problem than solution? Managing the practical challenges of PBL course delivery. In K. S. Coleman & A. Flood (Eds.), *Disciplines: The lenses of learning* (pp. 67–92). Common Ground Publishing LLC.

Wozniak, K. & Zagal, J. (2013). Finding evidence of metacognition in an ePortfolio community: Beyond text, across new media. School of Continuing and Professional Studies Faculty Publications, 36. https://via.library.depaul.edu/snl-faculty-pubs/36.

Chapter 7. The Learner-Teacher Portfolio Journey: Developing Self-Efficacy and Self-Determination in the Medical Sciences

Patsie Polly
UNIVERSITY OF NEW SOUTH WALES

Kathryn Coleman
UNIVERSITY OF MELBOURNE

Thomas Fath
MACQUARIE UNIVERSITY

Thuan Thai
UNIVERSITY OF NOTRE DAME AUSTRALIA

Jia-Lin Yang
UNIVERSITY OF NEW SOUTH WALES

The integration of learning and learner-centered tools such as an ePortfolio requires modeling and *scaffolding* of *folio thinking* to support *reflection, metacognition,* and digital literacy in order to develop skills and experience in reflective practice, career awareness, knowledge of graduate employability, and professional identity (see Sanborn & Ramirez, this collection). We have found through a number of studies that ePortfolios can assist learners in higher education to reflect upon the evidence of their claims to learning and demonstrate the development of skills that are life-long and life-wide. Anecdotal feedback from academic staff and students in this program suggested that high academic student performance did not always correlate with a strong understanding of professional skills development, career capability, and graduate employability. Career awareness and employability building were needed in tandem with disciplinary knowledge for assurance of graduate employability. Therefore, an *outcome-based design* was implemented in various Undergraduate Medical Science courses, where pathology, medical research practice-specific knowledge, and career development learning (CDL) were established (see Dellinger & Hanger, this collection). Importantly, reflection and CDL were integrated into the ePortfolio pedagogy. Through this unique approach, an "apprenticeship"-style professional knowledge and skills and career intervention were delivered, recorded, and reflected in a learning-centered ePortfolio. At the end of the program, the students were significantly more confident with career-associated self-efficacy and demonstrated autonomy (see Sanborn & Ramirez, this

DOI: https://doi.org/10.37514/PRA-B.2020.1084.2.07

collection). Teachers also experienced a greater sense of student engagement with *assessment* and reflection on skills building as well as more meaningful professional development. This chapter explores this learner-teacher ePortfolio journey and the role that creative thinking, teaching, and collaboration have played in developing self-efficacy and self-determination in the Medical Science degree program (BMedSc) at the University of New South Wales (UNSW), Sydney (Australia).

Reflections on Our Learner-Teacher Journey

Our team is an interesting one. We are an inter- and multi-disciplinary team of educators, researchers, and academics who place the learner at the heart of our learning and teaching design. As a professional learning community, we once found ourselves working closely together, navigating new pathways of portfolio practice for our students and ourselves. We have now developed these practices that grew from this early work (explored in this chapter) in new species and sites with new students and teaching teams. This reflective practice chapter captures a moment in time, as we paused to reflect on what we had learned and achieved. Our learner-teacher connection and collaboration began many years ago as we embarked on this journey together to develop and design new learning approaches for Medical Science students at UNSW Sydney. To do this, we iteratively designed an ePortfolio curriculum that developed reflection, identity, and digital literacy through folio thinking and the lens of the professional scientist (see Day, this collection). These skills and practices were developed across the program, transferable across program assessment and key employability capabilities. Our work was and has since been based on developing folio thinking through ongoing critical reflection (Allen & Coleman, 2011) and developing habits of mind (Costa & Kallick, 2009) in our learners as they progress through their learning journey.

This chapter is its own reflection, a space to practice what we have been teaching. A reflection on our learning journey as a multi-disciplinary team, designing a learner-centered curriculum and developing ePortfolio pedagogy that is now a cross- and inter-disciplinary active research space at UNSW Sydney. Here, we reflect on our academic and researcher journeys through published and chronicled papers that serve as milestones in our process, and how we have continued to ideate and design together despite such varied backgrounds through a commitment to both teaching and learning. In this chapter, we describe an important point in our practice at UNSW Sydney as a result of that body of work—to align assessments in the BMedSc program with graduate capabilities. In particular, this chapter explores standards-based criteria (UNSW[1]) and its relationship

---

1.   UNSW Standard-based assessment: *Standards-based* assessment depends on a set of predefined statements outlining different levels or standards of achievement in a program, course, or assessment component, and normally expressed in terms of the stated assessment criteria. https://teaching.unsw.edu.au/standards-based-assessment.

to folio thinking to explicitly teach and assess teamwork capabilities as well as our approach to aligning assessment tasks across a program that facilitate teamwork skills development over time. We also document the student and staff experience and describe our approach to facilitating skills and capability in capstone courses that build on skills such as teamwork and research practice. These courses continue to introduce and support work-integrated learning (WIL) (see Day, this collection), and integrative and experiential learning for undergraduates in the sciences.

What Is an ePortfolio at UNSW?

ePortfolio use and implementation in the Medical Sciences at UNSW has been a mechanism for supporting development of reflective practice on skills building and capabilities acquisition since 2012. Reflective practice in this sense, is the ability to reflect upon practice as a science professional in an iterative, ongoing, and systematic way. Developing this action takes time and needs to be *scaffolded* and modelled within *authentic* experiences. Reflective practice is an essential component of responsible professional practice (Coleman & Flood, 2016). Teaching reflective practice embedded within academic courses has been the co-curricular method of developing professional skills through an aligned and *backward designed* curriculum, supported by authentic curricular assessment. This integrated system of learning design and teaching has enabled students to develop their professional identities as medical scientists while developing the necessary skills and capabilities to provide evidence as graduates of this program of their leadership, scholarship, global citizenship, and professionalism (UNSW Sydney 2011, 2016).

In the School of Medical Sciences (SoMS) at UNSW, our pilot study implemented ePortfolio use as an educational tool for promoting student learning through reflective practice in a third-year undergraduate pathology course. We found that ePortfolios were an effective way to support student learning outcomes that aligned with the UNSW graduate attributes (Polly, Thai et al., 2013). Program-wide implementation and longitudinal use of ePortfolio has previously been suggested to facilitate learning, attainment of graduate attributes, employability skills, and professional competencies, as well as life-long learning (Clarke et al., 2009; Hallam et al., 2008; Polly, Thai et al., 2013). Since this initial trial, we have implemented ePortfolio pedagogy across other science courses in a four-year degree program curriculum as well as across various disciplines within SoMS at UNSW.

In 2013, our collaborative paper on use of ePortfolio in the sciences to support reflection of skills development in research communication discussed folio thinking and began to define an ePortfolio for our context and purpose (Polly, Thai et al., 2013). The definition of an electronic portfolio as "a digitized collection of artifacts including demonstrations, resources, and accomplishments that represent an individual, group, or institution" (Lorenzo & Ittelson, 2005, p.1) was developed as part of our practice as a professional learning community. We were keen to explore what a digital repository for a range of learning and teaching materials—including those produced for course-based assessment such as videos, images, and text-based reflections—might look like for learners at different year levels. Our platform at that time was Mahara ePortfolio in Moodle. Taking the Lorenzo and Ittelson (2005) definition further, we developed our assessment tasks to integrate ePortfolio pedagogy and practice on the notion that an ePortfolio is a personal digital space, a student-centric monitor of learning across disciplines that enables learners to both document learning and put themselves in a position where they can take charge of their own learning (Butler, 2007) through the selection of the *artifacts* for viewing or presentation to selected audiences.

Our further definition of the Lorenzo and Ittelson (2005) electronic portfolio is both contextual and purpose-driven, given that we found ourselves teaching in contemporary digital places of learning. As ePortfolio presentations are planned, designed, and curated by students rather than by the educator, they start to play an active role in developing life-long skills of reflection; selection of memories, experiences, and knowledge; and collection for students rather than simply serving as collections of static learning artifacts. Our collaborative research and practice led our team to investigate how ePortfolios have been utilized in many areas of international and national higher education spaces, spanning across assessment to career development. We were particularly interested in how they provide a space for learners to evidence their acquired attributes and capabilities for graduation. Our learning design and curriculum development have been influenced by this research and built on the evidence that reflection on learning has been found to facilitate both life-long and life-wide learning that enables learners to learn from their collections of evidence (Batson, 2015; Cambridge, 2008; Chen & Penny Light, 2010; Eynon & Gambino, 2015; Penny Light et al., 2012).

Our national research has focused on the use of ePortfolios in Australian higher education, which is characterized by portfolios for learning, assessment, and reflection (Australian ePortfolios Project, 2008; Oliver, 2015, 2016) and for professional development and graduate recruitment (Hallam et al., 2008; Leece, 2005; Oliver & Whelan, 2011). These national studies have indicated that the development of an ePortfolio for learning and assessment is supported by the life-wide approach to the technology because after submitting their ePortfolios for assessment, students "take" their learning with them after graduation as a career development tool (Leece, 2005). Interestingly, more than a decade after many of these studies were first published, we are still developing our own work towards the transformation of ePortfolios and enhancement of the curriculum in Australian universities. Our scholarly approaches continue to demonstrate to students and educators the connections among their learning, assessment criteria, program outcomes, and graduate capabilities (Barrett, 2005). A number of recent Australian studies explored the relationship between portfolios and graduate employability (Oliver, 2015, 2016; Vozzo et al., 2014; Watty et al., 2016). These studies, along with our own, have found that the clear alignment of assessment with learning outcomes encourages students to document their learning journey while reflecting on how the course assessment relates to the program of study and how the portfolio as both a collection and presentation of learning can be used beyond the course as a digital repository or collection space (Polly, Cox et al., 2015; Polly, Thai et al., 2013; Yang et al., 2015). Our practice is based on the important role that an ePortfolio plays in developing sustainable assessment (Boud, 2000) that goes beyond the unit of study as it enables students to present themselves in a number of ways, to a range of audiences, by empowering learners to shift identities in many instances.

Graduate Attributes and Professional Skills

Higher education has become increasingly interested in how students attain graduate attributes, how we can embed these skills and capabilities across programs of study and how these are evidenced and warranted. At UNSW Sydney, students must demonstrate proficiency in professional skills in order to satisfy the university graduate attributes. Currently in Australia, as well as globally, frameworks for university graduate attributes emphasize knowledge and skills that support graduate employability and global citizenship (Bosanquet et al., 2010). Furthermore, there has been a growing global desire to evaluate graduate generic and transferable skills such as communication and teamwork (Oliver, 2013, 2015). In Australia, several universities have begun to implement course-wide ePortfolios as a way for students to collect and evidence their achievement of university and discipline-specific graduate attributes (Hallam et al., 2008). In the BMedSc program at UNSW Sydney, we developed a mechanism for ePortfolio implementation and use to support students in reflective practice. In becoming reflective practitioners, students are able to recognize and build professional skills that underpin graduate attributes such as communication and teamwork. WIL through our research-intensive undergraduate courses has assisted, enabled, and engaged undergraduates in thinking and developing research practice skills and career learning.

Making Medical Science Students Employable Graduates and Competitive Professional Postgraduates

Within the Medical Science faculty, we recognize that students entering science undergraduate programs, such as the BMedSc, are generally unaware that professional, co-curricular skills such as communication are developed alongside academic curricular course requirements. It is these professional skills that will likely enhance their prospects for employability upon graduation in addition to increasing their competitiveness when applying for postgraduate programs (see Day, this collection).

The professional skills building journey in the BMedSc at UNSW Sydney started by scaffolding the development of research communication skills for undergraduates in the discipline of Pathology (Polly, Thai et al., 2013). Since this initial trial, we have moved toward a program-wide approach (Polly, Cox et al., 2015). The strategy was to begin this professional thinking and skills development early on in the first year, transfer these skills into the second year and then into third-year courses, in particular—including a third-year multidisciplinary biomedical research internship (School of Medical Sciences Research Internship— SOMS3001) that serves as a capstone course in the BMedSc program. Students were taught co-curricular skills by integrating activities such as skills-enabling workshops as part of their curricular academic assessment tasks (Jones & Polly, 2013; Polly & Jones, 2013). Embedded within courses, a series of academic literacy workshops focused on communication and research practice. Transfer of these communication skills (disciplinary and cross cutting transferable attributes) was longitudinal within the program and aligned across disciplines as research thinking and practice became the common thread. This teaching rationale enabled students to learn research practices and the associated professional skills attributed to the field and the needs of the professions they would enter.

We began our journey as a team to build ePortfolio pedagogy and reflective practice in research communication skills development throughout the undergraduate program. We aimed to align professional skills development with UNSW Sydney strategic priorities for graduates as global citizens, scholars, leaders, professionals (UNSW Sydney 2011, 2016). When considering the professionalization of the UNSW BMedSc, the focus was on self-directed learning to cultivate the students' sense of their professional identities as emerging medical scientists. Facilitating self-directed learning by undergraduate students has been foundational for "thinking, speaking and doing" like a professional in the medical science discipline (Polly, Cox et al., 2015; Polly & Jones, 2013; Polly, Thai et al., 2013).

Research Practice Learning and Transfer

The student learning journey within the program was supported by implementing a longitudinal approach to ePortfolio pedagogy so that skills transfer could be achieved by scaffolding skills development not only longitudinally but also transversely across years. This scaffolding would ideally result in transfer of skills from first- into second-, then second- into third-year (capstone) undergraduate stages and beyond into fourth-year honors. We focused on the transfer of communication, teamwork, and research practice skills as these skills cut across disciplines and result in graduate attributes desired by employers. In the discipline of pathology, for example, we targeted the oral and written research communication skills that had been initially developed in the second year by cultivating research thinking and communication in the third year. (Jones & Polly, 2013; Polly & Jones, 2013; Polly, Thai et al., 2013). As third- and fourth-year courses in the BMedSc program are designed to develop these skills through various assessment tasks, we recognized that year three was the critical point at which students would crystallize their skills development and use all of these research-related skills that they had acquired along the way. Those research skills could then be aligned across disciplines, despite having been learned in different contexts (Figure 7.1).

We made this longitudinal and cross-disciplinary approach explicit to students to show them how they were using the same skills across disciplines and in different contexts, which proved very powerful. Discussing this approach with students helped them to realize that the ways of thinking they learned in their second year could be transferred into the third year (for example in the medical science discipline of pathology), then across courses (for example between the disciplines of anatomy, physiology, and pharmacology), and beyond. The pinnacle of bringing these skills together was in the capstone third-year, cross-disciplinary biomedical research internship course, the School of Medical Sciences Research Internship (SOMS3001). This research internship is considered a pre-honors course in the BMedSc and is based on WIL, through which students get hands-on experience in real-world research lab settings. In other words, SOMS3001 is a course in which all of their research practice skills come together. These skills are based on elements of self-directed and transferable learning and are further developed according to their lab placements. In addition, students learn co-research practice within WIL, including aspects of working in a lab that has restraints in terms of work health and safety practices, research integrity, and working within a team.

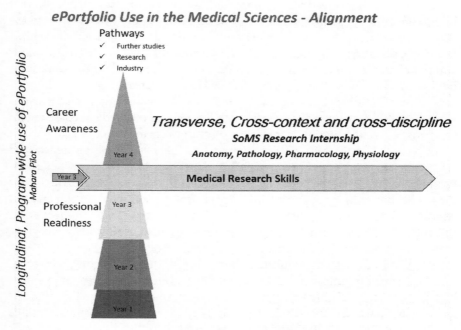

Figure 7.1. ePortfolio use to support research skills awareness in the medical science degree program at UNSW Sydney. The SoMS research internship requires integration and use of cross-context, cross-disciplinary medical research skills.

Scaffolded Reflective Practice and Building Awareness of Teamwork Skills

Although most Australian universities have included teamwork as a graduate attribute for the past 20 years, there is currently no way of evaluating or formally recognizing this attribute (Resort, 2011). Outside of validation and recognition of skills, capabilities, and competencies as a team member by peers, we felt that at the heart of the issue of teamwork was the explicit teaching of teamwork skills to students for *effective and affective* group work by the team leader (the research scientist in the lab). Ways of facilitating these communication skills include self-awareness, reflective practice, and authentic assessment. Authentic tasks offer students the opportunity to collaborate and reflect on real-world, ill-defined, and problem-based tasks (Herrington et al., 2003). However, reflective practice takes time—time to learn the necessary skills to reflect on the self and time to see what the individual has learned, time to evaluate and make appropriate revisions. In the team environment, self-reflection is an important skill and capability. Keeping this in mind, our aim in the learning and assessment design was to develop a system whereby we could collect learning analytics on undergraduate student teamwork capabilities in the biomedical sciences.

Our approach involved the program-wide alignment of assessment tasks that build teamwork skills through reflection and are easily quantified. Courses in the BMedSc program with assessment tasks that required and focused on explicit teamwork skills were identified, mapped, and aligned. Students' teamwork skills and performances against common standards in course-wide *rubrics* were standardized across courses and captured as students progressed through the program. The effect of this program-wide and cross-discipline approach for teamwork skills building through student reflective practice coupled with assessment was two-fold: 1) highlighting our teaching of teamwork and effective group work; 2) the potential for teaching reflective practice to scientists for self-awareness and self-efficacy in ePortfolios. This approach and ideology involved the wider establishment of the ePortfolio community of practice that was cross-disciplinary for the medical sciences by engaging disciplinary experts, academic developers, and educational designers (see Balthazor et al., Coleman et al., and Summers et al., this collection). Hence, teacher professional development in ePortfolio pedagogy, implementation, and use was enabled (see Day, this collection).

Based on our previous implementation of ePortfolio pedagogy, we recognized enhanced technical and transferable skills awareness in research practices by science students (Polly, Thai et al., 2013). Therefore, we proposed that ePortfolio use would also facilitate students' critical reflection on their teamwork skills development. In particular, students were asked to reflect on their teamwork skills development in their ePortfolio using WordPress, or any other online web creation tool. We believe scaffolding this process of ongoing and deep reflective practice via assessments is a key, a first-stage approach to building professional skills for science students that will have life-long benefits. This approach can be easily adopted and applied in other programs to support related skills development (Polly, Cox et al., 2015; Polly, Thai et al., 2013).

Work and Career Integrated Learning in the Medical Sciences

Interestingly, when developing professional skills either as part of a course-wide or even a program-wide approach, students ultimately see the linkage of skills development to career learning in courses that offer WIL. They are made aware explicitly through visible learning and teaching as they bring their professional skills development in core second-year subjects with them to new sites of learning and new contexts of knowledge in the BMedSc. This opportunity to teach themselves as reflective practitioners through the aligned learning of content and research practice in research-based capstone courses such as the School of Medical Sciences Research Internship (SOMS3001), Microscopy in Research (ANAT3212), and Honors Program (SOMS4001) has allowed students to link and integrate their skills and capabilities.

Research Internship

The School of Medical Sciences Research Internship (SOMS3001) is a third-year course presently offered to science undergraduate students throughout the year in semesters 1 and 2. Students who take this course intend and expect to experience "real-world" research laboratory learning in biomedical research techniques and associated research practice. This course has four key authentic assessment tasks that have been embedded to build research practice skills in oral and written communication (see Carpenter & Labissiere, this collection). The literature review, worth 20% of the course assessment schedule, facilitates development of capabilities in information searching, acquisition, evaluation, synthesis, higher order thinking, and contextualization regarding the student's research question. The research report, worth 40%, asks students to document and write about their research findings and to contextualize these findings within their research field. The key skills developed in this document refer to the student research experience and their understanding of their findings. Critical evaluation, synthesis, and understanding of research data, as well as higher-order thinking in order to analyze and interpret findings are also developed. Reflective practice underpins all of these capabilities. Skills in written research communication and critical evaluation are also developed (Jones & Polly, 2013). Both the research seminar presentation worth 20% of the course assessment schedule and the research report ask students to communicate their research findings in two different genres. Importantly, both tasks facilitate reflective practice in not only evaluating research findings but also recognizing development of skills in collaboration and teamwork in medical research (Polly & Jones, 2013; Polly, Thai et al., 2013). The researcher or academic in charge of the project assesses laboratory performance, worth 20%. This assessment item warrants academic endorsement of the undergraduate student's technical and analytic research skills and work ethic, as well as the student's development of workplace teamwork skills.

The skills developed through the SOMS3001 Research Internship have been foundational for undergraduate science students about to enter into workplaces and into postgraduate courses that require all of these professional skills. The driver of the ePortfolio as authentic assessment for/as/of learning was to facilitate an outward-facing professional self in order to become more attractive to prospective employers and increase the possibility of entry into competitive postgraduate programs such as medicine and dentistry. Students were able to identify the same practices in undergraduate subjects and the research internship. This awareness of skills and capabilities development was facilitated via reflective practice scaffolded within the ePortfolio space. This heightened awareness of their professional development also enabled them to view themselves as competitive candidates for entry into postgraduate programs such as medicine and dentistry as well as biomedical research apprentices to the profession or medical research upon entry into Honors.

Microscopy in Research

The School of Medical Sciences Microscopy in Research (ANAT3212) is a research-focused third-year course offered to science, advanced science, and medical science students. The majority of students have little or no practical experience in designing and performing experiments at the time they enroll in the course. The course combines the objective of providing students in-depth training in state-of-the-art imaging technologies with the aim of improving students' transferable skills such as teamwork, analytical thinking, and communication of research data.

Teaching methods in ANAT3212 encompass classic face-to-face lectures, an online virtual laboratory, and wet lab practical classes. The interactive environment of the virtual lab environment combined with the provision of ample online resources has been designed to stimulate students' self-directed learning prior to starting practical hands-on activities in a wet lab. Short research projects carried out in laboratories of active research-focused academics from different schools (including the School of Medical Sciences, the School of Biotechnology and Biological Sciences, and the Prince of Wales Clinical School) across the UNSW campus are a core feature of the current design of the course. This cross-disciplinary approach forms the basis of a strong research-integrated learning experience that inspires students to commence a research career and also embraces the graduate aspiration of training entrepreneurial leaders in research. Therefore, this course is ideally positioned to prepare students for a future workplace environment in the field of biomedical research. Assessments in this course are designed to foster a process of skills development equivalent to that described above for the Research

Internship program. To strengthen the learning process, oral presentations and report writing are scheduled in the first and second half of the course, supported by a feedback session of student performance after the assessment of the first oral presentation and report.

ePortfolio use and implementation were introduced in ANAT3212 in 2013 to facilitate students' reflection on the development of their skills during the course and consideration of how the skills developed in this course could be integrated into a life-long learning process. After successful implementation of reflective practice learning and doing in this course in 2013, the ePortfolio component became an assessable item in ANAT3212 the following year. The allocated total grade for the ePortfolio task contributed to 5% of the overall course grade. The value of ePortfolios in stimulating and supporting student engagement in reflective processes within ANAT3212 has been recognized both by students and those teaching the course over a period of three years in which ePortfolios have been used.

Honors Program

The School of Medical Sciences Honors Program has recently implemented ePortfolio use. The Honors program in the School of Medical Sciences (SOMS4001/ 4002) is a one-year program that aims to train students in research skills that are directly relevant to various Biomedical Science fields. The program runs as a fourth-year course and has an annual enrollment of approximately 60–80 students. The majority of the students have carried out undergraduate studies with a major in a biomedical (anatomy, pathology, physiology, or pharmacology) or related discipline. The Honors degree involves the following research-based assessment tasks: a literature review and an introductory seminar at the beginning of the project and a final oral presentation and a written manuscript at the end of the program. ePortfolios were introduced into the Honors program in 2015 to increase student reflection practice through an assessable, 500-word-long reflective essay, focusing on four key areas: (1) Building an awareness of skills learned, (2) Development of career awareness, (3) Identifying personal values, and (4) Self-reflective practice. Targeting students in the fourth year of their studies is important since this is the time when students are not only trained in skills directly relevant to their future workplaces, but are also increasingly engaging in career planning. Introducing ePortfolios into the Honors program is well integrated with the current practice of ePortfolio pedagogy in School of Medical Sciences undergraduate courses: in particular the research-focused third-year courses. Continuing reflective practices throughout the fourth year of their studies allows students to further refine their reflective skills.

In 2015, the reflective exercise was scheduled after the final oral presentation and the submission of the project manuscript to allow a reflective process that encompasses the entire journey from the start to the end of the students' Honors candidature. The reflective essay was then scored by members of the School of

Medical Sciences Honors committee, who are academics or biomedical research scientists. Approximately six to seven essays were assessed by each examiner, which allowed a comparison of the students' extent of reflective practice. This assessment technique allowed for a valuable level of benchmarking the students' reflective practices and comparison of students' performance. We then implemented a different approach in order to connect the assessment of the reflective practice with the assessment of the skills that were acquired throughout the candidature. To achieve this objective, the reflective exercise has now been incorporated as a reflective summary into the final manuscript. The examiners of the Honors students' research-based assessment tasks are School of Medical Sciences academic staff members. For each student, the same examiner marks all four assessment tasks (literature review, introductory seminar, final seminar, and project manuscript). Therefore, the examiner is able to correlate the student's reflection with the observed progression and performance of the student throughout the candidature. The new structure of the assessment process is expected to provide a more insightful assessment of the students' reflective practices.

Career Learning in the Medical Sciences

Connecting and Integrating Reflection, ePortfolio, Professional Skills, and Career Development

The development of career learning and professional identity interventions has been increasingly on our agendas in higher education. Career development learning (CDL) is a process that "empowers individuals to identify, develop and articulate the skills, qualifications, experiences, attributes and knowledge that will enable them to make an effective transition into their chosen futures, and manage their careers as life-long learners, with a realistic and positive attitude" (Stanbury, 2005). It is both a trans-disciplinary process and a subject discipline with its own history, evidence base, theoretical frameworks, and methodologies. The goal of CDL is to help students to acquire knowledge, concepts, skills, and attitudes that will equip them to manage their careers, and therefore their life-long progression in learning and work (Watts, 2006). Although there are different theories and developmental approaches to careers education, the most widely used framework by career centers around the world is the "DOTS" model (Figure 7.2). The basic assumption underpinning this model is that effective career learning is composed of a dynamic relationship between Decisions, Opportunities, Transitions, and Self (DOTS) (Watts, 2006). These four elements involve: Decision making—being able to weigh up personal factors to make a sound plan, Opportunity awareness—knowledge of opportunities and the ability to research them, Transition learning—understanding of how to seek and secure employment opportunities, and Self-awareness—the ability to identify and articulate motivations, skills, and personality as they affect career plans (Figure 7.2).

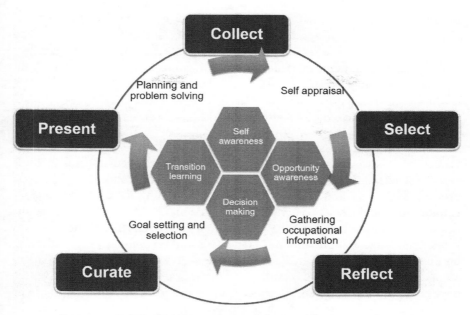

Figure 7.2, DOTS, CDMSE, and ePortfolio model (Yang et al., 2015).

These stages build iteratively upon each other, so, ideally, students move through the cycle more than once during their program and are afforded the opportunity to do so. An ePortfolio enables students to document their learning journey through ongoing deep reflection as they collect the artifacts that the DOTS model provokes. The ePortfolio in this instance is a space where they can collect their experiences, reflect on the connections between theory and practice, and present evidence of development of their graduate attributes, so that upon graduation they are well situated to make a successful transition into their chosen employment (Figure 7.2; Polly, Cox et al., 2015; Yang et al., 2015).

We found that when embedded in a curriculum that used CDL interventions alongside the DOTS model and a program-wide portfolio to collect evidence of learning generated in assessment, learners developed a narrative of their new disciplinary knowledge. We have utilized the ePortfolio to serve a range of these purposes, from career presentations for professional identity development to tools of learning and experimentation. Our ePortfolios, when designed with both DOTS and CDL, record past and current practice, provide opportunities for reflection upon practice to effect change, and act as a change agent by enabling long-term ongoing evaluation of performance and associated learning outcomes.

As CDL requires the student to undertake self-assessment and perform an appraisal of the context of their learning in relation to their discipline, it lends itself to learning and teaching methods that require reflection (McIlveen et al., 2009). David Boud, Rosemary Keogh, and David Walker (2013) suggest that reflecting on learning transforms experience into learning as it allows opportunity for the student to reassess an experience and make decisions on how to change or improve on the learning outcomes. As Boud (2000) shows, such reflection also enables students to: 1. identify their learning, 2. make judgments about their learning, and 3. prepare them for more learning.

Developing Self-efficacy and Self-determination in the Medical Sciences

Career awareness and employability building better equipped students to compete for scholarships and/or jobs (see Coleman et al., this collection). From our previous experience and Michael Tomlinson's 2008 study, we know that student employability is not solely determined by academic qualifications. Other qualities are also important, including generic graduate attributes and the ability to properly package and present one's credentials and capabilities. After reflecting on these findings, we designed a new course for third-year science students in 2012: Cancer Sciences (PATH3208). We were the first to deliver integrated career development learning (ICDL) in which both professional knowledge and career development learning were introduced in a learner-centered ePortfolio (a teaching ePortfolio in Moodle plus student ePortfolios in Mahara) utilizing emerging technologies (Yang et al., 2013, 2015) (see Castaño and Novo, this collection). We used the internationally recognized assessment tool, the Career Decision-Making Self-Efficacy (CDMSE) Scale, which seeks to measure student confidence in pursuing their career goals and to assess the longitudinal impact of interventions in career development education. The results from all thirty-two students in PATH3208 indicated that students were significantly more confident in four of the five aspects of self-efficacy: self-appraisal, obtaining occupational information, planning, and problem solving. However, even after the career intervention, students were no longer confident in the fifth aspect of goal selection (Figure 7.2). The outcomes of this pilot study support the extension of this approach to other third-year undergraduate science courses (Yang et al., 2015).

As educators within the higher education domain, we are keenly aware of the need to develop in our senior undergraduates the graduate capabilities, skills, and attributes necessary for them to reach their full potential in the graduate employment marketplace. ICDL is an "integrated learning approach specifically focusing on integrating professional knowledge and skills, career awareness and employability with disciplinary learning. ICDL is a self-directed learning component in these science classes" (Yang & Polly, 2015, p. 71). *Integrative learning*, according to the Association of American Colleges and Universities (AAC&U), is an understanding and a disposition that a student builds across the curriculum and co-curriculum, from making simple connections among ideas and experiences to synthesizing and transferring learning to new, complex situations within and beyond the campus (AAC&U, 2010). ICDL is therefore a process that empowers individuals to identify, develop, and articulate the skills, qualifications, experiences, attributes, and knowledge that will enable them to make an effective transition into their chosen futures and manage their careers as lifelong learners, with a realistic and positive attitude (Stanbury, 2005). ICDL makes student learning more meaningful by helping students to make the connection between their disciplinary studies, professional skills, and career aspirations. Success of the pilot study in the PATH3208 course led to application of the ICDL in four of the five third-year science courses in 2013: PATH3208: Cancer Sciences; PHAR3101: Drug Discovery, Design and Development; PHAR3202: Neuropharmacology; and ANAT3212: Microscopy in Research; the remaining course, NEUR3221: Neurophysiology, was used as a non-ICDL control. This approach enabled more students in third-year courses within the School of Medical Sciences to be engaged in an ICDL process in order to develop career awareness, employability, and professional skills. In addition, this approach allowed us to evaluate the ICDL in larger sample sizes and with proper controls.

As a result of our evaluation, we now propose our new ISA model (Yang & Azouz, 2015; Yang et al., 2016)—Image of potential own career, Self-directed lifelong and life-wide learning, Assessment and adjustment (see Figure 7.3)—as a mechanism for delivering ICDL. We developed this model as part of our study, as there have not been any previous single models that can comprehensively address this learning issue. The ISA model describes students' learning at the current time in which: 1. they can see their images of own potential career, 2. they can carry out a self-directed learning journey to pursue their career goals, and 3. they can assess and adjust their studies to get the most from them. Image pertains to professional and career goals and integrative learning tasks for obtaining knowledge, skills, and capabilities to achieve goals. Self-directed learning is a life-long and life-wide process since career goals may change in levels and/or directions due to opportunity or personal or socioeconomic reasons. The assessment and feedback from self, peer, and/or academic professional will frequently stimulate reflection and modification for appropriate personal learning (see Balthazor et al., this collection).

The ISA model stimulates students' intentional inquiry on personal learning issues, integration across isolated learning events, and reflection on previous learning experience. Therefore, it best describes this integrative learning and teaching approach and focuses on outcome-based active and reflective learning. The effective ICDL is composed of a dynamic relationship between self, opportunities, decisions, and transitions (Watts, 2006). Self-beliefs about career decision-making have been operationally defined using the concept of the CDMSE (Taylor & Betz, 1983), which highlights five relevant behaviors well matched with the DOTS model: self-appraisal, gathering occupational information, goal selection, planning, and problem solving. ICDL is part of integrative learning and focuses on professional knowledge and skills, career awareness, and employability learning. The ICDL is a life-long learning approach that is a "purposeful learning activity undertaken in an ongoing way with the aim of improving knowledge, skills and competence" (Eurostat, 2020) and thus it should be classified as self-directed and reflective learning.

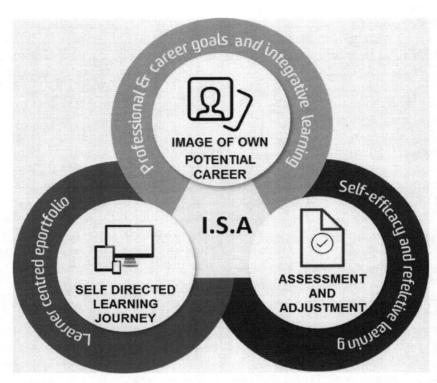

Figure 7.3: ISA Model: Image of own potential career, self-directed life-long and life-wide learning as well as assessment and adjustment model (Yang & Azouz, 2015; Yang et al., 2016).

Within the context of higher education, ePortfolios provide students with the opportunity to become owners of their learning as they collect, select, reflect, present, and curate their artifacts and evidence for assessment (Allen & Coleman, 2011) (see Coleman et al., this collection). ePortfolios also represent a useful vehicle for reflective practice—the process by which a student can transform experience into learning (Brookfield, 1995). Since effective ICDL requires the student to undertake self-assessment and perform an appraisal of the context of their discipline, ICDL lends itself to learning and teaching methods that require reflection (McIlveen et al., 2011). The capacity of ePortfolios to support reflection and selection makes their use a logical "best fit" tool for improving skills needed for graduate recruitment (Leece, 2005).

The ICDL intervention included but was not limited to following five broad areas:

- Guided and structured career development learning activities—including specific tutorials on how to use the Mahara/Moodle ePortfolio system; career opportunities associated with one's own profession; job-search strategies, goal setting, personal achievement recording, résumé writing, and interview techniques from video cases.

- Apprenticeship-style professional skills learning—including knowledge and experience gained through involvement in a real research group meeting and experiments; knowledge gained through invited seminar presentations by professionals; or knowledge gained through visits to research and practice facilities within or outside of the campus during which students had opportunities to talk with working professionals in fields of interest to them, or knowledge acquired from lectures, tutorials, and practicals. The "to do as a scientist does" approach to the practicals exposes students early in an apprenticeship/internship learning stage, which is critical for building independent research ability. Through the curriculum and co-curriculum activities, students, like scientists, construct cancer-specific knowledge, building upon previously obtained general knowledge to form a schema or brain knowledge network. Students work together to review current literature and identify a valid cancer research question in a group and, through collaborative learning, they design their project with hypotheses/aims, methods, and expected outcomes. Students then present and discuss their project with peers and write a literature review and project report.

- Student directed ICDL, using ePortfolio records and reflection on personal achievements in professional and career development learning through the completion of various written assignments, experiential activities, self-explorations, and group or class discussions.

- Development of a personal career plan in the ePortfolio "view" and a tailored résumé in Mahara, as well as participation in a mock interview.

- Participation in the pre- and post-course CDMSE surveys to further increase career awareness.

We then compared CDMSE subscales effects across four ICDL courses. Results indicated significant improvement in three or all five CDMSE subscales in all four ICDL courses. In contrast, there was no improvement in any CDMSE subscales in the non-ICDL (control) course. Comparing the ICDL group and the control group, a significant improvement in all five subscales was observed in the ICDL group but not the non-ICDL control group.

Outcomes from this study suggest that the incorporation of ICDL with the ISA model focusing on goal setting, ePortfolio career learning and reflection, and graduate capabilities can engage students in learning, teaching, and assessment to encourage and develop an understanding of professional identity in undergraduate science courses. This program-wide project proved successful in improving students' confidence in their abilities to seek positions of their choice as assessed by the Career Decision-making Self-efficacy Scale, and supports the extension of this approach to other senior undergraduate courses or programs in higher education.

Conclusion

The implementation and use of ePortfolio pedagogy to facilitate thinking, skills development, and research practice in the medical sciences is an important way to build reflective practice within a digital space. It has developed a program of learning, teaching, and assessment underpinned by a team who have in turn developed their own reflective practice and skills as learning designers. We have found that ePortfolio pedagogy that explicitly models and scaffolds authentic reflective practice is a foundational skill, developed over time as practice for preparing students to think critically and creatively as career aware, employable, and ready to enter postgraduate programs beyond their undergraduate medical science degree program. Linking ePortfolio thinking and assessment tasks that are authentic to the discipline has had the effect of improving student capabilities in research communication and practice, as well as teamwork and career learning as they develop their identity and sense of self as apprentice biomedical research scientists and future employees.

Acknowledgments

The studies presented here were funded by multiple UNSW Learning and Teaching Seed Grants and a UNSW Innovation grant and have received UNSW Sydney Human Ethics Approval, Ethics numbers HC13005, HC15134.

References

Abrami, P. & Barrett, H. (2005). Directions for research and development on electronic portfolios. *Canadian Journal of Learning and Technology/La revue canadienne de l'apprentissage et de la technologie, 31*(3), 1–15.

Allen, B. & Coleman, K. (2011). The creative graduate: Cultivating and assessing creativity with eportfolios [Conference presentation] *Changing Demands, Changing Directions. Proceedings ascilite Hobart,* 59–69. Australian Society for Computers in Learning in Tertiary Education.

Association of American Colleges and University. (2010). Integrative and applied learning VALUE rubric. https://www.aacu.org/value/rubrics/integrative-learning.

Australian ePortfolio Project. (2008). Final Report. https://research.qut.edu.au /eportfolio/australian-eportfolio-project-final-report/.

Barrett, H. (2005). Researching electronic portfolios: Learning, engagement, collaboration, through technology. http://electronicportfolios.org.

Batson, T. (2015). The significance of ePortfolio in education. Batson Blog, AAEEBL. http://www.aaeebl.org/blogpost/1008436/229349/The-Significance-of-ePortfolio -in-Education.

Bosanquet, A., Winchester-Seeto, T. & Rowe, A. (2010, July). Changing perceptions underpinning graduate attributes: A pilot study [Conference presentation]. Research and development in higher education> Reshaping Higher Education,

33, 105/115. https://www.researchgate.net/publication/272026146_Changing_per
ceptions_underpinning_graduate_attributes_A_pilot_study#fullTextFile
Content.

Boud, D. (2000). Sustainable assessment: Rethinking assessment for the learning
society. *Studies in Continuing Education, 22*(2), 151–167.

Boud, D., Keogh, R. & Walker, D. (2013). *Reflection: Turning experience into learning.*
Routledge.

Brookfield, S. (1995). The getting of wisdom:. *Becoming a critically reflective teacher.*
Jossey-Bass..

Butler, P. (2007). A review of the literature on portfolios and electronic portfolios.
https://uncw.edu/cas/assessment/docs/resources/eportfolioprojectresearch
report.pdf.

Cambridge, D. (2008). Audience, integrity, and the living document: eFolio Minnesota and lifelong and lifewide learning with ePortfolios. *Computers & Education,
51*(3), 1227–1246

Chen, H. L. & Penny Light, T. (2010). *Electronic portfolios and student success, effectiveness, efficiency, and learning.* Association of American Colleges and Universities.

Clarke, T., Housego, S. & Parker, N. (2009). Positioning ePortfolios in an integrated
curriculum.*Education + Training, 51*(5/6), 408–421.

Coleman, K. S. & Flood, A. (Eds.). (2016). *Enabling reflective thinking: Reflective
practice in learning and teaching.* Common Ground Publishing.

Costa, A. L. & Kallick, B. (2009). *Habits of mind across the curriculum: Practical
and creative strategies for teachers.* Association for Supervision and Curriculum
Development.

Eurostat, Adult Learning Statistics. (2020, May 12). https://ec.europa.eu/eurostat
/statistics-explained/index.php?title=Adult_learning_statistics.

Eynon, B. & Gambino, L. (2015). *The high impact eportfolio practice: A catalyst for
student, faculty and institutional learning.* Stylus.

Hallam, G. C., Harper, W. E., McCowan, C. R., Hauville, K. L., McAllister, L. M. &
Creagh, T. A. (2008). ePortfolio use by university students in Australia: Informing excellence in policy and practice. Australian ePortfolio Project final Report
http://www.eportfoliopractice.qut.edu.au/.

Herrington, J., Oliver, R. & Reeves, T. C. (2003a). "Cognitive realism" in online
authentic learning environments. In D. Lassner & C. McNaught (Eds.), *EdMedia
world conference on educational multimedia, hypermedia and telecommunications*
(pp. 2115–2121). Association for the Advancement of Computing in Education.

Herrington, J., Oliver, R. & Reeves, T.C. (2003b). Patterns of engagement in authentic onlinelearning environments. *Australian Journal of Educational Technology,
19*(1), 59–71.

Jones, G. & Polly, P. (2013). Scaffolding student learning by managing the development of academic literacys through an oral presentation assessment. In
K. Coleman & A. Flood (Eds.), *Marking time: Leading and managing the development of assessment in higher education.* The Learner Series.

Leece, R. (2005). The role of e-portfolios in graduate recruitment. *Australian Journal
of Career Development, 14*(2), 72–78.

Lorenzo, G. & Ittelson, J. (2005). An overview of e-portfolios. Educause learning initiative, 1, 1–27. Educause Learning Initiative Paper 1: 2005. https://library .educause.edu/-/media/files/library/2005/1/eli3001-pdf.pdf.

McIlveen, P., Brooks, S., Lichtenberg, A., Smith, M., Torjul, P. & Tyler, J. (2009, April). Career development learning and work-integrated learning practices in Australian universities [Conference presentation]. *Proceedings of the CDAA National Career Conference 2009.*

Oliver, B. (2010, July 20–21). The role of ePortfolios in mapping, assessing and evaluating graduate capabilities [Conference presentation]. *Proceedings of the Association of Authentic Experiential and Evidence-Based Learning Conference.* Boston, United States.

Oliver, B. (2013). Graduate attributes as a focus for institution-wide curriculum renewal: Innovations and challenges. *Higher Education Research & Development, 32*(3), 450–463.

Oliver, B. (2015). Redefining graduate employability and work-integrated learning: Proposals for effective higher education in disrupted economies. *Journal of Teaching and Learning for Graduate Employability, 6*(1), 56–65.

Oliver, B. (2016). Assuring graduate capabilities: Evidencing levels of achievement for graduate employability. Final Report. Office for Learning and Teaching (OLT), New South Wales. https://ltr.edu.au/resources/Oliver_Report_2015.pdf.

Oliver, B. & Whelan, B. (2011). Designing an e-portfolio for assurance of learning focusing on adoptability and learning analytics. *Australasian Journal of Educational Technology, 27*(6), 1026–1041.

Penny Light, T., Chen, H. & Ittelson, J. (2012). *Documenting learning with e-portfolios.* Jossey Bass.

Polly, P., Cox, J., Coleman, K., Yang, J. L. & Thai, T. (2015). Creative teaching, learning and assessment in Medical Science: ePortfolios to support skills development in scientists beyond just knowing their own discipline content. In K. Coleman & A. Flood (Eds.), *Capturing creativity through creative teaching:* The Learner Series.

Polly, P. & Jones, G. (2013). Enhancing student learning in written literacy through assessment and community of practice in a second year pathology course. In K. Coleman & A. Flood (Eds.), *Marking time: Leading and managing the development of assessment in higher education.* The Learner Series.

Polly, P., Thai, T., Flood, A., Coleman, K., Das, M., Yang, J. L. & Cox, J. (2013). Enhancement of scientific research and communication skills using assessment and ePortfolio in a third year pathology course. In H. Carter, M. Gosper & J. Hedberg (Eds.), *Electronic Dreams. Proceedings Ascilite 2013* (pp. 711–723). Australian Society for Computers in Learning in Tertiary Education.

Resort, R. (2011). Research and development in higher education [Paper presentation]. *Higher Education on the Edge 34.* 34th HERDSA Annual International Conference, Gold Coast, Queensland, Australia.

Stanbury, D. (2005). Careers education benchmark statement. *London: Association of Graduate Career Advisory Services.*

Taylor, K. M. & Betz, N. E. (1983). Applications of self-efficacy theory to the understanding and treatment of career indecision. *Journal of Vocational Behavior, 22*(1), 63–81.

Tomlinson, M. (2008). "The degree is not enough": Students' perceptions of the role of higher education credentials for graduate work and employability. *British Journal of Sociology of Education, 29*(1), 49–61

UNSW Sydney. (2011). Blueprint to beyond: UNSW strategic intent. https://www.unsw.edu.au/sites/default/files/documents/UNSW3268_B2B_Design_AW3.pdf.

UNSW Sydney. (2016). Our strategic priorities and themes—UNSW 2025. https://www.2025.unsw.edu.au/sites/default/files/uploads/unsw_2025strategy_201015.pdf.

Vozzo, L., Hatton, C., Reid, J., Pietsch, M., Bennet, M., Nanlohy, P., Moran, W. & Labone, E. (2014). Assessing professional teaching standards in practicum using digital technologies with Aboriginal and other pre-service teachers. Final Report. Office for Learning and Teaching (OLT), New South Wales. https://researchdirect.westernsydney.edu.au/islandora/object/uws:26942,

Watts, A. G. (2006). *Career development learning and employability.* The Higher Education Academy.

Watty, K., Leitch, S., McGuigan, N., Kavanagh, M., Holt, D., Ngo, L., McKay, J., Davies, J. & McCormick, T. (2015). Realising the potential: Assessing professional learning through the integration of ePortfolios in Australian business education. Final Report. Office for Learning and Teaching (OLT), New South Wales https://eprints.usq.edu.au/30917/2/ID13-2888_eportfolios_Final%20Report_2016.pdf.

Yang, J. L. & Azouz, L. (2015). A blended learning strategy encouraging active, life-long and life-wide learning. UNSW Medicine Learning and Teaching Forum 2015. https://d2xnkjysn6lg7q.cloudfront.net/files/unswPDF/1444175788979-2015-Posters-Booklet_final.pdf.

Yang, J. L., Coleman, K., Das, M. & Hawkins, N. (2015). Integrated career development learning and ePortfolios: Improving student self-efficacy in employability skills in an undergraduate science course. *The International Journal of Adult, Community and Professional Learning, 22*(1), 1–17.

Yang, J. L. & Polly, P. (2015, July 9–11). Career development learning across year three science courses—pedagogy and curriculum: Improving student self-efficacy in employability skills [Conference presentation]. The 22nd Learners Conference, Universidad CEU, San Pablo, Madrid, Spain.

Yang, J. L., Polly, P., Fath, T, Jones, N. & Power, J. (2016). ISA model and integrative career development learning in year three science course. *International Journal of Science, Mathematics, and Technology Learning, 23*(3), 33–46.

Chapter 8. A Learning Framework for ePortfolio based on Design Patterns

Andrea Ximena Castaño Sánchez
María Teresa Novo Molinero
Universidad Rovira i Virgili

This chapter proposes a process-learning framework for ePortfolios based on the learning design theory of Diana Laurillard, which aims at providing continuity between instruction and incidental learning in the classroom. We developed and mapped this approach after observing that instructors needed guidance on providing a sequence of ePortfolio-centered activities during the development stage. This concept of teaching and learning as a process also helped students create and identify *artifacts* to document their learning.[1]

In today's educational paradigm, teacher educators employ multiple approaches to convey the nature of iterative relationships among teaching methods, learning activities, and learners' needs. However, the documentation of these approaches, as well as the sharing of innovative strategies with one another represent a lingering concern. Diana Laurillard's (2012) design theory, specifically her *conversational framework*, provides the theoretical context for our model. The conversational framework provides a means for analysis of formal learning to establish an instructor's pedagogic design and the principles that underpin it through the affordances of technology. Indeed, the model's complexity provides the capacity to support sophisticated approaches to learning and *assessment*.

The second lens we use is "pedagogical patterns" (Bergin et al., 2007; Laurillard, 2012). Pedagogical patterns describe the best teaching practices of a given domain. Patterns are written down, shared, and revised, thereby providing templates for successful learning activities that help faculty teach writing based on process theories. Our pedagogical patterns emerged from empirical evidence of, and experience with, effective ePortfolio teaching in the field of teacher education. In the teacher education curriculum, providing pedagogical patterns informed by design theory served a double purpose. First, in using the design theory and pedagogical patterns in our curriculum, we were able to show the teacher candidates who were our students how we as instructors were following the principles we advocated. Second, in requiring the teacher candidates to apply

---

1. The learning framework with ePortfolios that we discuss in this chapter resulted from the design of "Pedagogical Patterns" using Laurillard's "Conversational Framework" model. For others who wish to pursue this approach, we recommend Laurillard's *Teaching as a Design Science: Building Pedagogical Patterns for Learning and Technology* (Routledge, 2012).

DOI: https://doi.org/10.37514/PRA-B.2020.1084.2.08

those principles and to include their learning artifacts in their teaching ePortfolios, they learned how ePortfolios could benefit their future students in the same way their ePortfolios were benefiting them as students in our courses.

The "Conversational Framework" for Learning with Technology

The conversational framework explains the teaching-learning cycle in formal learning derived from educational theories, pedagogical principles, and research findings (see Figure 8.1). In order to capture the principal elements of teaching and learning, the model requires implementation of methods and technologies: "The Conversational Framework specifies the roles to be played by teachers and learners in terms of the principal ideas in theories of learning, so the teaching-learning activities in a pedagogical pattern can be mapped to learning cycles in the framework" (Laurillard, 2012, p. 103).

The interaction among educators, learners, and peers defines a process of learning through concepts and practice, manifested in an iterative process of negotiation and co-construction of knowledge. At the same time, the learning cycles identified for each type of learning[2] are in play: a learning process of exchanging concepts and the outputs of their practice, either between teacher and learner, between learners, or even with oneself (Laurillard, 2012).

The learning cycles involved in the conversational framework are identified as teacher communication cycle (TCC), teacher practice cycle (TPC), teacher modeling cycle (TMC), peer communication cycle (PCC), peer modeling cycle (PMC), and the learner's internal learning cycle that modulates the learner's concepts (LC) and practices (LP). The TCC refers to the teacher's role in aligning goals, monitoring students' notions, and fostering conceptual knowledge. The teacher influences the learner's internal cycle at the conceptual level, while the TPC and TMC contribute to the learner's internal cycle through learning practices such as experiential learning, collaborative learning, or inquiry learning, etc. In a modeled environment, the teacher provides opportunities for learners to perform tasks related to the learning practice (e.g., posting artifacts in a *workspace ePortfolio*). The PCC and PMC include the learner's role in encouraging peers to exchange ideas and experiences; the learners complement the role of the teacher in encouraging *metacognition* and the exchange of ideas and practice among peers.

---

2.   Laurillard (2012) explains the model associated with learning through acquisition, learning through inquiry, learning through discussion, learning through practice, learning through collaboration.

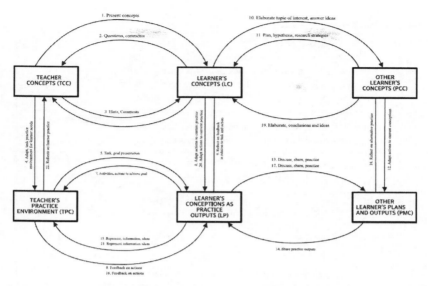

Figure 8.1. Conversational pattern mapped in the conversational framework.

These learning cycles appear in Laurillard's (2012) model as recursive loops that influence and contribute to the learner's internal learning cycle summed up by the base principles of learning in formal settings. The teacher designs a teaching and learning environment that provides the elements and design activities for each learning cycle, thus promoting the learners' capacity to develop their own concepts and practices. We mapped our ePortfolio onto the conversational framework to allow our students to evidence their learning by digital means. Our mapping process is described in Table 8.1, in which we indicate the learning cycle(s) involved and each LC's corresponding interaction according to the conversational model, as shown in Figure 8.1. We also include the number of students involved and the time allotted for each cycle. It is important to note each interaction between teacher and student can occur with just one student or a group of students.

Table 8.1. ePortfolio mapped to the conversational framework

Learning Cycles	Description of the Interaction	Group Size	Time
Teacher Communication Cycle TCC (1,2)	(1) The instructor introduces students to the concepts of the scientific method (the topic can vary if used in another subject) and technical and pedagogical specifications about ePortfolio for learning and through a flipped classroom using videos, tutorials, and learning by doing. (2) They provide activities to explore the ePortfolio platform and construct evaluation guides, *rubrics*, and provision of feedback with students. Students comment and ask questions they may have.	138 students	1 session ePortfolio concept 1 session KPSI

Table 8.1—*continued*

TCC (3) Teacher Practice Cycle TPC (4,5,6)	(3) Students individually practice using their personal ePortfolio and post examples of learning evidence, creating their personal ePortfolio according to their own interests. (4,5,6) Also, they complete a Knowledge Inventory that determines prior knowledge, and which they later publish and reflect on in their ePortfolios. Also, the teacher prepares the learning environment to promote students' conceptualization.	138 students	1 session
TCC (7, 8, 9) Peer Communication Cycle PCC (10, 11)	Students work in groups of 3 to 4 to: (7,8) explore and elaborate on their own topics of interest; (9) perform basic biological research with petri dishes, following the scientific method; access digital resources related to the scientific method to present and discuss the topic; (10,11) choose a topic, plan the setting and hypothesis, research strategies, and use digital tools for information resources, data collection, and data analysis.	43 groups	Through 4 sessions
Peer Modeling Cycle PMC (13,14)	(13,14) Students collect information and interpret data from experiments and select the most relevant results. Students create representations of the information using digital tools and record them using the ePortfolio.	43 groups	Through 4 sessions
PMC (15,16)	(15,16) Students work in topic-specific groups and mediate feedback with the instructor.	43 groups	Through 4 sessions
PCC (18,19)	(18,19) Students analyze and reflect on results with peers and elaborate conclusions.	43 groups	Through 4 sessions
TCC (20,21)	(20, 21) Students publish results in varied digital forms (images, videos, text, blog entries) in their group ePortfolio.	43 groups	Through 4 sessions
TPC (22,23)	(22,23) Students individually post reflections in their ePortfolios and choose evidence from the activities to be published, acknowledging cooperative efforts with their peers.	183 students	Through 4 sessions
Designers' Reflections	It is important to know that the interaction between teacher and student can be to one student or to a group of students. Large groups of students require a lot of the instructor's time. It is necessary to group students to facilitate extrinsic feedback and peer interaction.		

Table 8.1—*continued*	
Designers' Reflections continued	Also, providing the ePortfolio rubric in advance, along with all other course scoring rubrics (Appendix 2), may influence learners as far as evidence collecting. But this approach may be counterproductive as it discourages students from exploring other forms of doing.
	The strict time limit and reactions triggered by activities within the classroom can be positive as far as the instructor's feedback, but it would be valuable to know how this time frame suits each student's own pace.

Pedagogical Patterns

A pedagogical pattern can be defined as a detailed description of an educational practice that proposes a general solution for an educational problem, according to a set of determined characteristics within the learning environment. The goal is to effectively troubleshoot problems in similar educational situations. The pattern must follow a "problem-solving template" associated with each contextual and discipline settings (Bergin et al., 2007; Derntl, 2006; Derntl et al., 2009; Laurillard, 2012).

Pedagogical patterns differ from design patterns. In this case, "pedagogy" refers to formal learning; the instructor must be able to employ the pedagogy that proves most effective. The essence of a pattern is to solve a problem that recurs in different contexts, keeping in mind that a problem can reappear in a slightly different form each time. Teaching and learning activities are mapped in the range of learning cycles within the conversational framework. Each activity must play its part in prompting other activities to ensure interaction among cycles of learning. Therefore, this process represents modeling practices based on the characteristics of the learning environment and students as active learners (Laurillard, 2007).

A pedagogical pattern is presented in a formal description to capture sound pedagogy; this format identifies teaching design in terms of "general descriptors" or "context descriptors," which provide sufficient information linked to pedagogic design principles so that other instructors can use this information in other contexts. "Pedagogy descriptors" provide the information about the effectiveness of the teaching and learning design with technology, while the "evaluative descriptors" identify ways in which to improve the pattern.

Laurillard (2012) has categorized the general descriptors as: origin, referencing the source of the pattern; summary, a brief description of what is being taught and how; topics, or keywords to help other instructors to apply the pattern; learning outcomes, what the learner will know or be able to do by the end; rationale, the learning approach or pedagogic design principle; duration, time spent on the activities (not necessarily continuous); learner characteristics, educational experiences, interests, etc.; setting, face-to-face, blended, or online learning; and group size. The pedagogy descriptors comprise both "teaching information" and "comments," which are categorized as: resources and tools, any physical and digital materials, as well as any conventional or digital technologies; learning cycles, the sequence of teaching-learning activities according to the conversational framework; the designer's *reflection*; and student feedback. We formulated our pedagogical pattern using "general descriptors" and "pedagogical descriptors" to explain the purpose of the model in teaching the scientific method (see Table 8.2)

In Table 8.3, we summarize the learning design features of ePortfolio development into a generic pedagogical pattern. The description of every design feature identified is linked to its specific source in Table 8.4.

Table 8.2. Pedagogical pattern for evidencing learning with ePortfolio in the context of teaching the scientific method

Title	Evidencing learning to teach the scientific method
Source	Spanish university class for pre-service teachers training during the course "Teaching and learning experimental sciences, social sciences and math" degree in Elementary Education.
Summary	Using ePortfolios to document and track students' products and reflection on learning activities carried out during instructional time; involving individual and group work on learning how to teach children the scientific method with petri dish experiments.
Topics	Evidence of learning, ePortfolio, teaching natural sciences, pre-service teacher education, collaborative work.
Learning Outcomes (forces)	To evidence knowledge of the scientific method, and to demonstrate teaching skills by developing strategies for conducting classroom experiments following the scientific method.
Rationale	Constructivist pedagogy, *inquiry-based learning*, learning by doing.
Duration	Four weeks
Learner Characteristics	Pre-service teachers in the Elementary Education Program and the Teaching and learning experimental sciences, social sciences, and math course.
Setting (context)	Classroom, computer lab, and learning environments in practicum.
Group size	138 third-year undergraduate students in the Elementary Education Program.
Resource and Tools	Mahara ePortfolio Platform, Moodle, KPSI[3] test, handouts with general instructions, bibliographical sources, videos, blogs, social media, documents online.

---

3. KPSI i Knowledge and Prior Study Inventory (Giné, N. y Parcerisa, A., 2003)

Table 8.3. Learning design features of ePortfolio

Learning Design Features of ePortfolio				
Agency				
Taking different skill levels, interests, and participations into account.		Identifying learner's goals		
Managing Self and Interaction				
Journal-Reflection	Learners' interaction on social media and connection to ePortfolio.	Peer interaction/ collaboration	Content knowl-edge (theory)	Collaborative teamwork
Scaffolding				
Student-centered teaching	Problem-based learning	Learning activities	Assessment	
Identification of Evidence				
Evidencing learning		Making the learning process visible		

Additionally, the use of digital technologies is transversal to the design features. These design features add value by informing designers, instructors, and the target student population about the details of learning interaction with media technology. In this sense, the proposed pattern makes demands on the affordances of ePortfolio technology/platforms, so that stakeholders can adapt the same to suit their demands. ePortfolio technology may consist of platforms that might be augmented through the incorporation of social media, productive tools, reflective tools, LMS outputs, and ePortfolio software, as well as asynchronous online discussions, blog entries, website feeds, social media, publications from authoring tools, and tools for recording data and reflections, file sharing, and manipulation of documents (Presant, 2016; Ravet, 2015).

Table 8.4. Mapping of learning-associated patterns for ePortfolio to design solutions

ePortfolio for Learning Design Features	
Agency	
Take different skill levels and interests into account	Engaging students in *active learning*; the thought is to motivate students, driven by their own interests, to produce new information.
	Reference patterns: "Expand the known world," "explore for yourself" and "students decide" (Bergin et al., 2002).
	Highlighting the idea that in student-centered settings, the learner ought to be effectively included in characterizing general learning goals in addition their own singular objectives for the course. In this sense, the educator can adjust the learning process to student-identified objectives.
	Reference patterns: "Elaborating goals and expectations" (Derntl, 2005, p 322).

Table 8.4—*continued*	
Managing Self and Interaction	
Journal-Reflection	Allowing students access to online platforms that facilitate journaling where students record changes in thinking and attitude, information gathering, ways of knowing, and express alignment of the content with their personal goals.
	Providing the conditions for students to search for solutions by exploring problems encountered during educational experiences.
	Motivating students through their own experiences.
	Identifying learning and the synthesis of evidence accompanied by the detection of learning gaps.
	Reference patterns: "Diary" pattern (Derntl, 2006, p. 272). "Reflection" pattern (Bergin et al., 2002)
Learner interaction via social media and connections to ePortfolio	Taking advantage of the open nature of social participatory media.
	Promoting networking among students with social media web tools or connected with ePortfolios, promoting the creation of a coherent presentation instead of disconnected pieces of text—giving value to this type of evidence.
	Managing digital media and online presence.
	Being aware of the managing of digital identity related with the ePortfolio, the criteria to consider something private or public.
	Most of these design features are referenced in the related framework for building and scaffolding interaction in social spaces, which denotes three group patterns: design of a social environment; supporting interaction inside (virtual) communities; and managing channel communications also related to patterns developed in the Rhizome project on digital identity (Warburton, 2012).
	Reference patterns: "Social Media and Learning Interaction in social spaces" (Warburton, 2014, pp. 151–158).
Peer inter-action/Collaboration	Supporting meaningful academic conversations about learning.
	Facilitating asynchronous online communication among participants, instructors, tutors.
	Facilitating synchronous online interaction which is embedded to a certain learning activity.
	Asking learners to comment on each other's work.
	Allowing participants to discuss their contributions, resources, and ideas online and face-to-face.
	Reference patterns: "Chat," "Online discussions," "exchange of contributions" (Derntl, 2005, pp. 310, 377).

Table 8.4—*continued*	
Content knowledge (theory)	Promoting information gathering, supported by instructor and peers.
	Elaborating on content associated with learning as a concept.
	Discussing gathered information and subsequent results.
	Motivating participants to collect information such as examples, theories, brainstorming, results which could be gathered in collaboration and shares among peers.
	Reflecting on appropriate information within a given context.
	Maximizing learning by engaging students.
	Reference patterns: "Brainstorming," "Theory elaboration," "Information Gathering" (Derntl, 2005, p. 329). "Test Tube"; "Try it yourself" (Bergin et al., 2002).
Collaborative teamwork	Providing opportunities for participants to choose their team partner(s) and to work in teams (e.g., publishing in group ePortfolios).
	Providing social media tools to work collaboratively.
	Supporting authentic, organized team tasks.
	Encouraging peer support by information exchange, reciprocal inspiration, and social interaction, learning, and teaching to peers that can evolve into communities of learning and practice.
	Supporting team-initiated decisions.
	Determining team size on the basis of task requirements.
	Reference patterns: "Student group management" (Avgeriou et al., 2004). "Team building" (Derntl, 2005, p. 363). "Groups work" "Study groups" (Bergin et al., 2002).
Scaffolding	
Student-centered instruction	Providing scaffolding to ensure a student-centered environment and opportunities for interaction.
	Facilitating learners' assimilation of concepts and theory.
	Increasing participation gradually.
	Reference pattern: "Interactive lecture" (Derntl, 2005, p. 172): "Active Student" (Bergin et al., 2002)
Problem proposals	Allowing learners to choose between solving personal or assigned problems. To this end, learners can follow a method.
	Providing a specific, proven methodology to employ in project- or problem-based learning activities.
	Facilitating learners' active involvement in and dedication to the problem-solving process.
	Reference patterns: "Problem proposals" (Derntl, 2005, p. 356); "Real world experience," "Problem solving machine," "Students design sprints" (Bergin et al., 2002).

Table 8.4—*continued*	
Learning activities	These are related to agency as methodologies and problem proposals..
Assessment	Providing a space where learners share their work and refer to it during the learning activity.
	The following objectives associated with assessment patterns may not be graded as part of an ePortfolio, but their use may improve evidence throughout the ePortfolio process:
	- Grade teams fairly, ensure fair individual grading.
	- Ensure participants learn from their own experience.
	- Require participants to be less dependent on the instructor.
	- Require participants to apply theory.
	- Ensure participants understand the topic.
	- Suggesting tasks, activities that produce evidence of learning on ePortfolios.
	Reference patterns: "try it yourself," "self-test," "fair grading," "fair project grading," "peer grading," "key ideas dominate grading," "online ePortfolios" (Bergin et al., 2002); "Classroom display" (Pachler et al., 2009, p. 46). "Blended evaluation" (Comber, 2014, p. 293).
Feedback	Providing feedback characterized by given opportunities for learners to internalize concepts and ways of knowing.
	Offering constructive feedback.
	Tutors/teachers receiving feedback.
	Ensuring feedback can improve evidence in ePortfolio.
	Reference patterns: "Feedback on feedback," "differentiated feedback," "feedback," "feedback sandwich," "embrace correction," "acquire participants feedback," "anonymous feedback" (Bergin et al., 2002), (Derntl, 2006, p. 221, Whitlock & Mellar, 2014, p. 311).
Identification Use of Evidence	
Evidence learning	Guiding effective discussions, tasks, and activities that elicit evidence of learning.
	Keeping in mind that although this pattern resembles an ePortfolio scenario, it presents subtle differences in not being only an informal communication channel via a blog, as in the original source, but a persistent collection of personal assets.
	Providing an option to have an assignment that is created specifically for web presentation.
	Creating assignments that can be displayed in ePortfolios.
	Recognizing evidence and justifying criteria for credentialing and open *badges* (Ravet).*
	Reference patterns: "Showcase learning," (Robertson, 2014, p. 67); "Online portfolios" (Bergin et al., 2002).

Table 8.4—*continued*	
Make the learning process visible	Allowing learners to express themselves in a narrative form. - Learners make sense of events and observations. - Learners can use digital objects to converse about a common learning activity. - The student must reflect either on a blog or a dedicated element embedded in an ePortfolio. - Learners comment and interact with each other. Reference patterns: "Narrative spaces," (Pachler et al., 2010, p. 51). "Spotlighting the learning process," (Derntl, 2014), "Object to talk with" (Pachler et al., 2010, p. 54).

Note: Badges "were created to capture learning whenever and wherever that learning occurs: formal, informal, public, private, group, individual" and Open badges "can be designed to represent a small thing, such as fundamental principle or a single competency or to represent a large thing like a competency set, license, or a degree."

Instructors can map ePortfolio elements to all learning cycles described in the conversational framework, depending on how they incorporate technology in instruction and assessment.

Design Pattern for Evidencing Learning in ePortfolios

When married to learning strategies for ePortfolio, design patterns have the potential to link course activities and students' reflections in order to evidence students' learning during formal instruction. The mapping of learning-associated patterns, independent of learning outcomes and methodology, serves to (1) facilitate participants' trust in their own knowledge, (2) make the value of gained knowledge visible and (3) make learners reflect on their own participation in classroom/course activities.

A problem may occur when students need to evidence their learning either for recognition in a *showcase ePortfolio* or to recall aspects of learning in a workspace model, or both. At the same time, instructors need access to student evidence to follow up on their learning paths, to ensure formative assessment complements summative assessment, and to provide feedback and support. Also, teachers need to identify pedagogical challenges about ePortfolio implementation during formative moments.

Students may not be able to place certain traces of digital interaction in their ePortfolios, such as responses during simulations or immersive virtual worlds, mainly due to digital incompatibility. However, there is the possibility of validating the evidence originated in these kind of learning environments. This feedback is provided by considering different learning paths as methods developed; therefore, its importance relies on the moments the learner or the mentor acknowledge the need to evidence learning.

Solution

Through the exploitation and interconnection of digital spaces, the ePortfolio allows richer and more diverse opportunities for interaction among stakeholders. For this purpose, the technology should offer "simplicity, immediacy, transparency, customizability and support for intuitively structured instructor-student and peer interaction" (Derntl, 2014, p. 61). The ePortfolio may provide evidence of learning during instructional time, such as when the student constructs their (digital) personal identity in their ePortfolio (Barrett 2005, 2016). Also, learners collect and construct evidence all the time by reflecting on their learning needs, considering their previous experiences in a subject area, keeping track of social media interactions, working with other students, gathering information from the content area, completing scaffolded learning activities, retaining feedback (which can occur online and face-to-face, during evaluation, co-evaluation, self-evaluation) designing their own learning, and so on.

Theoretical Justification

The functional elements of ePortfolio can serve as a display of learning at many consecutive moments during the flow of learning activities. Learning activities display different actions at different moments of the learning cycles, as seen in the conversational framework pattern (Figure 8.1). The student is constantly performing some type of action, even if that action is perceived as passive (e.g., observing/listening to their partners when engaged in teamwork). In these moments, students create evidence that comes inherently from the course design and from intrinsic motivation, depending on the educational experience. These learning activities have been described in terms of design patterns (Derntl, 2005; Mor et al., 2014), which happen at different moments during formal learning. The instructor and/or other instructors can recycle these patterns in subsequent course designs.

As well, complementary learning activities associated with ePortfolio integration and implementation foster the manifestation of design patterns associated with ePortfolio for learning, especially reflective elements within the ePortfolio, the use of evidence based on artifacts, and reflection supported by social media. New patterns can be derived from related patterns already implemented, thereby supporting the learning design. In our case, we identified the relationship between the patterns we had gathered as part of the solution and the five key aspects for ePortfolio integration: situational factors, learning goals, feedback, assessment, and teaching and learning activities (Fink, 2013), knowing that every ePortfolio has a different purpose and every discipline has its own timing and resources (see Coleman et al., this collection).[4] Therefore, instructors must articulate ePortfolio

---

4. Fink (2013, p. 76) has identified the situational factors as class, size, level of the course, time structure; general context: curriculum, traditional or online; nature of the

components with the course design, based on the mapping of course activities and assessment.

Teaching and learning activities should align with the learning outcomes. These activities must reflect the principles of active learning and reflective dialogue for (personal) learning goals. To understand the integrative nature of the learning ePortfolio, Fink (2013) points explicitly to the relationship between effective teaching and learning activities, on one hand, and meaningful feedback and assessment procedures on the other: "this is the relation between feedback and assessment activities that enhance the learning process" (p. 94).

Feedback and assessment components provide students and instructors a qualitative measure for how well they are achieving their goals, and also provide value and meaning to what is being taught (Castaño et al., 2015). Instructors should provide frequent and immediate feedback, caringly delivered in accordance with the principles of positive feedback (Nicol & Macfarlane-Dick, 2006). Assessment procedures should also have clear criteria for showcasing skills and achievement and provide opportunities for self-assessment and peer assessment (Abrami & Barrett, 2005; Derntl, 2014). Feedback and assessment procedures should be included in the design of student-centered ePortfolios in which students showcase collected evidence of what they know from diverse educational experiences and contexts. Through this intentional design, students are more likely to engage in meaningful reflection, which should lead to the identification of learning, the synthesis of evidence, as well as the identification of gaps in learning (Borman & Dowling, 2006; Johnson et al., 2006). ePortfolios for assessment should likewise include students, instructors, and peers in the evaluation process. K. Chang Barker (2006, p. 312) affirms that ePortfolios for assessment must include some form of "student achievement by teachers" and assessment of "student progress and changes in knowledge, skills and abilities." This assessment model provides a bigger picture of students' work over time.

Therefore, the success of ePortfolio-mediated learning is dependent on appropriate ePortfolio-mediated pedagogy, which, with careful design, may facilitate learners' ability to identify significant evidence of their progress and sense of value for their learning. Some ePortfolio course integration proposals have promoted the use of specific activities at various points in the learning cycles such as: encouraging students to engage with the learning outcomes of the course so these become their own goals; teaching students how to evidence their learning achievements; providing opportunities to gain awareness of their strengths and weaknesses through self-reflection, peer review, and teacher feedback; providing opportunities for students to share their work; encouraging group work; showcasing students' work in class; evaluating a learner's own work and his/her peers'

---

subject: convergent or divergent physical skills; student characteristics: prior knowledge, attitudes, personal situation, reason for enrolling; and teacher characteristics: level of development, course expertise.

work based on common criteria; and making room for learners to question content while providing evidence (CityU, 2011).

Additionally, ePortfolio creators need to weigh a number of factors when they prepare to publish their ePortfolio (Castaño, 2014). As technologies, ePortfolios offer many options for how they can be constructed. For example, they offer an array of technological components such as pages, menus, navigation options, feeds, social media integrations, and so on. Given these rich choices, each ePortfolio can be tailored to meet a particular need such as applying for a teaching position as compared to showcasing consulting work.

In this regard, students face challenges when crafting online identities, mostly in terms of their self-representation in a context with conflicting cultural influences (Yancey, 2006). Social media and learner interaction allow for the creation and exchange of user-generated content by means of social software supports that add value through human social behavior, message boards, social networking, etc., which are the technologies that support more democratic and distributed interaction and production on the web (Coates, 2005; O'Really, 2005). This influence in education is significantly altering ways of accessing information and is facilitating multiple forms for dialogue among educators and students and among students themselves (Siemens, 2008).

A Learning Framework for ePortfolio

According to the Joint Information Services Committee (JISC), ePortfolios should offer pedagogic support for action planning especially because different disciplines adhere to different processes for reflection on and presentation of learning (2008, p. 6) (see Coleman et al., this collection). Therefore, integrating ePortfolio into a course requires careful implementation of an action plan. Several authors have proposed different models and guidelines to map the interactions among students, instructors, and content with ePortfolios (Fink, 2013). However, every ePortfolio has a different purpose and every course, program, or discipline has its own time and resources. Likewise, every ePortfolio model should be integrated with its own map of activities and assessments (see Coleman et al., this collection), with reflection as its core component and instructions to ensure students know how and when to evidence their learning (Barrett, 2009).

A learning framework can be conceptualized by grouping patterns in relation to main concepts associated with ePortfolio learning that center on evidence produced during the learning process and showcased in the ePortfolio publication. The cross-cutting themes in group patterns that may influence the ePortfolio process and publication can be linked to or embedded in the ePortfolio (Jankowski et al., 2011; Johnsen, 2012; Light et al., 2012). They include agency, managing self and interaction, *scaffolding*, and identification of evidence. These concepts pertain in turn, to topics and are designed for very specific purposes such as *active learning*, experiential learning, assessment, feedback, and so on, but are also part of the learning process that can be evidenced in the ePortfolio in forms of digital artifacts such videos, images, podcasts, texts, maps, graphics, etc. (see Table 8.3).

Conclusion

The framework challenges instructors to incorporate the concepts and technology of ePortfolio in the classroom and questions the notion that instruction on the ePortfolio concept and related technology must happen outside the classroom, due to time limitations and curricular demands. However, the intentions of ePortfolio for learning is to document learning that can happen at any time. Although our ePortfolio model originates as a practice in pre-service teacher education, the ePortfolio for learning extends beyond academic time and spaces to incorporate life experiences in addition to evidence from a course or academic program. In this sense, the framework acts as an answer to many ePortfolio practitioners who ask how to support course activities to benefit learners, mainly in lectures and learning contexts influenced by social media and digital narratives. The pattern-based methodology has the potential to address the complexity and fluidity of the ePortfolio scope approached by social science research (Bryant & Chittum, 2013). For this reason, the framework is based on the pedagogical pattern mapped by the conversational framework in a specific educational practice and then proposed as a generalization for educational practices where learning evidence is connected or embedded in the ePortfolio. Therefore, the continuous validation of patterns can be classified by the theoretical justification. The validity of the framework relies on quality specifications of the referenced design patterns that have been deployed in relevant projects by main pattern design authors such as those who led the Rhizome Project (Warburton, 2014) and the JISC Project (2008) "Scoping a vision for formative e-assessment."

Producing and collecting evidence of learning is transferable in most educational contexts and an essential part of the process of learning. Representing a pattern to evidence learning through educational technology via ePortfolio or its evolution into an open passport for credentials presents endless possibilities; that is, production in learning design relies on constructing multiple practices to map and combining documented pedagogical patterns. We note that this work is not finished but represents a continuum. We do not offer a prescribed way to "perform" and evidence learning with ePortfolios, but rather broaden the possibilities for a dynamic ePortfolio that complements other representations of learning (learning designs, pedagogical patterns). It is important to note a certain level of flexibility in teacher's guidance of constructing and collecting evidence, making it more personal to the student. However, too much freedom could eventually result in a situation in which students may not demonstrate attainment of the learning outcomes. A balance must be found between flexibility and guidance, key for the learning design and pedagogical intentions and decisions.

We hope to influence future studies on the facilitation of evidencing learning through ePortfolio as well as other future systems and technologies for recognition, such as Open Badges and Open Passport, to connect ePortfolio process and product towards accreditation of each individual's learning path. We look forward to new technological platforms or systems that support flexible management of artifacts and other evidence of learning that enable students to select their learning tools and make evidence of their learning available to different audiences.

References

Abrami, P. & Barrett, H. (2005). Directions for research and development on electronic portfolios. Canadian Journal of Learning and Technology/La Revue Canadienne de L'apprentissage et de La Technologie, 31(3). https://www.eduhk.hk/obl/files/Directions%20for%20Research%20and%20Development%20on%20Electronic%20Portfolios.pdf.

Avgeriou, P., Retalis, S. & Papasalouros, A. (2004). Pattern student group management. http://www2.tisip.no/E-LEN/patterns_show.php?nr=27.

Barker, K. (2006). ePortfolio for skilled immigrants and employers: LIfIA project phase one final report. http://www.futured.com/documents/ePortfoliotoConnectSkilledImmigrantsandEmployers.pdf.

Barrett, H. (2005). White paper: Researching electronic portfolios and learner engagement. https://electronicportfolios.org/reflect/whitepaper.pdf.

Barrett, H. (2016). Digital identity through digital storytelling in ePortfolioss. http://www.slideshare.net/eportfolios/digital-storytellingdublin2016.

Barrett, H. C. & Garrett, N. (2009). Online personal learning environments: structuring electronic portfolios for lifelong and life-wide learning. On the Horizon, 17(2), 142–152.

Belshaw, D. (2016). Doug Belshaws' Blog—What is a "credential" anyway? http://dougbelshaw.com/blog/2016/04/06/what-is-a-credential/.

Bergin, J., Eckstein, J., Manns, M.-L., Sharp, H., Voelter, M., Wallingford, E. (2007). The pedagogical patterns project. http://www.pedagogicalpatterns.org/.

Bergin, J., Manns, M. L. & Sharp, H. (2002). Patterns for Active Learning. http://hillside.net/plop/plop2002/final/ActiveLearningV1[1].8.doc.

Bergin, J., Marquardt, K., Manns, M. L., Eckstein, J., Sharp, H. & Wallingford, E. (2004). Patterns for Experiential Learning. http://www.pedagogicalpatterns.org/current/experientiallearning.pdf.

Borman, G. D. & Dowling, N. M. (2006). Longitudinal achievement effects of multiyear summer school: Evidence from the Teach Baltimore randomized field trial. Educational Evaluation and Policy Analysis, 28(1), 25–48.

Bryant, L. H. & Chittum, J. R. (2013). ePortfolio effectiveness: A(n ill-fated) search for empirical support. International Journal of ePortfolio, 3(2), 189–198.

Castaño Sánchez, A. X. (2014). The application of eportfolio in higher education: implications on students' learning. https://www.researchgate.net/publication/315856918_The_Application_of_Eportfolio_in_Higher_Education_implications_for_Student_Learning.

Castaño, A. X., González, Á. P. & Jiménez, J. M. (2015). Factors influencing e-Portfolio use and students' approaches to learning in higher education. *International Journal of Information and Communication Technology Education (IJICTE)*, *11*(3), 39–52.

Chang, C.-C., Tseng, K. H. & Lou, S. J. (2012). A comparative analysis of the consistency and difference among teacher-assessment, student self-assessment and peer-assessment in a web-based portfolio assessment environment for high school students. *Computers & Education*, *58*(1), 303–320.

CityU. (n.d.). ePortfolio-pedagogy. https://sites.google.com/site/officialwebsite teachers/eportfolio-pedagogy.

Coates, T. (2005). An addendum to a definition of social software. Plasticbag.org. http://plasticbag.org/archives/2005/01/an_addendum_to_a_definition_of _social_software/.

Comber, O. (2014). Pattern blended evaluation. In Mor, Y., Mellar, H., Warbuton, S. & Winters, N. (Eds.)*Practical design patterns for teaching and learning with technology* (pp. 293–300). Sense Publishers.

Dalziel, J. (2015). *Learning design: Conceptualizing a framework for teaching and learning online*. Routledge.

Denise, W. & Mellar, H. (2014). Pattern feedback on feedback. In Y. Mor, S. Warburton, N. Winters & H. Mellar (Eds.), *Practical design patterns for teaching and learning with technology* (pp. 311–314). Sense Publishers.

Derntl, M. (2005). *Patterns for person centered e-learning*. Citeseer.

Derntl, M. (2014). Spotlighting learning processes. In Y. Mor, S. Warburton, N. Winters & H. Mellar (Eds.), *Practical design patterns for teaching and learning with technology* (pp. 61–66). Sense Publishers.

Derntl, M., Neumann, S., Oberhuemer, P., Tattersall, C., Verpoorten, D. & Klemke, R. (2009). *Report on the standardized description of instructional models*. University of Vienna.

Eckstein, J., Bergin, J. & Sharp, H. (2002). Feedback Patterns. Proceedings of EuroPLoP 2002, (Jan 4, 2003), 1–31. http://csis.pace.edu/~bergin/patterns/Feed backPatterns.html .

Fink, L. D. (2013). *Creating significant learning experiences: An integrated approach to designing college courses*. John Wiley & Sons. (pp. 92–99).

Hatzipanagos, S. (2015). What do MOOCs contribute to the debate on learning design of online courses? Elearning Papers, 1(42). https://www.researchgate.net /publication/299976151_What_do_MOOCs_contribute_to_the_debate_on_ learning_design_of_online_courses.

Hsieh, P.-H., Lee, C.-I. & Chen, W.-F. (2015). Students' perspectives on e-portfolio development and implementation: A case study in Taiwanese higher education. *Australasian Journal of Educational Technology*, *31*(6), 641–656.

Jankowski, N. A. & Provezis, S. J. (2011). Making student learning evidence transparent: The state of the art. University of Illinois and Indiana University, National Institute for Learning Outcomes Assessment (NILOA). https://www.learningout comeassessment.org/documents/TransparencyOfEvidence.pdf.

JISC. (2008). Effective practices with e-portfolios. Joint Information Systems Committee. http://repository.jisc.ac.uk/5997/1/effectivepracticeeportfolios.pdf.

Johnsen, H. L. (2012). Making learning visible with ePortfolios: Coupling the right pedagogy with the right technology. *International Journal of ePortfolio*, 2(2), 139–148.

Johnson, R. S., Mims-Cox, J. S. & Doyle-Nichols, A. (2006). *Developing portfolios in education: A guide to reflection, inquiry, and assessment.* Sage.

Jovanovic, J. & Devedzic, V. (2015). Open badges: Novel means to motivate, scaffold and recognize learning. *Technology, Knowledge and Learning*, 20(1), 115–122.

Laurillard, D. (2002). *Rethinking university education: A conversational framework for the effective use of learning technologies.* Routledge Falmer.

Laurillard, D. (2007). Pedagogical forms for mobile learning. In N. Pachler (Ed.), *Mobile Learning: towards a research agenda* (pp. 153–176). Work-based learning for education professionals Centre.

Laurillard, D. (2012). Teaching as a design science: Building pedagogical patterns for learning and technology. *Routledge, Taylor & Francis Group.*

Laurillard, D. & Derntl, M. (2014). Learner centered design—Overview. In Y. Mor, H. Mellar., S. Warburton, N. Winters & H. Mellar & N. Winters (Eds.), *Practical design patterns for teaching and learning with technology* (pp. 13–16). Springer.

Mellar, H. & Patchlet, N. (2014). Assessment and feedback—Overview. In Y. Mor, H. Mellar., S. Warburton, N. Winters & H. Mellar & N. Winters (Eds.), *Practical design patterns for teaching and learning with technology* (pp. 239–244). Springer.

Mor, Y., Craft, B. & Hernández-Leo, D. (2013). The art and science of learning design. Research in Learning Technology, 21. http://oro.open.ac.uk/38313/1/Mor-Craft-HL.pdf.

Y. Mor, H. Mellar., S. Warburton, N. Winters & H. Mellar & N. Winters (Eds.) (2014). *Practical design patterns for teaching and learning with technology.* Springer.

Mor, Y., Winters, N. & Warburton, S. (2010). Participatory pattern workshops resource kit. HAL archives ouvertes. https://hal.archives-ouvertes.fr/hal-00593 108wnload/pdf/47723811.pdf.

O'Reilly, T. (2005). What is Web 2.0: Design patterns and business models for the next generation of software. O'Reilly. https://www.oreilly.com/pub/a/web2/archive/what-is-web-20.html.

Pachler, N., Mellar, H., Daly, C., Mor, Y., Wiliam, D. & Laurillard, D. (2009). Scoping a vision for formative e-assessment: a project report for JISC. HAL archives ouvertes. https://core.ac.uk/download/pdf/47761683.pdf.

Penny Light, T., Chen, H. L. & Ittelson, J. C. (2011). *Documenting learning with ePortfolios: A guide for college instructors.* John Wiley & Sons.

Presant, D. (2016). Litoraly Blog. https://littoraly.wordpress.com/2016/01/17/do-open-badges-make-eportfolios-obsolete/.

Ravet, S. (2015) #OpenLegers – via #OpenBadges and #BlockChains. Learning futures. http://www.learningfutures.eu/2015/12/from-eportfolios-to-openledgers-via-openbadges-and-blockchains/.

Robertson, J. (2014). Pattern: Showcase learning. In Y. Mor, H. Mellar., S. Warburton, N. Winters & H. Mellar & N. Winters (Eds.), *Practical design patterns for teaching and learning with technology* (pp. 67–72). Springer.

Siemens, G. (2008). Learning and knowing in networks: Changing roles for educators and designers. *Academia*. https://www.academia.edu/2857165/Learning_and_knowing_in_networks_Changing_roles_for_educators_and_designers.

Warburton, S. (2012). *Digital Identity and Social Media*. (IGI Global., Ed.).

Warburton, S. (2014). Social media and learner interaction in social spaces-overview. Y. Mor, H. Mellar., S. Warburton, N. Winters & H. Mellar & N. Winters (Eds.), *Practical design patterns for teaching and learning with technology* (pp. 151–157). Springer.

Yancey, K. B. (2006, January 12). An exercise in absence: Notes on the past and future of digital portfolios and student learning. *SmartClassroom*. https://campustechnology.com/articles/2006/01/an-exercise-in-absence.aspx.

Zhang, S. X., Olfman, L. & Ractham, P. (2007). Designing eportfolio 2.0: Integrating and coordinating web 2.0 services with eportfolio systems for enhancing users' learning. *Journal of Information Systems Education, 18*(2), 203.

Part 3. Assessing Performance

Chapter 9. Strategies for ePortfolio Adoption and Sustainability across Administrative, Faculty, and Student Stakeholders

Teggin Summers
Jessica Pederson
Deb Perry
Rachel Kow
Constance Ulasewicz
Crystal O. Wong
San Francisco State University

Factors for ePortfolio Adoption and Growth

The use and enthusiasm for electronic portfolios has been steadily increasing over the past several decades, building on a rich history of traditional paper portfolios, which have been used in K–12 and professional disciplines for hundreds of years (Challis, 1999; Johnson et al., 2006; Taylor et al., 1999). The study and use of ePortfolios has matured as a discipline in its own right, with over fifty percent of colleges and universities availing themselves of this learning technology approach (Dahlstrom et al., 2013). Additionally, professional organizations, such as the Association for Authentic, Experiential, and Evidence-Based Learning (AAEEBL), and journals, such as the *International Journal of Electronic Portfolios* (IJeP), have emerged to further instantiate the value and impact of ePortfolios. Indeed, research is showing that students in some ePortfolio programs have higher grade point averages, credit accumulation, and retention rates (Hakel & Smith, 2009). For example, data from La Guardia Community College show students in ePortfolio courses as having higher pass and retention rates than those in comparable non-ePortfolio courses (Eynon et al., 2014). La Guardia has also seen that the composite one-semester retention or graduate rate for students in impacted courses [in 2011–2012] was 80.4%, versus 61.7% for students in comparison courses. Likewise, students enrolled in impacted courses had higher course completion (96.4%, + 1.8 percentage points), course pass (79.7% + 8.2 percentage points) and high pass—C and above (77.7% + 9.9 percentage points)—rates than students in comparison courses (as cited in Eynon et al., 2014, p. 96).

DOI: https://doi.org/10.37514/PRA-B.2020.1084.2.09

And yet, despite this growing body of research and application of ePortfolio programs, this pedagogical process that is so inextricably bound with its corresponding technology platforms continues to present very real and complex challenges for adoption, implementation, and sustainability. While some of these issues can be attributed to the basic challenges associated with any technology adoption cycle (see Richardson et al., this collection), the pedagogical substance and importance of ePortfolios adds an additional layer of complexity to the already difficult task of planning and executing successful ePortfolio adoption, implementation, and sustainability.

Like other learning technologies, ePortfolios present nuanced challenges to adoption, largely because they represent both a pedagogical process, such as *folio thinking* (Chen, 2004, 2012) and a technological counterpart. Perhaps even more than comparable learning technologies, ePortfolios are deeply pedagogy-heavy. Folio thinking, the pedagogic process that is at the core of ePortfolios, involves *reflection* on self and identity, as well as personal and professional development (Chen, 2012). ePortfolios are iterative, process-oriented, and *authentic*. These pedagogical approaches can be new to many instructors and administrators, and considering adopting a new pedagogical approach can be a challenge, especially when it is compounded by also implementing and supporting a new technology (see Garriott, this collection).

An additional complicating factor is that ePortfolios mean so many different things to different students, faculty, stakeholders, and constituents. For some, they are considered tools for program *assessment*; for others, they are considered reflective learning portfolios, often being integrated at a course level; and for yet others, they are seen as professional websites, showcasing students' skills, experiences, and best work products (see Carpenter & Labissiere, Terry & Whillock, and Coleman et al., this collection). Achieving faculty buy-in can be difficult amidst so many different definitions and approaches for ePortfolios. In all cases, if ePortfolios are being implemented in ways that truly leverage their potential to imbue reflection, self-assessment, and metacognition into the learning process, they have the potential to act as a high impact practice and catalyst for learning and transformation.

As a high impact practice and catalyst for learning-centered institutional change, ePortfolios can be even more difficult to successfully adopt and to continue to scale and support. Ultimately, ePortfolios represent a great deal of potential for positive impact, and consequently require thoughtful planning and development that continuously includes multiple stakeholders and multiple perspectives on adoption. When Bret Eynon and Laura Gambino (2017) propose that ePortfolio initiatives can advance student success; support reflection, social pedagogy, and deep learning; and act as catalysts for learning-centered institutional change, they emphasize an important qualifier: ePortfolio initiatives have this potential when they are done well. Throughout their publications, Eynon and Gambino maintain the importance of planning and thoughtful, collaborative approaches to ePortfolio implementation (see Dellinger & Hanger, this collection). Ultimately, ePortfolios present challenges to adoption, scalability, and sustainability because they are exponentially complex, representing both new pedagogical approaches and new technology adoptions. In order to have successful ePortfolio adoption and growth, institutions and programs need administrative advocacy and support; faculty programming and support; and meaningful, authentic purposes in order for faculty and students to truly value and use them.

Administrative Support and Resources

Successful ePortfolio adoption and growth is contingent on the contribution of upper-level administrative support and resources. An institutional level of support and resources dedicated to ePortfolio pedagogy and infrastructure must exist in order for the initiative to successfully grow on a college campus. Drawing from author experience at both Virginia Tech and San Francisco State University, we suggest that having one or two full-time position(s), along with at least one part-time position (perhaps a student assistant) dedicated to ePortfolio strategy and implementation can result in a local initiative growing to be a campus-wide program. If the ePortfolio initiative is technology-heavy, meaning that much of the ePortfolio architecture and systems are developed and supported in-house, it may also be helpful to have a full-time technical lead position.

Administrative support also includes the allocation of funds to pay for and support an ePortfolio platform, whether that is part of the LMS or a standalone system. This is largely necessary if departments, programs, or the institution as a whole have an interest in using ePortfolios for any type of course, programmatic, or institutional assessment. If it is important to the school to keep ePortfolio *artifacts* or reflections for any type of overarching evaluation or assessment needs, it is best to invest in a platform that enables institutional ownership, including student-centered co-ownership, of that assessment data. This is often only possible through the use of a vendor-supplied platform; however, it is important to negotiate university ownership of the platform data. Moreover, having a central, campus-supported ePortfolio platform creates a sense of cohesion for students between their portfolios and the rest of their academic activities associated with the university (see Terry & Whillock, this collection). A central platform makes it easier for students to access their portfolios and keeps the process integrated with their coursework and other learning activities. As has been described in much of the literature around ePortfolio adoption, it is important for the pedagogical uses of the ePortfolios to dictate any decisions made about ePortfolio technologies or platforms, which requires cross-university strategic thinking and planning (Jafari, 2004; Johnsen, 2012; Meyer, 2016) (see Richardson et al., this collection). Administrative support can help seed and facilitate the formation and work of these groups.

Administrative support also comes in the form of tying ePortfolio development and implementation to strategic, university-wide initiatives (see Sanborn

& Ramirez and Polly et al., this collection). This is true not only in terms of any type of institutional-level educational approach or technology adoption, but also because ePortfolios actually have the potential to provide an added value to institutional initiatives whenever areas such as student engagement, student identity development, authentic assessment, closing the achievement gap, and student success are concerned. ePortfolios, when applied thoughtfully and strategically, have the potential to act as high impact practices and increase gains in all of the aforementioned areas (Watson et al., 2016). When tied to a key initiative (see Terry & Whillock and Day, this collection), ePortfolios can contribute to the achievement of milestones, while also resulting in growth and adoption across the university. The secret ingredient for this success, however, is that ePortfolio initiatives need high-level advocacy and support coupled with grassroots-level customization and authentic use.

We saw success with this coordinated effort when Virginia Tech included the use of ePortfolios for assessment of learning outcomes within the First Year Experience (FYE) program, which was a key component of their Quality Enhancement Plan for their institutional accreditation (see Richardson et al. and Dellinger & Hanger, this collection). Attaching ePortfolios to this key initiative necessitated the involvement of administrators whose advocacy subsequently paved the way and created conditions for adoption, growth, and sustainability. In this example, any course or department participating in the FYE program was required to have students complete ePortfolios that included artifacts and related reflections demonstrating the achievement of three learning outcomes (drawn from the VALUE Rubrics developed through the Association of American Colleges and Universities). This goal to collect assessment data for accreditation created the impetus for high-level administrative support, including funds for participating departments and the development of a cross-institutional support team comprised of the Office of First Year Experience, the Center for Instructional Development and Educational Research, the Office of Assessment, and the ePortfolio Initiatives program. This funding also included built-in support for faculty professional development. Additionally, the ePortfolio Initiatives office worked at a grassroots level with programs to customize their ePortfolio experience to meet departmental learning outcomes and incorporate activities addressing student identity and growth as future professionals in their major (see Polly et al., this collection). The ePortfolio Initiatives team also worked with programs to customize their ePortfolio assignments and prompts. Because they included institutional assessment, along with activities for reflecting on learning and personal and professional development, the ePortfolios were able to meet areas of growth for students and contribute to continuous improvement for the university. This approach addressed the needs of many of the stakeholders and was highly successful for the programs that leveraged the multiple levels of ePortfolio functionality.

Across all of the uses for ePortfolios within an institution (including connections to institution-wide initiatives, as well as co-curricular, programmatic, and course level uses), another level of administrative support pertains to procuring funding and creating resources for faculty and student ePortfolio development, use, and support. The allocation of funds must include monies for the staffing discussed above, as well as related faculty development programming and support.

Faculty Programming and Consultative Support

Faculty programming and support for ePortfolios has to cover the rich combination of pedagogy and technology that is so representative of ePortfolios. ePortfolios include inherently authentic, non-disposable assignments that matter outside of the classroom; however, as with all technology for teaching and learning, it is vital to explicitly articulate the goals of and reasons for the ePortfolio platform to students (Jagger & Xu, 2016; Pacansky-Brock, 2017). Faculty can provide explicit rationale when they explain the purpose of the ePortfolio assignment. At San Francisco State University, the Center for Equity and Excellence in Teaching and Learning (CEETL) offers ePortfolio workshops to sustain and deepen this discussion, often speaking to the value of folio thinking.

The CEETL team leads 30 to 40 workshops per semester, reaching approximately 750 students per term. We begin the workshops by engaging students in a conversation around ePortfolios and asking students to describe their academic and/or professional online presence. Strikingly, if anecdotally, approximately 85% of students in gateway courses and 50% of students in capstone courses (most of whom are graduating) report that they have no digital academic or professional presence at all. In other words, many of our students have no online space in which to share their work: no LinkedIn, personal website, ePortfolio, or blog, to name a few avenues. Our informal surveying of the room by show of hands opens up the conversation further. We ask students where they want to go next (employment, graduate school, travel, or volunteer experiences) and to consider how they will construct the narrative for themselves and other audiences that connects where they have been (college) to where they want to go. We ask them to reflect on how they will communicate who they are (their style and philosophy) to someone who has never met them and is looking at a stack of applicants.

We then move into hands-on worktime in our campus' ePortfolio platform. We begin by sharing the ePortfolio of one of our ePortfolio Student Ambassadors (see Garriott, this collection) and modeling best practices in action. Our ePortfolio platform tends to be user-friendly, dynamic, and engaging. Nevertheless, we explicitly communicate to our students that even if they never use our ePortfolio system again after their course, the act of reflecting on their narrative arc will be of value to them in future interviews and conversations. Regardless of the platform they might choose for themselves, we aim to leave them convinced of the value of actively constructing their online academic and professional presence. We view this as one of the digital literacies our students will need in order to succeed.

CEETL offers an array of other support for ePortfolios on our campus as well, including faculty Lunch & Learn events where faculty share a meal and discuss their best practices with their peers; Open ePortfolio Lab hours where students can take advantage of one-on-one feedback and help with their ePortfolios; and a self-starter guide for faculty and students (https://docs.google.com/document/d/1Zs8fywRo9pKWna9km5fQ69BGmp5BUKjSfzsVs99jWhg/edit?usp=sharing) who prefer to work independently. We have developed an ePortfolio resource website (http://eportfolio.sfsu.edu/) to support a deeper dive into folio thinking, which includes a gallery of student ePortfolios and a discussion of ethical image use and Creative Commons licensing. At SF State, ePortfolios are a doorway to twenty-first century digital citizenship for our students.

SF State has only a small number of staff hours to dedicate to ePortfolio support, and we manage to provide significant assistance by being strategic in our resources and support offerings. Over the last several years, we have focused our support largely on programs and departments. Such focused support helps to assure that the group has some buy-in and the support may be more sustainable over time, and it allows for a small staff to be able to provide services in a scalable or sustainable way. We have found that when a department adopts an ePortfolio project or initiative across its program, there is often broader communication across the department about the uses and value of using ePortfolios within its courses (see Coleman et al., this collection). Students see that their department values the portfolio process when ePortfolio touchstones are embedded within multiple courses and their instructors are all on the same page about the use of ePortfolios within their program. Additionally, integrating the use of ePortfolios within the department also contributes to continuity whenever there is turnover of department heads or chairs. If possible, it is best to be able to offer tiers of support, which is the approach we are taking at SF State. Our current model is to provide workshops each semester to departments and programs that are adopting ePortfolios. We are also providing workshops for individual courses for two semesters, along with support materials and train-the-trainer sessions with instructors and GTAs so that after two semesters, instructors are prepared to orient their students to ePortfolios on their own. This approach is allowing us to foster growth of ePortfolios at our university, while still operating within the capacity of a very small unit. At SF State, we have one lead instructional designer and one deputy instructional designer who focus primarily on managing and growing ePortfolios. These positions split their time providing faculty instructional design consultations and faculty development across a variety of teaching and learning topics with their ePortfolio duties (including developing support materials and scheduling and delivering workshops to ePortfolio classes and programs). Additionally, our two other instructional designers, as well as student assistants (see Terry & Whillock and Garriott, this collection), also offer ePortfolio workshops and staff ePortfolio Open Lab hours.

Finding Your Purpose and Cultivating Buy-In

Even with administrative advocacy and support in terms of infrastructure and resources, many universities and institutions unexpectedly struggle to successfully implement ePortfolios (Straumsheim, 2014). Even as increasing numbers of universities are looking to ePortfolios to address systemic issues of retention, accreditation, and assessment (Dahlstrom, 2012; Kahn, 2014; Knight et al., 2008; Ring & Ramirez, 2012), we have to consider the additional conditions for successful adoption.

While we know that obtaining stakeholder buy-in is key to the ultimate success or failure of its institutional adoption (Seldin & Miller, 2009) (see Dellinger & Hanger and Richardson et al., this collection), an equally important contributor to cultivating buy-in and eventual adoption is a unifying purpose among faculty, students, and administrators (Coleman et al., 2017; Knight et al., 2008; Ring & Ramirez, 2012). While coming to a consensus is one of the most prolific hurdles to ePortfolio adoption (Reis & Villaume, 2002; Strudler & Wetzler, 2008), large-scale implementation is possible and examples are well-documented, even with diverse, urban, and high-risk populations (Eynon, 2011). This mutual, unified purpose is critical because "unless students and faculty see value in creating an ePortfolio, it will be viewed as an add-on and as a result will not include quality evidence" (Ring & Ramirez, 2012, p. 312). George Siemens (2004) also outlined several conditions necessary for cultivating buy-in, stressing the importance of stakeholders' perceptions, the institution's culture, and the availability of both technical and pedagogical resources and support for ePortfolio (as cited in Knight et al., 2008). In Carl Straumsheim's coverage of the e-Portfolio Forum during the 2014 Association of American Colleges and Universities' annual meeting, he cautions readers, saying, "Investing in the tool for the sake of keeping up with the trend is a recipe for failure" (2014, para. 3). It cannot be understated that a successful ePortfolio implementation requires a clear, unifying purpose to propel and sustain ePortfolio adoption.

Unfortunately, reaching a consensus on the driving purpose of ePortfolios can be difficult and arduous (Swan, 2009). It often requires considerable student and faculty time and effort (Knight et al., 2008) and whole-hearted administrative support through a strategic plan (see Day, this collection). Peter Seldin and J. Elizabeth Miller (2010) make several suggestions on how to cultivate buy-in and facilitate institutional adoption, stressing the importance of not rushing the process of adoption, which may take up to two years. They recommend starting small, involving the institution's most respected faculty members from the beginning, not forcing anyone to participate, and allowing space for individual teaching and learning differences. Seldin and Miller (2010) also speak to the significance of candidness around the process, faculty ownership, and clear evaluation criteria and standards.

Authentic Reflective Practices

We want to suggest that reflection can be a strong unifying purpose behind ePortfolio buy-in, adoption, and use at university-wide, programmatic, and course levels. Reflection can be thought of as an opportunity for learners to evaluate their own work and "is both process and product" (Desmet et al., 2008, p. 19). It is a critical thinking skill (Ring & Ramirez, 2012; Ring et al., 2015), and reflection is how learners make sense of standards and the underlying purpose of their curriculum (Rickards et al., 2008). As the Alverno College Faculty (2000) explain, "both reflection and self assessment [sic] depend on careful observation, but the purpose of self-reflection is understanding, in contrast to the judgment, the evaluation of performance on the basis of criteria, that is the purpose of assessment" (p. 7). They add that "the reflection becomes the evidence of the identity and learning that are transferred across situations" (p. 35). Reflection has many benefits for learners, involving the student as an active participant in assessment (Knight et al., 2008). It also encourages students to combine their learning experiences, received feedback, and course content in a personalized way (Rickards et al., 2008).

ePortfolios are a powerful reflection tool, and they "bring to the forefront the richness of student work and teacher practice. E-portfolios celebrate the body of student work, as well as show the reflection and dialogue generated between students and teachers" (Ahn, 2004, para. 17). They also inherently foster reflection on the process of learning, in addition to the artifacts and tangible products of learning, which often amplifies and blends their learning (Watson et al., 2016). However, to fully receive the reflective and metacognitive benefits of ePortfolios, they must be considered by stakeholders as a key part of the curriculum; when viewed as an additional, incongruous task, ePortfolios are rarely as effective for learners (Coleman et al., 2017; Ring & Ramirez, 2012; Siemens, 2004; Tzeng, 2010; Watson et al., 2016).

The case studies that follow show examples of ePortfolio reflection across courses, as well as one student's experience with her ePortfolio. The role of reflection is a theme, showing its potential as a unifying purpose. These case studies highlight a student's perspective, as well as programmatic and course ePortfolios in practice, including challenges and strategies for success, culminating in suggestions for best practices and resources for faculty success with ePortfolios. When faculty have a clear purpose for use of ePortfolios and are prepared with strategies to overcome challenges, there is a stronger chance of cultivating buy-in, adoption, and successful use of ePortfolios.

ePortfolios in Practice

A Student Perspective (Rachel)

As a graduate student in math education at San Francisco State University, with a year teaching in a classroom and my own educational career on the horizon, I have had significant exposure to electronic portfolios and have spent a great deal of time reflecting on and building my ePortfolio. Building my ePortfolio prompted me to reflect and think deeply on my own learning and practice. Teaching reflective practice is a difficult task and putting together a portfolio also allowed me to reflect on and think deeply about the purpose and intent of the work I selected. Finally, as I continue to hone my skills as an educator, the ePortfolio has given me the tools to be reflective and intentional, and it has helped me revise and guide the construction of new ideas.

My instructors taught the ePortfolio as a process of reflective practice as well as a tool for seeking employment and applying to various programs, such as graduate school or internships. The instructors that best helped me understand the purpose of an ePortfolio believed that it was a process of learning and not just a project to be completed. I think if these professors did not honestly foster this belief in themselves, then I would not have gained so much insight and actualized reflective practices within myself.

The instructor plays a large part in helping students understand the purpose of an ePortfolio. On the surface, many instructors tend to describe the ePortfolio as similar to a traditional, paper portfolio. The idea of a traditional portfolio is to collect assignments to curate evidence that you have completed work in the applicable field. However, an ePortfolio is not simply intended to gather completed work; it is a teaching tool, which must have some academic rigor and purpose. Many instructors who are simply told by their department to implement these ePortfolios may not find academic purpose or rigor and just see the ePortfolio requirement as part of a checklist of items to be completed (see Dellinger & Hanger, this collection). Another challenge that many students face is that an ePortfolio, at least at a department level, needs to be implemented and communicated early so that students may save their work and begin to curate their proud achievements. Many of the students in my program had difficulty obtaining work from a few years prior since the expectation was not clearly communicated by all professors far enough in advance.

From my perspective as both a student and future educator, I encourage instructors to think about how the ePortfolio is a teaching tool and what makes it an academically purposeful project. Like any other assignment, an ePortfolio must have a purpose for the course and/or program. Additionally, in order for any project to be meaningful for students, instructors must first believe that the assignment is meaningful in some way.

Case Study 1: Family Interiors Nutrition & Apparel ePortfolio

In the Family Interiors Nutrition & Apparel (FINA) department, there are four separate content areas: Family & Consumer Sciences, Interior Design, Nutrition & Dietetics, and Apparel Design & Merchandising. All of these programs share a Professional Development Class in which students enroll in the spring of their senior year. One of the requirements of this course is the development of a portfolio that contains and is reflective of work completed throughout a student's undergraduate education. Until 2016, students had the option to turn in this portfolio in a paper or online format. In 2018, all 160 portfolios were turned in online via the university ePortfolio platform or a blogging/website building system.

Strategies for Success

The concept of strategies for success with an ePortfolio assignment are many, with three being: 1) a clearly described grading rubric, 2) access to software, and 3) peer evaluation.

Grading Rubric

In the FINA department, when we ask students to *showcase* their best work, we emphasize that it is not the students' work and assignments that are being evaluated; rather, their means of visually displaying this work is being graded. FINA has four distinctly different content areas represented by students within a class, and faculty teaching the Professional Development course have not taught nor are proficient in each of the four content areas. A rubric (see Appendix A) is essential for clearly informing the students about requirements and grading expectations for the ePortfolio. The rubric is where the objective of the ePortfolio must be clearly defined. The objective for our department reads as follows: "Your final semester portfolio is intended to be utilized as an ongoing professional tool for job interviews, publicizing your skills, and other professional uses. As such it is designed so that it can be further modified to meet your future and changing needs." We further go on to explain that a high-quality portfolio tells a cohesive story, has a good narrative, and actually describes the skill set of the student and soon-to-be industry professional.

Access to ePortfolio Software

As students become aware of the importance of the storytelling aspect of the ePortfolio, the importance of the ePortfolio platform shouts out to them. If faculty have not experienced the tools offered through various sites, we strongly suggest that they take the time to at least investigate before expecting their students to understand the various functions, features, and creation processes. We are fortunate that the university's Center for Equity and Excellence in Teaching and Learning has developed guidelines and fully supports questions from both faculty and students for using the SF State ePortfolio platform. Because of this support, our faculty members are able to focus largely on content and how students best represent themselves through the platform. Some students have shared that they feel constricted by the layout and storytelling aspect offered to them through the portfolio tool, while others totally enjoyed the parameters. When constrained students (mostly in the Interior Design and Apparel Design & Merchandising program areas) were given the option of finding other sites (free portfolio and blog platforms), they gladly did, and this option offered them full ownership of their ePortfolio assignment.

Peer Evaluation

Access to review student ePortfolios along the way from initial to final development via the web is an intrinsic part of the beauty of this assignment. Students tend to be more successful when fellow students are given the opportunity to view and comment on their work in progress. Research supports that students report significantly higher awareness of growth and development as learners when receiving feedback on their ePortfolios (Eynon et al., 2017). As the ePortfolio represents work and personal growth outside of the Professional Development class, it is presented as an assignment due for online review at two predetermined dates throughout the semester. For the assignment, ePortfolios are posted online and fellow students must choose to view three portfolios and comment on three strengths and three areas that require greater clarity. This peer evaluation offers students within a content area the ability to offer suggestions of alternative artifacts because they actually are aware of the work required from other classes throughout the curriculum. Peer evaluation also offers students the ability to view other portfolios and find images, labeling, explanations, or other elements that they like and will then possibly integrate into their own ePortfolio.

Challenges for Success

The challenges for success within an ePortfolio assignment are many, including lack of time, content, and creativity.

Lack of Time

It is imperative that students understand that the creation of an ePortfolio takes time. For this particular assignment, it is more than an accumulation or compilation of work, but rather a thoughtful progression that tells a story about an individual. The creation of such a work takes reflective time for self-assessment, as well as time for peer evaluation. As many students tend to wait until the last possible moments to complete an assignment, the two peer reflection assignments throughout the semester offer firm deadlines that allow for helpful and creative feedback.

Lack of Content

Often students report that they do not save assignments, that their images are not clear enough, or that they do not feel that what they have is representative of who they are. For each of these potential stumbling blocks, there is a possible solution. Generally, an entire assignment, such as the entire paper or reflective analysis, is not required. Instead, students may need to create an abstract for a paper or summarize their reflections and add an image or graph or diagram. When images are not clear, a photo editing program can help students crop an image or add color and brightness. As of this writing, some free programs students can use to edit images include Microsoft Word, Microsoft PowerPoint, GNU Image Manipulation Program (a free, open source program referred to as GIMP that is similar to Photoshop), PicMonkey (a free drag-and-drop web application) or applications for their phones, such as one called Aviary. When the work is not representative of the student, a narrative is key to explaining the pathway or journey to where or who they currently are. These issues also connect to lack of time, because it takes time to develop the content, to post that content in the ePortfolio, and to reflect back and analyze if the selected content tells the student's story accurately.

Lack of Creativity

Not all careers require creativity, but if an ePortfolio is a tool for obtaining a job, it must be viewed through the eyes of a manager whose attention the prospective employee must grab. One example is the student who has discovered new combinations of food components to create recipes for those with food allergies. Writing a paper is the academic assessment piece, but for the ePortfolio, an image of the food components or of the student measuring out products will make the accompanying text abstract come alive. Similarly, for students working in the community, a reflective analysis is an integral academic requirement. Within the ePortfolio, however, this assignment is enhanced by adding an image of the poster, a link to a website, or a picture of the student engaged in the activity. Lastly, our ePortfolio platform comes preloaded with a banner image of San Francisco State University. While a good image, some students have shared that this is an image of where they have been, not where they are going (see Polly et al. and Coleman et al., this collection). To enable the creative response here, the portfolio site allows the student to upload a new banner image, one that is representative of who they are or where they want to go.

Case Study 2: English Freshman Composition ePortfolio

At SF State, English 114, Freshman Composition, is the first sequence of a "First Year Experience" composition course. This class focuses on writing for inquiry, belonging, and self-development; developing rhetorical knowledge and information literacy; and using reflection and metacognition to enhance writing, critical reading, and the habits of mind. These learning goals are accomplished through a shared curricular framework that includes a variety of student-centered projects, one of which is the digital portfolio project (see Terry & Whillock, this collection).

Strategies for Success

In English 114, ePortfolios are used as an invitation for students to showcase and reflect on their best works. To accomplish this objective, students are guided through the building blocks of ePortfolios via the portfolio platform. However, before ePortfolios are introduced to students, faculty are encouraged to explore the technology themselves, as instructors tend to be more confident in the classroom if they have experience with the tools that they want students to use (see Desmet et al. and Garriott, this collection). Once the self-learning has been accomplished, faculty can then imagine how to support students in using ePortfolios as a learning technology.

Emphasize Pedagogy and Reflection

One success strategy is to place emphasis not on the platform but on the kind of thinking behind the creation of an ePortfolio: folio thinking. This term was coined by Helen Chen (2004) when she was trying to address an institutional learning problem. Since then, the pedagogy of folio thinking has been redefined, refined, and tailored to specific disciplines. Within the context of our composition classroom, however, folio thinking refers to the process of collecting, reflecting, and connecting assignments that allow students to articulate their competence and new learning experiences (Suter, n.d.). When this concept is applied to ePortfolios, students are not simply collecting completed/graded assignments and then depositing them into their ePortfolio. Instead, they are using a student-centered approach to capture their learning and make their learning visible. Specifically, students are asked to *select* projects that are meaningful to them to showcase and share publicly. Then, they are asked to *reflect* on the projects, to describe their selected projects and the learning and engagement process behind them. Lastly, students are asked to *connect*, to explain their new learning and competence and to explain how their projects, holistically, show their growth as students, writers, and learners in the first year.

Scaffold Assignments

Another strategy for success is to appropriately scaffold the ePortfolio assignments into the 16-week semester so that students don't perceive ePortfolios as a stand-alone, value-less project. To start, the creation of an ePortfolio and the discussion of its importance, benefits, and value occurs early in the semester (Weeks 1–2) along with an assignment page (see Appendix B), so students know what to expect from the ePortfolio project. Then, throughout the semester, depending on the timing of other major assignments, students are asked to submit artifacts (from the first-year composition class and other classes) in intervals, one each from the beginning (Weeks 1–5), middle (Weeks 6–11), and end (12–15). Students are reminded that these artifacts are not fixed and can be modified or deleted. While the submissions are taking place, students receive oral and written feedback on their ongoing submissions, either through peer or teacher feedback. As Week 16 approaches, students write a cover letter that includes reflection and connection; that is, they describe their new understanding, engagement, and habits of mind and explain how their new learning shaped them as students and writers. During finals week, the assessment takes place at the ePortfolio Party—an in-class party scheduled on the last day of class where students introduce their ePortfolios to the class, view each other's portfolios, leave feedback, and connect digitally with peers.

By the end of the semester, these students' ePortfolios not only provide opportunities to display their accomplishments, but they also give students a way to capture their learning and growth that enhances their development as lifelong learners.

Challenges for Success: Balancing Creativity with Technological Complexity

Challenges vary from one student to another, depending on the digital writing and technology experience students bring to the classroom and the approach to learning they exhibit. Quite often, the design-minded students find our ePortfolio platform constraining because it does not have as much functionality as they would like it to have in order to express their authentic selves. These students resist the predefined templates and tabs that box in their creativity or identity. On the other hand, another group of students have a hard time picking up all of the components of the ePortfolio and its related assignments, even when they are scaffolded carefully. For these students, the reasons are varied too: it could be that their class attendance is spotty, their engagement lacking, or that this is their first exposure to digital text. For them, repetition, practice, exposure, and feedback are key, but given the short 16-week semester along with the many additional outcomes that need to be taught, once again time can be a real challenge. Lastly, for unknown reasons, there will always be a tiny percentage of students asking this question during Week 15, "What is the digital portfolio assignment?"

Best Practices and Resources for Adoption and Growth of ePortfolios

Several overarching themes emerge when considering adopting and growing ePortfolios in practice at the course level, which is where most student ePortfolio engagement occurs. From the student perspective, we see that instructor attitude and emphasis on reflection has a strong impact on how students view and use their portfolios. This is reinforced in the English Department's emphasis on pedagogy and reflection and making those values transparent to students. Additionally, instructor and peer feedback, transparent expectations (including providing rubrics), and scaffolded assignments are all strategies used in both case studies that make ePortfolio implementations more effective.

Both case studies also represent overarching themes of challenges for ePortfolio implementation, including lack of time and content, as well as the ways in which ePortfolio platforms can be difficult to use or can limit creativity. The importance of *scaffolding* assignments underscores an effective way to address time management, which is a real concern for teachers and students when working with ePortfolios. It is helpful to build in time throughout the semester for students to work on their portfolios, as well as time for students to engage in peer review and feedback, both in terms of reviewing the artifacts and showcasing the ePortfolios. Another strategy to achieve greater effectiveness and to maximize potential is to introduce the ePortfolio at the beginning of the semester, along with the course learning outcomes or objectives (see Coleman et al., this collection). Doing so early shows students that the ePortfolio is a valued course activity, and it creates transparency in terms of the learning goals. Introducing the portfolio assignment alongside the course objectives also provides students a clear reference when it comes time for them to produce their reflections throughout the semester and compose their self-assessments on how they are progressing towards and achieving course outcomes.

Planning Matrix for Adoption and Supporting ePortfolios

Drawing on our experiences across institutions that are seeing success with ePortfolios based on a variety of strategies and approaches, we created the matrix seen in Table 9.1. Its purpose is to highlight important questions that can help guide stakeholders involved in ePortfolio planning, implementation, and support. It can also serve as a useful metric for assessing where a department or institution is in terms of developing and sustaining a successful ePortfolio program. The assessment categories are:

- Developing: Campus and faculty interest is expressed in ePortfolios and use is happening sporadically across the institution.
- Partially Developed: ePortfolios have some level of staffing and resources dedicated to the program and portfolios are used in pilot or a small number of programs and courses across the institution.
- Fully Developed: ePortfolios have strong staffing and resources and are used across multiple programs or tied with a key initiative on campus. Robust support is in place.

Stakeholders can use the guiding questions and matrix (see Table 9.1) to gauge where they are in terms of ePortfolio adoption, growth, and support. The matrix can also be used as a guide to address areas for success, describe what has been accomplished, and identify which pieces still need more attention.

Guiding Questions

Where do you think ePortfolios would be most useful or impactful at your institution? Check all that apply.

- ☐ Institutional initiative
- ☐ Institutional assessment
- ☐ Program general use
- ☐ Program assessment
- ☐ Co-curricular and experiential learning programs
- ☐ Individual courses

Rank the ePortfolio uses/approaches in order of your highest priorities or needs

_   ePortfolios for Learning
_   ePortfolios for Assessment
_   ePortfolios for Professional Development

Table 9.1. ePortfolio planning matrix, developed at San Francisco State University

Areas for Success	Developing	Partially Developed	Fully Developed
Administrative Resources and Support: What resources has or can your university dedicate to advancing and supporting ePortfolios?			
Staffing (below are some possible staffing models): • Percentage of a full-time staff position • One full-time dedicated position • 2+ full time dedicated positions • 1 or more graduate student assistants • 1 or more undergraduate interns	Based on the size and goals of your institution, you are planning for dedicated staff positions.	Based on the size and goals of your institution, there is enough staffing to support pilots and small projects/programs.	Based on the size and goals of your institution, one or more dedicated staff members support programs and university-wide initiatives.
Technology platform: this will vary based on your school size and identified needs. The more institutionally-based and assessment prioritized, the more need for an institutionally-provided and supported platform. The more that learning and student identity are prioritized, the more possible it is to use free, more creative, and open blogging and website building platforms.	Projects and programs use external, third-party platforms. The institution may be considering purchasing a university license.	The institution provides some form of technology for building ePortfolios, with limited documentation and support.	The institution provides an ePortfolio platform and some projects/programs use third-party platforms when appropriate. Technology support is robust.

Areas for Success	Developing	Partially Developed	Fully Developed
Administrative Resources and Support, continued			
Inclusion in working groups and planning committees.	ePortfolios and related staff are rarely considered or invited within planning committee.	ePortfolios and related staff are occasionally considered or invited within planning committees, often added at the end of the process.	ePortfolios and related staff are considered and included within planning committees from the beginning and are built into strategic planning.
Resources to provide faculty development workshops and student support.	There is planning for or a small amount of staff and funds for faculty development, help documentation, and student support.	The institution has at least one staff member to provide a limited amount of faculty development, create support documentation, and provide student support.	The institution has enough staff to provide faculty development and student workshops that meet the demands of the university, with robust help documentation.
Faculty Buy-in: What is the level of faculty participation and buy-in? And what are you doing to garner support and buy-in?			
Involve faculty in development and planning.	Faculty are minimally involved in planning.	Faculty are frequently included in the development of the ePortfolio initiative, once the planning is underway.	Faculty are included in the beginning stages of planning for the ePortfolio initiative and contribute to regular feedback and development.
Provide choices for faculty design of ePortfolio components.	The ePortfolio platform and approaches are highly templated and leave little room for faculty choice in design.	The ePortfolio platform and approaches have space for faculty to customize the ePortfolio assignments to match their curriculum.	Faculty use of ePortfolio and their related assignments are taken into consideration with the platform and ePortfolio approaches. The platform and approaches can be customized to meet goals.

Areas for Success	Developing	Partially Developed	Fully Developed
Faculty Buy-in, continued			
Facilitate faculty identification of authentic uses and meaningful assignments and purpose for ePortfolios at the course and program levels.	ePortfolio design has little inclusion of reflection or meaningful assignments beyond fulfilling requirements.	Much of the purpose of the ePortfolio is to meet requirements but there are some specific moments for reflection and meaningful assignments.	The ePortfolio balances needs for requirements with multiple moments of reflection and a variety of meaningful assignments. Students have choice for selecting ePortfolio artifacts.
ePortfolios in Practice: On a practical level, have these considerations been met?			
ePortfolios are introduced early in the course/program/ePortfolio experience.	ePortfolios are introduced at the end of the curriculum as a final or culminating experience.	ePortfolios are introduced early-to-mid-curriculum, with some explanation of the pedagogical purpose.	ePortfolios are introduced early and often throughout the curriculum, with explanation of the pedagogical purpose.
Learning outcomes and goals for ePortfolio experience are introduced early and across periodic time intervals to students.	Learning outcomes and goals of ePortfolios are introduced at the end of the curriculum as a final or culminating experience.	Learning outcomes and goals of ePortfolios are introduced early-to-mid-curriculum.	Learning outcomes and goals of ePortfolios are introduced early and often throughout the curriculum.
Instructors promote value of ePortfolio and reflective pedagogy.	Faculty rarely discuss the value of ePortfolio and reflective pedagogy.	Faculty occasionally discuss the value of ePortfolio and reflective pedagogy.	Faculty frequently discuss the value of ePortfolio and reflective pedagogy, including related assignments.
Considerations for time are included within course/program/ePortfolio experience to create space for working on ePortfolios.	ePortfolios are assigned at the end of the curriculum, with much of the work happening outside of class.	The curriculum is designed for students to develop ePortfolios over time, with opportunities for feedback.	ePortfolios are embedded throughout the curriculum, with many opportunities for development, feedback, revision, and showcasing.

Areas for Success	Developing	Partially Developed	Fully Developed
ePortfolios in Practice, continued			
Touchpoints are built into ePortfolio courses/programs/experiences to create opportunities for instructor and/or peer feedback.	ePortfolios are assigned at the end of the curriculum, with much of the work happening outside of class.	The curriculum is designed for students to develop ePortfolios over time, with opportunities for feedback.	ePortfolios are embedded throughout the curriculum, with many opportunities for development, feedback, revision, and showcasing.
ePortfolio assignments and experiences are appropriately scaffolded to promote learning development.	ePortfolio assignments provide little scaffolding to promote learning development.	ePortfolio assignments are more structured in the beginning and build up over time in complexity and student creativity and choice.	ePortfolio assignments are more structured in the beginning and build up over time in complexity and student creativity and choice, culminating in more collaborative ePortfolio experiences with authentic audiences.
ePortfolio platform and technology meets three criteria: (1) it meets your institutional, programmatic, and/or course priorities around learning, assessment, and professional development; (2) it has a relatively intuitive interface; and (3) it provides space for student creativity and personalization.	The ePortfolio platform and technology only meets one of the criteria.	The ePortfolio platform and technology meet two of the criteria.	The ePortfolio platform and technology meet all three of the criteria.

Conclusion

While the above considerations may seem overwhelming, a helpful approach may be to view the ePortfolio process (an iterative cycle of self-assessment and reflection) as a metaphor for the ePortfolio development, implementation, and support at your institution. The components involved in building portfolios, such as identifying goals; reflecting on achievements; seeking and receiving feedback; revising; and continuing to build upon ongoing work, are the very same processes that contribute to successful ePortfolio initiatives. These successes happen over time, in iterative ways that are enhanced by being student-centered and including multiple perspectives and stakeholders.

The contributions and connections between stakeholders contribute to the richness of the impact of ePortfolios. When administrative stakeholders see the value of portfolio processes for student success and contribute resources and advocacy, this empowers learning technology specialists to promote and support ePortfolio use within departments, programs, and at the faculty level. When programs and faculty feel supported and can engage in conversations and planning around integrating ePortfolios into the curriculum, the space is created for them to consider the meaningful purpose behind their own use of ePortfolios. Ultimately, students should see that the university places value on portfolio processes. Once that significance is more transparent to students, it increases opportunities for them to engage in folio thinking. ePortfolio initiatives that have the highest chance for success have administrative support coupled with faculty participation in emphasizing meaningful reflection. ePortfolio initiatives may ebb and flow depending upon the availability or scarcity of these various avenues of support and engagement, but this cyclical process parallels the folio thinking process. Instructors, educational technology staff, and university members who continue to pursue ePortfolio growth will learn and grow themselves throughout their journeys with ePortfolios on their campus.

References

Ahn, J. (2004). Electronic portfolios: Blending technology, accountability & assessment. *T.H.E. Journal, 31*(9).

Alverno College Faculty. (2000). *Self assessment at Alverno College* (G. Loacker, Ed.). Alverno College Institute.

Challis, M. (1999). AMEE medical education guide no. 11 (revised): Portfolio-based learning and assessment in medical education. Medical Teacher, 21(4), 370–386. https://doi.org/10.1080/01421599979310.

Chen, H. L. (2004, January 27). *Supporting individual folio learning: Folio thinking in practice* [Poster presentation]. NLII Annual Meeting, San Diego, California.

Chen, H. L. (2012, January 19–20). Electronic portfolios and student success: A framework for effective implementation [Conference presentation]. WASC Resource Fair. https://www.slideshare.net/WascSenior/helen-chen-electronic-portfolios-and-student-success-a-framework-for-effective-implementation.

Coleman, K., Harver, A., Watson, C. E., Rhodes, T., Batson, T. & Chen, H. (2017). *Field guide to eportfolio*. Association of American Colleges and Universities.

Dahlstrom, E. (2012). *ECAR study of undergraduate students and information technology, 2012*. EDUCAUSE Center for Applied Research.

Dahlstrom, E., Walker, J. D. & Dziuban, C. (2013). *ECAR study of undergraduate students and information technology, 2013.* EDUCAUSE Center for Applied Research.

Desmet, C., Miller, D. C., Griffin, J., Balthazor, R. & Cummings, R. E. (2008). Reflection, revision, and assessment in first-year composition ePortfolios. *The Journal of General Education, 57*(1), 15–30.

Eynon, B. (2011). Making connections: The LaGuardia ePortfolio. In D. Cambridge, B. L. Cambridge & K. B. Yancey (Eds.), *Electronic portfolios 2.0: Emergent research on implementation and impact* (pp. 59–68). Stylus; AAC&U.

Eynon, B., Gambino, L. & Torok, J. (2014). What difference can ePortfolio make? A field report from the connect to learning project. *International Journal of EPortfolio, 4*(1), 94–114.

Eynon, B. & Gambino, L. (2017). *High-impact ePortfolio practice: A catalyst for student, faculty, and institutional learning.* Stylus; AAC&U.

Jafari, A. (2004). The "sticky" ePortfolio system: Tackling challenges and identifying attributes. *EDUCAUSE Review, 38–48.*

Johnsen, H. L. (2012). Making learning visible with ePortfolios: Coupling the right pedagogy with the right technology. *International Journal of ePortfolios, 2,* 139–148.

Johnson, R. S., Mims-Cox, J. S. & Doyle-Nichols, A. (2006). *Developing portfolios in education: A guide to reflection, inquiry, and assessment.* SAGE Publications.

Kahn, S. (2014). E-Portfolios: A look at where we've been, where we are now, and where we're (possibly) going. *Peer Review, 16*(1), 4–7.

Knight, W. E., Hakel, M. D. & Gromko, M. (2008). *The relationship between electronic portfolio participation and student success.* Association for Institutional Research. https://eric.ed.gov/?id=ED504411

Meyer, L. (2016). How to select the right e-portfolio platform. Campus Technology. https://campustechnology.com/articles/2016/11/16/how-to-select-the-right -e-portfolio-platform.aspx.

Pacansky-Brock, M. (2017). *Best practices for teaching with emerging technologies.* Routledge.

Reis, N. K. & Villaume, S. K. (2002). The benefits, tensions, and visions of portfolios as a wide scale assessment for teacher education. *Action in Teacher Education, 23*(4), 10–17.

Rickards, W. H., Diez, M. E., Ehley, L., Guilbault, L. F., Loacker, G., Hart, J. R. & Smith, P. C. (2008). Learning, reflection, and electronic portfolios: Stepping toward an assessment practice. *The Journal of General Education, 57*(1), 31–50.

Ring, G. & Ramirez, B. (2012). Implementing ePortfolios for the assessment of general education competencies. *International Journal of EPortfolio, 2*(1), 87–97.

Ring, G. L., Waugaman, C. & Broadwell Jackson, D. (2015). Using ePortfolios to assess and improve the general education curriculum. The Journal of General Education, 64(4), 310–333. https://doi.org/10.1353/jge.2015.0027.

Seldin, P. & Miller, J. E. (2010). *The academic portfolio: A practical guide to documenting teaching, research and service.* Jossey-Bass.

Siemens, G. (2004). ePortfolios. elearnspace. http://www.elearnspace.org/Articles /eportfolios.htm.

Straumsheim, C. (2014). Promising portfolios. Inside HigherEd. https://www.inside
highered.com/news/2014/01/27/aacu-conference-shows-plenty-uses-e-portfolios
-also-pitfalls-hype.

Strudler, N. & Wetzel, K. (2008). Costs and benefits of electronic portfolios in
teacher education: Faculty perspectives. *Journal of Computing in Teacher Education, 24*(4), 135–141.

Suter, V. (n.d.) Folio thinking. https://vsuter.org/eportfolios/.

Swan, G. (2009). Examining barriers in faculty adoption of an e-portfolio system.
Australasian Journal of Educational Technology, 25(5). https://ajet.org.au/index
.php/AJET/article/view/1112.

Taylor, I., Thomas, J. & Sage, H. (1999). Portfolios for learning and assessment:
Laying the foundations for continuing professional development. *Social Work
Education, 18*(2), 147–160.

Tzeng, J.-Y. (2010). Perceived values and prospective users' acceptance of prospective technology: The case of a career eportfolio system. *Computers & Education,
56*(1), 157–165.

Watson, C. E., Kuh, G. D., Rhodes, T., Light, T. P. & Chen, H. L. (2016). Editorial:
ePortfolios—The eleventh high impact practice. *International Journal of EPortfolio, 6*(2), 65–69.

Appendix A. FINA Department Portfolio Rubric

Your final semester portfolio is intended to be utilized as an ongoing professional
tool for job interviews, publicizing your skills, and other professional uses. As
such it is designed so that it can be further modified to meet your future and
changing needs. A high quality portfolio will:

- tell a cohesive story,
- have good narratives,
- be appropriate for your industry, and describe your skill set.

Instructions:

- From your major area options below, select a minimum of eight (8)
  examples of your best works/projects to include in your portfolio. You
  may add as many additional items as you like.
- Written essays should be reduced to an abstract and include a visual such
  as a picture or graph. Full essays/papers may be included as downloads
  for further readings.
- Please include clear well written narratives describing what the viewer is
  looking at.

	MISSING OR NEEDS IMPROVEMENT				EXCELLENT
MEETS 8 WORK/PROJECTS REQUIREMENT	0	4	6	8	10
WORK/PROJECTS VISUALS INCLUDED	0	2	4	6	8
WORK/PROJECTS NARRATIVES INCLUDED	0	2	4	6	8
PHILOSOPHY STATEMENT INCLUDED	0	1	2	3	4
OVERALL COHESIVENESS	0	2	4	6	8

Appendix B. Assignment Sheet

The Digital Portfolio Project: Showcasing Your Writing

English 114 | C. Wong

This assignment is an invitation to polish and showcase your writing. You can design your portfolio in a way that captures your sense of yourself and your growth and accomplishments as a student and as a writer.

Task: Create a digital portfolio of your favorite pieces of writing from this semester using Portfolium. Writings can be of varying length and should showcase some of your best work. Design your portfolio so that it represents your authentic self, using images, titles, and blurbs as you see fit.

Grade Distribution

50 points total	Expectations	Check off when complete
25 points	Personalize your ePortfolio (**profile tab**) • Showcase at least 3 artifacts—one from the beginning, middle, and end of semester—that show your growth as a student and as a writer (**portfolio tab**)	⊓
	• Reflect on your artifacts, that is, to describe what they are, what they say about you, and what kinds of learning / competence you achieved as a result of creating them (**portfolio tab**)	⊓
	• Make connections with at least 3 people (**connections tab**)	⊓

Continued on next page

50 points total	Expectations	Check off when complete
25 points	Attend our ePortfolio party—this is scheduled on the last day of class	
	• At the party, say a few words about your ePortfolio: your intentions, what you want the viewer to know about you, how you decided on images, etc.	❐
	• View at least 3 ePortfolios and leave feedback (suggestion: you might want to comment on their visual and/or rhetorical devices)	❐

Chapter 10. Artifacts in ePortfolios: Moving from a Repository of Assessment to Linkages for Learning

Howard B. Sanborn

VIRGINIA MILITARY INSTITUTE

Jenny Ramirez

MARY BALDWIN UNIVERSITY/JAMES MADISON UNIVERSITY

As a collection of *artifacts* presented and curated by students in the digital space, ePortfolios offer students a means to trace the building of their knowledge and *showcase* their talents and abilities. They permit both students and instructors to explore new types of assignments that can be submitted as evidence of student learning over time. Yet, as willing as many students are to try their hand at assignments beyond the typical essay, they often do not have an understanding of how to draw out sophisticated observations about their own learning that take place in and between assignments.

In this chapter, we explore the linkages across ePortfolio artifacts made possible by explicit reflection at discrete moments in the semester. In particular, we demonstrate how the guidance of humanities professors who require assignments with implicit reflection, such as artist statements and the design and creation of artistic pieces, can help professors in the social sciences gain insights into how to teach reflection about other cultures to students. Structured reflection can encourage students to think deeply about their work on a specific artifact. More importantly, it can allow them to more easily connect their artifacts together into a sophisticated narrative about their learning. A statistical data analysis illustrates the improvements students made in analyzing *artifacts* in summative reflective essays that they included in their ePortfolios. As students were asked to reflect alongside their artifacts, they gained the skills that allowed them to more competently evaluate the appropriateness of various types of assignments to their learning.

Background and Literature

ePortfolios serve many purposes, from the *assessment* of student learning and the marketing of skills to an employer to the showcase of student work and the development of learning in a course or program (Barrett, 2007). In particular, there is great traction gained from the use of ePortfolios in assessment *for* learning (Black & Wiliam, 1998) (see Coleman et al., this collection). Students are not only

DOI: https://doi.org/10.37514/PRA-B.2020.1084.2.10

afforded the space for displaying their work but also given the opportunity to form their ideas once they see an artifact uploaded to their ePortfolio. They may even feel greater facility in solving larger, substantive questions about coursework when given the time to craft an answer while, at the same time, not competing with other students to speak during class time (Black & Wiliam, 2004). These efforts are an attempt to promote learning that "should be thoughtful, reflective, focused to evoke and explore understanding, and conducted so that all pupils have an opportunity to think and to express their ideas" (Black & Wiliam, 1998, p. 8). ePortfolios, then, are a means to create this space for exploration and reflection, both at discrete moments during the semester and at the culmination of a project or course.

Dellinger et al. (2013) detail the importance of Schön's (1983) reflection-in-action in a study of reflective captions, referred to in their piece as "reflective tags," which students submitted along with their artifacts in an ePortfolio. Explicit contextualization provided students an increased ability to reflect on the lessons learned about cultures and groups. At the end of the semester, students who had curated their ePortfolios with these tags also tended to perform better in their summative assessment: a reflective essay in which they evaluated their processes of learning.

Individuals can engage in increasing levels of reflection, ranging from the simple contrast of what one once knew and what one now knows to the textured and complex insights of an individual weaving empathy, insight, and knowledge into a deeper understanding of a particular topic. Indeed, there have been studies of the quality of reflection in ePortfolios (Dellinger et al., 2013; Parkes et al., 2013), but the evaluation of reflection atomized to the artifact-level is often difficult to conceptualize and measure.

Student artifacts are the elemental components of the ePortfolio. The digital space allows for greater experimentation in the composition of assignments, as well as a means to draw connections that demonstrate learning as it happens (Bhattacharya & Hartnett, 2007). Yet, the practice of effective *reflection* can be a challenge for students. Faculty do not often recognize the frustration their students have in learning how to learn (see Polly et al., this collection). They fail to provide them guidance on how to reflect that is tailored to the goals of a particular ePortfolio (Landis et al., 2015). As a result, it becomes easy for students to turn their ePortfolios into digital repositories, akin to a collection of links one might find in Dropbox or Google Drive, rather than spaces for reflection and synthesis of their work.

Another related pitfall is the competing goal of implementing both formative and summative assessments in student coursework (Barrett & Carney, 2005). ePortfolios should be a collection of "unique linkages, connections, and reflections among multiple experiences and artifacts in ways that would not otherwise be possible with a traditional paper portfolio" (Parkes et al., 2013, p. 101). Yet, many professors ask students to produce a final product for the class that can be used as a means to evaluate whether one has met program leaning outcomes. The linking of artifacts provides a thread that holds the ePortfolio together, but this attempt to scaffold reflection throughout a course can be lost in the desire for a more straightforward assessment.

In sum, ePortfolios can offer students an effective means to synthesize the lessons of a course or program by not only asking them to showcase their work but also to draw out the connections between artifacts in an effort to reinforce their learning and, perhaps, even spur on the creation of knowledge. Unfortunately, students are not often prepared to link ePortfolio artifacts together in a manner that encourages the reflection that results in deep learning desired by professors. As a result, professors must make efforts to incentivize reflection from students as they submit artifacts so as to draw out the "linkages, connections, and reflections" that will cultivate a richer engagement with the lessons from the classroom.

Case Study: Artifact Analysis in the Study of Asia

Students were asked to take two classes as part of a general education requirement (see Terry & Whillock and Carpenter & Labissiere, this collection) to teach them about the "civilizations and cultures" (C&C) of the world. For each class, their guidance was the same; they were to upload artifacts, tagged with reflective annotations, to their ePortfolios alongside a summative, reflective essay. This reflective essay was subsequently assessed by a team of faculty for student achievement in three categories: Cultural Understanding, Reflection, and Artifact Analysis.[1]

Two of the classes included in the C&C program were drawn from the Department of International Studies and Political Science: Politics in East Asia and Politics in China. These two courses were junior-level seminars without pre-requisites and were open to students of all majors. The subject matter of the two courses centered on government institutions and political processes. In the East Asia course, these elements were compared across Japan, China, Taiwan, and the Koreas. In the China course, students learned about the post-Mao reforms that took place during the 1980s and how the authoritarian government led by the Communist Party has evolved since it came to power in 1949.

Initially, students were asked to complete response essays as part of the requirements for these classes, in line with the typical assignments for a regional political science survey course. In these essays, students were asked to relate current events to the lessons of the class. These assignments formed the bulk of the artifacts from which a student could choose for their ePortfolio and write about in their summative reflective essay. However, even though students performed well in lessons about government and politics, their assessment scores in cultural understanding and reflection consistently fell below benchmark, indicating that

---

1. The first assessment instrument was a *holistic rubric*, which was later replaced by this three-category scale.

they did not seem to adequately grasp lessons about culture that prompted the creation of the civilizations and cultures component of the core curriculum. This poor performance was seen in C&C classes drawn from across the curriculum, particularly in the natural and social sciences, as well as in engineering courses.

Consequently, in 2012, professors from humanities courses held workshops designed to promote the functionality of ePortfolios, particularly the ability to create projects that were not possible outside of the digital space. In both the Politics in East Asia and Politics in China courses, the professor introduced one such project: a propaganda poster. Students could be creative in using software to design posters or scan in handmade drawings, while illustrating the messaging techniques of government propaganda and marketing bureaucracies in places like China, using materials purchased from the Shanghai Propaganda Poster Art Center as guides, and North Korea (Myers 2010). Students in these courses were also given the opportunity to upload podcasts or videos as descriptions of the cultures they were learning about; one assignment asked students to create a tourism ad encouraging visitors from the West to visit an East Asian country using lessons about culture from the class. However, despite these efforts to encourage students to complete a variety of *multimodal* assignments, students still did not appear to grasp the lessons on and nuances of similarity and difference in cultures across the region. Results from the 2013 assessment of these courses largely supports this conclusion.

It is not surprising, then, that these "creative" artifacts did not produce a sophisticated understanding of the course lessons on democracy and governance in Asia. Students composed creative assignments without context—without much thought on how their work at this one moment connected to others across the entirety of the course. Asia, in particular, serves as a challenging topic for study; as important and increasingly relevant as the region is, it is often quite "foreign" to Western students (Bahree, 1986). In terms of government, students are often limited by their personal conceptualizations of ideas like democracy and culture, defaulting to their own perspectives and even stereotypes to answer questions about places like China and Japan. This lacuna between showcasing academic work and drawing connections between artifacts and beyond the subject matter revealed the shortcomings of summative reflection. Indeed, reflection at discrete moments in the semester can help students to lay their views bare and contrast them with the views of citizens of other countries (see Balthazor et al., this collection).

Previous research has detailed the efforts to teach political science students more effectively about Asia by borrowing lessons from the humanities (Sanborn & Ramirez, 2017). As many of the multimodal assignments for the Politics in East Asia and Politics in China courses were drawn from ideas spurred on by professors from the humanities, so, too, were the solutions on how to contextualize lessons about democracy and Asian politics with reflection at discrete moments. In C&C art history classes, for example, students created artifacts that asked them to envision "sacred spaces" based on lectures and discussions about spirituality in Asian art. While these projects often involved creative expression in the form of graphic design, they also positioned the learner at the center of the lessons. Students would discuss their process of creating these unique assignments and reflect on their choices. In doing so, students personalized their learning of complex subjects, drawing links across artifacts in a more sophisticated way in their summative reflective essays.[2]

Thus, in revising the politics courses, the focus became less on creating multimodal assignments and more on incorporating reflection into students' composition of propaganda posters and podcasts. The students in the courses even participated in Skype exchanges with students from Hong Kong who were protesting for greater democracy in the city. However, these artifacts were bounded by specific requirements to reflect on a concept, such as democracy or accountability, from their own point-of-view. Then, after completing the assignment, the students were asked about what they perceived as different, or how their views had changed, and then they were charged with tracking that gain of knowledge in their reflective essay later in the semester.

For example, in 2015, students were asked to create a free form blog post about interactions with their own governments, followed by a second blog post, informed by readings and class discussions, about how citizens of China hold their government accountable. Then, they engaged in their video conference with students in Hong Kong, asking questions about democracy, armed with their baseline views of what democracy meant to them and what they thought democracy meant to individuals in Asia. Based on this discussion, students were asked to explain what the necessary components of democratic governance were, with the idea that they could glean the similarities and differences of conceptions of this regime type having both talked with students in Hong Kong about democracy and having reflected on their own conceptions of accountability, liberty, and equality.

In addition, students were still given the opportunity to create propaganda posters. However, they were directed to reflect explicitly on their process of creation, rather than simply summarize what they hoped to achieve in their messaging. As a result, students could make connections among artifacts in a more sophisticated manner than they had in earlier iterations of the course.

To test the effectiveness of this approach, we drew summative reflective essays from ePortfolios for each of the classes included in this study: the 2013 pre-revision versions of Politics in East Asia and Politics in China, the 2014 post-revision version of Politics in East Asia, and the 2015 post-revision version of Politics in China. We also assessed essays from two art history courses offered in 2013 on which the revisions were based: History of Asian Art and Chinese Art & Culture. These

---

2. For more information on the types of assignments discussed here, see Ramirez and Sanborn (2015) and Sanborn and Ramirez (2017).

essays were scored by two raters using an analytical *rubric* created for the C&C program (Figure 10.1); classes had ended months before and the points given by the raters did not count in students' grades. An essay was scored from 1 to 5 along the Cultural Understanding, Reflection, and Artifact Analysis scales, respectively, and these points were summed for a rating, out of a total of 15 points. If the total score awarded by each of the two raters for an essay differed by more than three points, the raters discussed their allocation of points for the essay before coming to a consensus. The scores of the two raters were summed for a final overall score out of 30 points, including a score out of 10 points for artifact analysis.

ANALYSIS OF ePORTFOLIO ARTIFACTS	
"5" RATING	Presents a complex, insightful analysis of a selection of substantive, varied, and revealing artifacts which fully support and develop the essay's thesis/focus.
"4" RATING	Presents an effective analysis of a selection of relevant and varied artifacts which effectively support and develop the essay's thesis/focus.
"3" RATING	Presents a clear analysis of a selection of appropriate and varied artifacts, which loosely support and develop the essay's thesis/focus.
"2" RATING	A weak analysis, which may be attributed to a poor selection of artifacts either in terms of relevance, diversity, or quality.
"1" RATING	Fails to include or discuss artifacts.

Figure 10.1 Artifact Analysis Scores. Source: Virginia Military Institute (VMI) Core Curriculum Oversight Committee, guidance for Civilizations and Cultures summative reflective essays.

This analysis of quantitative data is limited by the constraints of a rubric that attempts to quantify reflection and analytical abilities. In addition, there are a small number of observations for each of the classes included in this study, limiting generalizability. However, with clear calls for empiricism in the study of effective practices for the use of ePortfolios by faculty and administrators (Bryant & Chittum 2013; Rhodes et al., 2014), we proceed with this analysis, aided by the use of statistical techniques designed to detect significant differences across small samples.

Table 10.1 features a summary of data on the analysis of artifacts by students enrolled in six courses from 2013–2015. In 2013, one can clearly see the difference in the evaluation of ePortfolio artifacts for both pan-Asia and China-specific courses, by discipline. Students in the Asian and Chinese Art classes scored, on average, a 7.3 out of 10 points. The benchmark for the C&C program, for the sake of comparison, was a total score of 18 points, or 6 points per category. At the same time, the Asian (3 of 10) and Chinese (4.8) politics classes fell well below the standard for the program.

Table 10.1. Analysis of student ePortfolio artifacts in summative reflective essays, 2013–2015

	Artifact Analysis (out of 10)	Standard Deviation	Number of Essays
Pan-Asia courses			
2013 History of Asian Art	7.3	1.30	20
2013 Politics in East Asia	3.0	1.41	14
2014 Politics in East Asia	7.1	1.39	15
p-value of difference between politics courses	**0.0000**		
China courses			
2013 Chinese Art and Culture	7.3	1.35	16
2013 Politics in China	4.8	2.24	17
2015 Politics in China	6.0	1.56	15
p-value of difference between politics courses	**0.0497**		

Notes: To test for the significance of the difference of the scores across politics classes, a two-sample t-test is conducted with equal variances assumed. One-tailed statistical significance (p <.05).

In 2014 and 2015, after the revisions to the politics coursework described above, the scores improved significantly. Students in the revamped Politics in East Asia course scored a 7.1 out of 10, on average, while students in the updated Politics in China class scored a 6 of 10. To test whether this improvement in scores met the threshold for statistical significance, we conducted a two-sample t-test comparing the scores of the 2013 politics classes to their later counterparts. In both cases, we were able to reject the null hypothesis of no difference between the two sets of classes; the roughly 4-point average improvement in scores for the Politics in East Asia course was significant at the .001 level, while the 1.2-point improvement in the Politics in China course just crossed the threshold of significance at the .05 level. Students, thus, performed better when the artifacts were explicitly tied to reflection, rather than simply a collection of multi-modal assignments without explicit analysis of their purpose in the student learning process.

Conclusion

The initial motivation for the revision of these politics courses, based on lessons from the humanities, was to promote in students a greater appreciation for culture and sophisticated reflection on how they came to know what they now knew (Sanborn & Ramirez, 2017). A somewhat intended, but certainly fortuitous, outcome was the thoughtful evaluation of artifacts that they included in their ePortfolios. Students drew on different artifacts to make the case for their learning in the summative reflective essays as they had for years before. They linked together artifacts, however, in a more persuasive narrative, tied to the reflection and learning they developed over the course of the semester.

A simple, perhaps obvious, lesson of this study is that professors should encourage reflection as part of the artifact-selection process. The digital space affords a flexibility and creativity in assignments that many educators are willing to explore with their students. It is the reflection that occurs alongside this exploration that produces deep learning and allows students to develop their thinking about complex subjects as it happens and sort out the lessons of a course upon reflection at the end of the term.

References

Bahree, P. (1986). Teaching about Asia. *Western European Education, 18*(4), 31–59.

Barrett, H. C. (2007). Researching electronic portfolios and learner engagement: The REFLECT initiative. *Journal of Adolescent & Adult Literacy, 50*(6), 436–449.

Barrett, H. C. & Carney, J. (2005). Conflicting paradigms and competing purposes in electronic portfolio development. http://electronicportfolios.com/portfolios /LEAJournal-BarrettCarney.pdf.

Bhattacharya, M. & Hartnett, M. (2007, October 10–13). E-portfolio assessment in higher education [Conference presentation]. 37th ASEE/IEEE Frontiers in Education Conference, Milwaukee, Wisconsin.

Black, P. & Wiliam, D. (1998). Inside the black box: Raising standards through classroom assessment. *Phi Delta Kappan, 80*(2), 139–148.

Black, P. & Wiliam, D. (2004). The formative purpose: Assessment must first promote learning. *Yearbook of the National Society for the Study of Education, 103*(2), 20–50.

Bryant, L. H. & Chittum, J. (2013). ePortfolio effectiveness: A(n ill-fated) search for empirical support. *International Journal of ePortfolio, 3*(2), 189–198.

Dellinger, M. A., Koons, K. & McDonald, C. (2013). *ePortfolios and the study of civilizations and cultures* [White paper]. Inter/National Coalition for Electronic Portfolio Research, Cohort VI.

Myers, B. R. (2010). *The cleanest race: How North Koreans see themselves and why it matters.* Melville House.

Parkes, K. A., Dredger, K. S. & Hicks, D. (2013). ePortfolio as a measure of reflective practice. *International Journal of ePortfolio, 3*(2), 99–119.

Ramirez, J. & Sanborn, H. (2015). Creativity and reflection through multi-modal learning: Measuring creative expression in student ePortfolios. In K. Coleman & A. Flood (Eds.). *Capturing creativity through creative teaching.* Common Ground Publishing.

Sanborn, H. & Ramirez, J. (2017). Reflections on Asia: Borrowing lessons from art history in East Asia and China coursework. *ASIANetwork: A Journal for Asian Studies in the Liberal Art,s 24*(2), 70–88.

Schön, D. A. (1983). *The Reflective Practitioner.* Basic.

Chapter 11. Accountability and Actionable Data: A Comparison of Three Approaches to Program Assessment using ePortfolios

Rowanna Carpenter
Yves Labissiere
PORTLAND STATE UNIVERSITY

As increasing numbers of higher education institutions adopt and assess ePortfolios, programs and departments within those institutions must balance calls for accountability with the need to generate useful evidence. General education programs, in particular, need to provide external audiences with credible evidence that they advance students' skills in areas such as critical thinking and written communication. At the same time, faculty must be able to use data for program improvement. *Assessment* using ePortfolios makes it possible to meet both internal and external demands; however, programs need to plan carefully to do both well.

Calls for higher education accountability have proliferated in recent years. Assurances from educational institutions or accreditors claiming that universities and colleges successfully educate their students do not satisfy policy makers and the larger public. Books such as *Academically Adrift* (Arum & Roksa, 2011) claim universities fail to develop students' critical thinking skills. Efforts such as the Voluntary System of Accountability, internal to the higher education community, call on colleges and universities to present evidence of student learning publicly so potential students and other stakeholders can evaluate the outcomes of higher education. Some suggest standardized tests are the best way to provide such evidence, arguing that tests are easily administered, valid, reliable, and allow comparison across institutions (Arum & Roksa, 2011; Benjamin, et. al, 2012).

However, many assessment experts insist that standardized tests are disconnected from the work that students produce in the classroom and thus do not result in actionable data (Walvoord, 2010). In fact, one of the major critiques of standardized tests is that faculty are not able to use the resulting data to inform program improvement (Linn et al., 1991; McCollum, 2011). As Trudy Banta and her colleagues assert, "educators and policy makers in postsecondary education are interested in assessment processes that improve student learning and at the same time provide institutional data that may be used to demonstrate accountability" (Banta, Griffin et al., 2009). The Association of American Colleges and Universities' (AAC&U) Valid Assessment of Learning in Undergraduate Education (VALUE) initiative directly challenges the idea that standardized tests

DOI: https://doi.org/10.37514/PRA-B.2020.1084.2.11

are the only way to produce valid, reliable, and comparable information about student learning in higher education. As opposed to standardized tests, which often have no connection to students' course work, the VALUE *rubrics*, developed by teams of national experts, are meant to assess authentic student work—work such as ePortfolios generated in the context of a course. Tracy Penny Light, Helen Chen, and John Ittleson (2012) argue that ePortfolios can "support student self-assessment but also inform and contribute to institutional improvement and educational effectiveness, involving all campus stakeholders ranging from senior leadership to individual students" (p. 98) (see Richardson et al., this collection).

This chapter focuses on reviewing ePortfolios for a program-level assessment that centers on whether the program as a whole is meeting its goals related to student learning, rather than investigating an individual student's or a particular faculty member's performance (Suskie, 2009; Walvoord, 2010). Examining ePortfolio assessment at the program level reveals the tensions between the demands for external accountability and the need to engage faculty to produce actionable data using limited resources (see Day, this collection). Based on assessment literature and our experience reviewing ePortfolios for program-level assessment, we propose the following key criteria for programs that are developing ePortfolio assessment processes.

- Reliability: Acceptable levels of reliability help ensure that any data produced can be viewed with confidence.
- Comparability: External audiences are often interested in comparing measures of student learning across institutions.
- Usability: In order to complete an assessment cycle, programs must be able to interpret findings in ways that help them identify areas for improvement.

As programs consider adopting rigorous ePortfolio assessment practices, factors beyond usability, reliability, and comparability should be considered. Programs must also seek:

- Efficiency: Portfolio review processes require resources in the form of funds and human time. It is important to acknowledge the resource and infrastructure requirements for any assessment process and to be sure that the investment of resources yields actionable information (Banta et al., 2009; Cooper & Terrell, 2013; Suskie, 2009).
- Rater Experience: It is important that any assessment process is seen as valuable, meaningful, and worthwhile to the faculty who participate.

These considerations (reliability, usability, comparability, efficiency, and rater experience) constitute the RUCER framework we propose for programs building ePortfolio assessment processes. In the next section, we explore each criterion in more depth. We then use the framework to compare three approaches to ePortfolio assessment. Finally, taking into account all of the criteria discussed above, we advance some recommendations for programs considering implementing assessment with ePortfolios.

A Framework of Key Criteria

Reliability

Reliability in an ePortfolio assessment process refers to the extent to which, given the same piece of student work, different raters converge on the same score (see Sanborn & Ramirez, this collection). Acceptable levels of reliability help ensure that any data produced can be viewed with confidence. When assessing ePortfolios, rubrics help establish a scoring process that is consistent and unbiased (Suskie, 2009). In order to improve reliability, assessment approaches using rubrics usually incorporate a training session during which reviewers become familiar with the rubric, practice applying it to a particular piece of student work, and discuss any discrepancies in scoring so that they make scoring decisions consistently with each other. This type of training increases agreement among raters (Penny Light et al., 2012). While several measures of reliability for ePortfolio assessment processes exist, inter-rater agreement—how well two scores on the same piece of student work converge—is a common approach used by many universities (Finley, 2011).

Usability

Successful assessment processes are not only reliable, they must also result in meaningful data (Banta et al., 2009; Peterson & Einarson, 2001). If faculty cannot use the resulting data to inform program improvement, the process is not useful, regardless of reliability. Linda Suskie (2009) outlines four characteristics of useful assessments:

- They yield reasonably accurate and truthful information about what students have learned.
- They have a clear purpose so that assessment results are valued and don't end up sitting on a shelf.
- They engage faculty and staff.
- They focus on clear and important student learning goals. (p. 37)

As program faculty or staff are planning assessment, they should consider what type of data are produced, how those data relate to faculty work, and how the data can be used to inform action and improvement.

Comparability

Calls for accountability often include questions of whether evidence of student learning for a given program is comparable to evidence for other programs or institutions (Banta et al., 2009). Assessments of embedded, authentic assignments such as ePortfolios are often not appropriate for comparison because they vary so much from institution to institution (Suskie, 2009). Because such assessment approaches connect intimately to program practice and pedagogy and reflect the learning experiences of students in a particular program, we have to acknowledge the challenge to comparability that arises when adopting such localized practices. Nationally recognized rubrics, such as the VALUE rubrics, help mitigate these concerns because they were designed to provide for comparability without standardization (Rhodes, 2011).

Efficiency

It is important to acknowledge the resource and infrastructure requirements for any assessment process and to be sure that the investment of resources yields actionable information (Banta et al., 2009; Cooper & Terrell, 2013; Suskie, 2009). While some assessment or ePortfolio processes involve grading ePortfolios in the context of a course and aggregating those judgments to the program level, many program-level processes select a few samples of student work from key courses and review those in a process that takes place outside of regular classroom parameters. Taking the process outside of the classroom allows for a focus on a single goal or learning outcome, creates opportunities to involve faculty beyond those who teach the course in question, and addresses the problems that can arise when instructors across courses do not use the same assessment practices within their courses (Johnstone et al., 2001; Miller & Leskes, 2005; Suskie, 2009). An approach that takes assessment outside of the classroom uses resources beyond those required to deliver the course material and grade the student work from the course (Banta et al., 2009; Linn et al., 1991; Suskie, 2009). These resources include faculty time, any specific software requirements, and stipends for faculty participants (if applicable).

As a proxy for the resources needed for an assessment process, we use efficiency, including the time it takes to read ePortfolios, the number of ePortfolios reasonably possible to assess in a single day, and the time it takes to calibrate or train raters. Each of these measures relates to the overall resources—funds and human time—required to complete the task.

Rater Experience

It is important that any assessment process is seen as valuable, meaningful, and worthwhile to the faculty who participate. In addition to producing data that serve accountability purposes, an assessment process can provide the occasion for in-depth conversations about student learning and expectations for students within a program (Briggs, 2007; Hutchings, 2010; Suskie, 2009). Such conversations are only valuable, however, if faculty are invested in the process and the outcomes. Any changes supported by assessment results cannot be implemented without faculty participation (Banta et al., 2009). With the use of embedded assessments, such as ePortfolios, faculty can make a direct link between assessment conversations and their classroom practices (McCollum, 2011; Suskie, 2009). Such conversations are also an opportunity to reinforce using assessment for improvement and not for individual faculty evaluation, a practice that promotes trust and continued engagement in the assessment process (Suskie, 2009; Walvoord, 2010). For faculty to learn from their experience reviewing portfolios, they need time to read the ePortfolios, have conversations with each other, and reflect on the results for their own classroom practices. An important consideration is the balance between the efficient production of assessment data and the time required for faculty to feel engaged and energized by the process.

Method

Given higher education institutions' need to respond to calls for accountability, including providing valid and reliable evidence of student learning, we want to inform the conversation about ePortfolio assessment by offering a comparison of three approaches to assessing ePortfolios using the framework we have presented above. We are interested in examining the reliability and usability of each process alongside a consideration of the efficiency of the process (how much does it cost to generate results?), the faculty experience in the process, and the comparability of the data across programs and institutions.

To examine our framework and learn about the potential contributions of alternative assessment strategies, we compared an approach using a *holistic rubric*, an approach using *adaptive comparative judgment*, and an approach using an *analytic rubric* (one of the VALUE rubrics), each described below (see Sanborn & Ramirez, this collection). We invited ten experienced reviewers to participate in our project. These faculty taught the freshman general education course from which we drew the ePortfolios or taught at other levels of the general education program. Each of them had participated in our established portfolio review process at least five times. All faculty were familiar with program learning goals and existing ePortfolio review processes.

Each assessment process took place on a single day. Because we value the conversation and collective experience of convening a group of faculty in one place, we did not examine asynchronous review processes. However, we believe our framework can help inform other assessment approaches as well. We conducted the review processes on three successive days. On each day, the faculty met in the morning to receive orientation to the day's task, spent the bulk of the day reviewing portfolios, and reconvened at the end of the day to provide feedback on the process. These review processes took place during the summer and each faculty reviewer was compensated for participation. Following the review, we analyzed reliability data, the ePortfolio score data, data on the length of time the reviews took, and our notes on the reviewers' experiences with each process.

Approach 1: Local Holistic Critical Thinking Rubric

During the first review process, the ten "expert" reviewers participated as part of an established ePortfolio review process with 25 other reviewers. The larger process involved scoring 265 student portfolios. All reviewers, including our experts, received orientation and training in the morning, during which they were introduced to a locally-developed six-point holistic critical thinking rubric (see Appendix A. Note: Since the writing of this chapter, the rubric has been revised substantially.). All reviewers read and scored one ePortfolio and convened for a conversation about the scores. Following a question and answer session during which reviewers worked toward consensus about how to score the first sample ePortfolio, the reviewers scored a second ePortfolio. After a second discussion, reviewers read and scored the rest of the ePortfolios.

Each ePortfolio was read by at least two people. If the two scores were the same or only one score apart, the average of the two scores was used as a final ePortfolio score. When the difference between the first two scores was two or more, a third reviewer read and scored the ePortfolio. To avoid having this process influence subsequent ratings, our expert reviewers read a sample of portfolios that were not included in the ACJ or VALUE processes.

Reliability for this approach was measured through inter-rater agreement, calculated by determining the number of ePortfolios needing a third review and dividing by the total.

Approach 2: Adaptive Comparative Judgment (ACJ)

On the second day, our expert reviewers participated in an Adaptive Comparative Judgment (ACJ) process. For this process, we included a set of 100 portfolios that had not already been read by our reviewers. ACJ is an approach to rating ePortfolios that involves comparing two ePortfolios and selecting a "winner" between the two. In this case, raters were asked to select the ePortfolio that represented the better example of critical thinking, as defined by our holistic rubric, and declare it a winner. After making their selection, the judges made notes about why they made that decision. We were curious about ACJ as an assessment technique for several reasons. First, this approach promises superior reliability coefficients—well above .9 (Pollitt, 2012)—thus addressing one of the concerns with traditional rubric approaches to ePortfolio assessment. Second, this approach also involves a different way of reading student work. Rather than comparing the work with a set of criteria from a rubric, the ACJ approach asks reviewers only to compare two portfolios and make one choice. Each portfolio is then compared with several others over the course of the day and each portfolio is read by more judges than in a standard holistic rubric scoring approach. For details on this approach, see Pollitt (2012).

The ACJ software tracks agreement for each portfolio. As consensus forms on a particular portfolio, it is removed from the subsequent pair presentation. In other words, if portfolio A is consistently judged better than other portfolios, it is removed from subsequent trials. The ACJ process relies on a modified Rasch model to calculate reliability (Pollitt, 2012).

Approach 3: VALUE Integrated Learning

We chose to use one of the AAC&U VALUE rubrics as a third assessment approach: the *Integrative Learning* rubric (see Appendix B). Having previously piloted several VALUE rubrics, we found that the Integrative Learning rubric correlated most closely with our local critical thinking rubric. The VALUE rubric also offered an opportunity to compare a holistic rubric approach with an analytic rubric approach.

The group of reviewers met in the morning to review the rubric. Because the rubric is analytic and includes five categories each associated with a four-point rating scale, the scoring conversation took longer than the comparable conversation for the holistic rubric. To have time to score the ePortfolios, we only scored one *calibration* ePortfolio and had a single conversation before asking the reviewers to proceed with reading the rest of the ePortfolios. Two reviewers read and scored each ePortfolio. We included the same sample of 100 portfolios that were reviewed during the ACJ process. Reviewers were instructed to skip any portfolio they had previously viewed, so we were getting fresh reads for each portfolio. We reconvened at the end of day for a conversation about the process.

Reliability for this approach was measured through inter-rater agreement for each of the five rubric criteria.

Findings

In this section, we compare our existing approach to ePortfolio assessment (Existing/Holistic), adaptive comparative judgment (ACJ), and an approach using a VALUE rubric (VALUE/Analytic) using the framework we have proposed and outline our findings for each criterion below. Table 11.1 summarizes the primary findings for each of our three assessment processes for the five criteria.

Existing/Holistic

Efficiency

Training raters in our existing holistic rubric approach takes approximately 90 minutes. This session includes an overview of the process and review and discussion of two calibration portfolios.

Because our "experts" were embedded as part of a larger ePortfolio review process, we could compare the time it took them to rate ePortfolios with the time clocked by other reviewers who participated in scoring ePortfolios that day. We found that our experienced reviewers took an average of 9.8 minutes for a first review and 6.5

minutes for a second review. Our less experienced reviewers took an average of 13 minutes for a first review and 8.7 minutes for a second review. In addition, our experienced reviewers assessed 64 portfolios, reading an average of 13 portfolios each.

We had not considered that our experienced reviewers would take so much less time to review portfolios than our less experienced reviewers. The result makes sense, but it also suggests that the rest of our findings need to be considered in light of this discovery. We are referring to processes as performed by faculty experienced in reading and scoring ePortfolios.

Reliability

Overall reliability, as measured by inter-rater agreement was 83%.

Usefulness of Data

The data produced through this process are an overall mean rubric score for the program and mean scores for faculty teams (generally consisting of three to five faculty members). We also produced distributions of portfolio scores at the program and team levels. These data are useful in that they are derived based on a rubric that was developed in house by our faculty and therefore align closely with the program definition of critical thinking. These data are also the basis of the assessment reports that faculty have received each year for more than a decade. Faculty are familiar with those reports and the underlying data and are accustomed to having conversations about the findings (see Appendix C).

A holistic rubric score gives an overall sense of student achievement, but does not pinpoint specific areas for development as an analytic rubric score would do. When faculty are presented with an aggregate team or overall score that has risen or declined, they must make some assumptions about the factors that may have played a role in that change. This shift in scores prompts discussion of pedagogical practices, assignments, and student responses to those as faculty work to explain and contextualize the results of the assessment process.

Comparability

Because we are using a locally developed rubric, we are not able to compare our critical thinking scores with any group beyond our institution. This emphasis on a local instrument can be problematic when faced with questions about accountability. However, because we have been using this rubric for an extended period, we do have historical data. We can compare scores over many years internally.

Raters' Experience

Our experienced reviewers enjoyed the opportunity to read student work and discuss that work with colleagues. Some raters expressed frustration with the process of scoring using a holistic rubric because an ePortfolio containing several artifacts may exhibit evidence from more than one scoring level. Because of the volume of ePortfolios that need to be read in a day, reviewers can feel pressured to base their judgment on the first appropriate piece of evidence they find rather than spend time reading the entire ePortfolio. Generally though, reviewers enjoy the aspects of academic community, discussion, and deep reading of student work that are present in our current practice.

Adaptive Comparative Judgement (ACJ)

Efficiency

Training scorers for the ACJ approach took approximately 60 minutes. This included an overview of the process and practice sessions using a sample of portfolios during which reviewers practiced selecting the winner among pairs of ePortfolios based on the representation of critical thinking in the holistic rubric. Thus, speed was tacitly encouraged in the task. Reviewers knew that since the judgment of any one portfolio was a communal one, they could get away with a more "impressionistic" glance and get the job done. The reviewers were able to rank all 100 sample portfolios in one day. The average time spent making a comparison was 5.4 minutes and reviewers made an average of 41 comparisons each over the course of the day.

Reliability

Calculated using a modified Rasch model, overall reliability using ACJ was 93%. We predicted the reliability coefficient would reach 98%, had our reviewers been able to complete one more round of comparisons.

Usefulness of Data

The data produced through this process are a rank-ordered list of portfolios. While this ranked distribution tells us how well each student does relative to the other students in the sample, there is no "objective" or independent assessment of quality such as in the other two methods. There is no way to know if the top ePortfolio in the sample represents a 6 on the rubric or a 3. There is no way to tell whether scores tend to cluster around a particular point or are widely distributed across a range of scores. A possible way to ameliorate this problem would be to use "anchor" portfolios that represent each point on our rubrics (these are ePortfolios that score a 1, 2, 3, 4, 5 or 6) and see where they fall on the distribution. That, we hope, would provide a sense of the quality of the distribution. However, without that additional scoring process to identify the *anchor ePortfolios*, this assessment procedure produces a rank-order list without reference to specific levels of learning that might be represented. Along with the rank, the data also consist of reviewers' comments about why they made particular judgments. These comments are available for each portfolio. These qualitative data provide insight into the important aspects of critical thinking present in the samples that reviewers are using to make their judgments. The data can provide information about the tacit criteria that are in play during a scoring session. Combined with the ranks, they provide descriptors of the top and bottom ePortfolios, an interesting addition that is not currently available from the other approaches examined here (see Appendix D).

Thinking about how we might present this data back to faculty also raised challenges. Given the ranking data, we could provide faculty teams a distribution of where their student portfolios fell across the ranks, but unless their students' scores were clustered toward the top or bottom, we are not sure how faculty would interpret these data. Without additional information such as anchor portfolios suggested above, faculty might not have enough information to make sense of the findings and identify areas for change or improvement.

Comparability

Since what we generate from this process is a relative distribution of scores of local samples of ePortfolios, our results cannot be generalized to another sample—local, non-local, internal, or external. What may be promising, however, may be the use of anchor ePortfolios shared across time within an institution (and perhaps even between institutions with common artifact types and rubrics). If this were possible, it might create an opportunity for comparability across institutions, while maintaining a superior inter-rater reliability.

Raters' Experience

The experience of our ACJ reviewers was mixed. As predicted, they found it easier to make the pairwise comparisons and select the winner among two portfolios. However, many expressed disappointment with not "having to get close" to the student's work. In other words, for many comparisons, the work to select the "winner" was somewhat shallow, easy, and therefore not as satisfying as reading to get a holistic sense of the student's work. The experience felt more impersonal to many raters, as if they were primarily "scorers" or rankers, a task that could be performed without connecting to the "meaning" in the work. Some reviewers also expressed feeling pressure to make a quick judgment. While some preferred the user friendliness of the task, others bemoaned the distancing (to the student's work) nature of the experience. This process also offered less opportunity for collegial conversation than the other two. In an ACJ process, all reviewers must engage in the comparison process at the same time to complete a round. In this way speed was incentivized and some reviewers reported feeling pressure to move quickly. In order to finish the scoring process, we needed to move quickly between rounds of comparisons. Reviewers did not have the self-pacing and breaks for conversation available in the other two processes.

VALUE Analytic
Efficiency

The calibration process took considerably longer for the VALUE rubric than for our existing holistic rubric calibration process. While the goal was to review two test ePortfolios, the process of reviewing the VALUE rubric, which was unfamiliar to these reviewers, only allowed for one test portfolio and one calibration conversation within the 90 minutes we had allotted. We expect that if we were to adopt the rubric and use it consistently over several years, the time required for calibration would be reduced. We expect it would still be longer than the time required for a holistic rubric, but would be less than what we experienced in this study.

While reviewing ePortfolios using the VALUE Integrative Learning rubric, reviewers took an average of 12.3 minutes for a first review and 12.5 minutes for a second review. This is 2.5 and six minutes longer than our standard process, respectively. The reviewers were able to complete reviews of 46 ePortfolios (two reviews each) for an average of nine portfolios per reviewer.

Reliability

Inter-rater agreement varied across the rubric subcategories. Three categories reached or almost reached acceptable agreement levels: Connection to Discipline (78%); Transfer (80%); and Integrated Communication (83%). The two categories that related to how well students integrated their own experiences into their ePortfolios had lower levels of inter-rater agreement: Connection to Experience (71%); and *Reflection* and Self-Assessment (66%). Some of these lower levels of agreement would likely have increased with additional rounds of calibration.

Usefulness of Data

The VALUE rubric data are mean scores and score frequency distributions for the program and for each team on each of five rubric categories. The data are more nuanced than a holistic rubric score and can give some indication of specific areas in which the program is doing well and specific skills that may need more attention. Whereas the conversation following a holistic rubric scoring session may be fruitful, faculty may have a hard time pinpointing activities that could help improve the score if they feel that is appropriate because a global score does not offer the detail of a set of analytic rubric scores. The VALUE rubric data provide more specific information, which allows for more targeted conversations about specific skills students may need assistance in developing.

Comparability

The data produced through an assessment process using a VALUE rubric are not strictly comparable to any other university, even if they are using the same VALUE rubric because most universities adapt the rubrics to their uses and in fact are encouraged to do so (Finley, 2012). However, several states are participating in the Multi-State Collaborative to Advance Learning Outcome Assessment, which aims to use the VALUE rubrics to "produce valid data summarizing faculty judgments of students' own work, and also seeks to aggregate results in a way that allows for benchmarking across institutions and states" (State Higher Education Executive Officers Association, 2015). As a growing number of universities use the rubrics for various projects, programs that use the rubrics join a national conversation about student learning and have a similar starting point for talking about critical thinking or integrative learning across campuses.

Raters' Experience

Generally, raters reported that they appreciated the additional time they got to spend with student ePortfolios in the VALUE rubric assessment process. Because they were rating students' work across five criteria, they needed to read more of the ePortfolio to determine their ratings.

Some raters liked the experience of using a rubric (VALUE or internal) less than the ACJ process. For these raters, the rubric seemed somewhat artificial, and they felt it could be difficult to distinguish among categories. Other raters liked that they were able to focus on specific elements of the portfolio to determine a rating and were not asked to compare other portfolios as part of the process.

Table 11.1. Summary of findings

Holistic	ACJ	VALUE
Reliability		
Acceptable	Highest	3/5 Acceptable 2/5 Not acceptable
Usability of Data		
One score requires assumptions and interpretation Have historical data Faculty developed the rubric—they understand the score	Ranking of ePortfolios highest to lowest is most difficult to interpret	5 scores result in more specific information about particular skills
Comparability		
Internal history No external comparability	No external comparability	This is the most comparable with other institutions Many universities are using the rubrics
Efficiency		
Middle in terms of training and rating times 64 ePortfolios scored	Quickest judgment process Most ePortfolios scored (100)	Longest training process Fewest ePortfolios scored (46)
Reviewer Experience		
One score can be difficult to determine Like the interaction with colleagues	Some liked the comparison process Least interactive process Less connection to student work	Mixed Some liked the anchor points Liked the time necessary to read and score

Discussion

This research study offered an opportunity to take a close look at three ePortfolio assessment practices using our proposed RUCER five-criteria framework. As a result, we better understand each process and the framework of criteria that we suggest institutions need to balance as they consider implementing ePortfolio assessment practices. Our framework, which adds a consideration for the quality of evidence, faculty experience, and the resources required to run each process to more common considerations of reliability and comparability, gives institutions a realistic view of what each of these approaches can offer. The framework and its criteria represent the complexity of considerations institutions should entertain when making decisions about any ePortfolio assessment process, synchronous or asynchronous, using many types of scoring schemes. We weigh each process below to provide an example of the way our framework can play out as a decision-making tool.

If the only considerations on the table were reliability and efficiency, and the institution has decided against a standardized test, then the ACJ approach is promising. During that review process, reviewers completed comparisons of all 100 ePortfolios with the highest reliability. The VALUE rubric and holistic rubric processes offer similar measures of reliability, and the holistic rubric was the second most efficient. Not surprisingly, the process in which reviewers had to make the largest number of judgments, the VALUE process, resulted in the fewest number of portfolios being read, indicating that it would cost the most to produce the data.

If comparability beyond the institution is important, the only process offering that possibility is one using a VALUE, or other nationally developed, rubric. Although the data may not be strictly comparable across programs or institutions, an approach using a VALUE rubric makes it possible to have cross-campus and cross-institutional conversations about our students' strengths and weaknesses.

However, if an institution or department wishes to implement a robust and meaningful assessment cycle, it must look beyond reliability, efficiency, and comparability to considerations of data usefulness and rater experience, considerations both squarely anchored in the experience of faculty. Assessment planners must consider, even before any data are collected, what type of data will be produced by a given process, how those data might be presented to faculty for consideration, and whether those data will be considered meaningful by the faculty in question.

Although the ACJ process was most efficient and reliable, the rank-ordered data are not, in and of themselves, meaningful. We had difficulty envisioning how faculty could interpret the data in ways that led to meaningful shifts in practice and improvement in student learning. The holistic rubric, on the other hand, is based on our program's definition of critical thinking, so it is closely connected to our program and the data are meaningful to our faculty who have worked with them for several years. The VALUE rubric process produces the most detailed data related to student work, pinpointing specific skills that emerge as strengths for our students and others that may need work.

Any of these three sets of data can be improved by aligning them with other program data about students and their learning. For example, we often supplement our holistic rubric score with an inventory of the types of student work included in ePortfolios or student responses to aligned items from course evaluations. The ACJ process would be enhanced by having a few of the ePortfolios reviewed using a rubric and including those as anchor portfolios.

Conversations related to assessment and faculty support are converging (e.g., Carpenter & Fitzmaurice, 2019; Stanny, 2018) with increased recognition that assessment processes serve as rich opportunities for faculty support, not just data gathering activities, supporting our inclusion of reviewer experience as a criterion for consideration. ePortfolio review processes give faculty a glimpse into each other's courses through the work students produce. Gathering faculty on an ePortfolio review day offers many opportunities for conversation about the meaning and manifestation of program learning outcomes, the strengths and challenges observed in the student artifacts, and collegial conversation about assignment and curricular design. These are outcomes that are not captured in measures of efficiency, but certainly matter if we want to be accountable for improving student learning outcomes.

As part of this research project, we had conversations with experienced ePortfolio reviewers. They provided important insight into the experience with each ePortfolio assessment process, information programs should consider before adopting new practices. Although they did not articulate it as such, these faculty members helped us see the importance of the human aspects of an assessment process. Reviewers are not data production tools. As reviewers, they agreed to be part of a social process that is focused on students' experiences and learning. When they were not able to interact with each other as much (as in the ACJ process), they were less satisfied with their personal experience of the day. Any assessment process must take these human needs into account (Briggs, 2007). Because of these candid conversations with our reviewers, we have a much clearer sense of the ways in which people seem to prefer to read ePortfolios and interact with other raters, the rubric or task, and the ePortfolio.

These conversations with faculty help illuminate the workings of the assessment process itself, contribute to a deeper understanding of the process, and allow assessment practitioners to improve the quality of future assessment endeavors. The conversations and interactions can also contribute to deeper faculty engagement with the learning outcomes and more authentic buy-in for any improvement effort that results.

The framework proposed in this project proved to be a useful set of criteria for evaluating ePortfolio assessment processes. The criteria, taken together, highlight the need to center the human aspects of the process (review and meaning making) while weighing important considerations of reliability, efficiency, and comparability. Practitioners who are tasked with developing an ePortfolio review process can use these criteria to weigh the relative importance of all factors. We argue that adding a focus on the usability of the results, the experience of the reviewers, and resources helps ensure that the process will produce assessment that both supports program improvement and provides for accountability.

References

Arum, R. & Roksa, J. (2011). *Academically adrift: Limited learning on college campuses.* The University of Chicago Press.

Banta, T. W., Griffin, M., Flateby, T. L. & Kahn, S. (2009). *Three promising alternatives for assessing college students' knowledge and skills.* University of Illinois and Indiana University, National Institute for Learning Outcomes Assessment.

Banta, T. W., Jones, E. A. & Black, K. E. (2009). *Designing effective assessment: Principles and profiles of good practice.* Jossey-Bass.

Benjamin, R., Miller, M. A., Rhodes, T. L., Banta, T. W., Pike, G. R. & Davies, G. (2012). *The seven red herrings about standardized assessments in higher education.* University of Illinois and Indiana University, National Institute for Learning Outcomes Assessment.

Briggs, D. C. (2007). Assessing what students know, how they know it, or both? *Measurement: Interdisciplinary Research and Perspectives, 5*(1), 62–65.

Carpenter, R. & Fitzmaurice, C. (2019). Assessment and faculty support: Fostering collegial community to strengthen professional practice. *The Journal of General Education, 67*(1–2), 90–108.

Cooper, T. & Terrell, T. (2013). *What are institutions spending on assessment? Is it worth the cost?.* University of Illinois and Indiana University, National Institute for Learning Outcomes Assessment.

Finley, A. (2011). How reliable are the value rubrics? *Peer Review, 13*(1), 31–33.

Hutchings, P. (2010). *Opening doors to faculty involvement in assessment.* University of Illinois and Indiana University, National Institute for Learning Outcomes Assessment.

Johnstone, S. M., Ewell, P. & Paulson, K. (2001). *Student learning as academic currency.* American Council on Education.

Linn, R. L., Baker, E. L. & Dunbar, S. B. (1991). Complex performance-based assessment: Expectations and validation criteria. *Educational Researcher, 20*(8), 15–21.

McCollum, D. L. (2011). The deficits of standardized tests: Countering the culture of easy numbers. *Assessment Update, 23*(2), 3–5.

Miller, R. & Leskes, A. (2005). *Levels of assessment: From the student to the institution.* Association of American Colleges and Universities.

Miller, R. & Morgaine, W. (2009). The benefits of e-portfolios for students and faculty in their own words. *Peer Review, 11*(1), 8–12.

Penny Light, T., Chen, H. L. & Ittleson, J. C. (2012). *Documenting learning with eportfolios: A guide for college instructors.* Jossey-Bass.

Peterson, M. W. & Einarson, M. K. (2001). What are colleges doing about student assessment? Does it make a difference? *Journal of Higher Education, 72,* 629–669.

Pollitt, A. (2012). The method of adaptive comparative judgement. *Assessment in Education: Principles, Policy & Practice, 19*(3), 281–300.

Rhodes, T. (2009). The VALUE project overview. *Peer Review, 11*(1), 3–7.

Rhodes, T. (2011). Emerging evidence on using rubrics. *Peer Review, 13*(4), 4–5.

Stanny, C. (Ed.) (2018). Special issue: Assessment in action: Evidence-based discussions about teaching, learning, and curriculum. *New Directions for Teaching & Learning, 2018*(155), 1–116.

State Higher Education Executive Officers Association (2015) MSC: A Multi-state collaborative to advance learning outcomes assessment (Pamphlet). https://www.aacu.org/sites/default/files/files/VALUE/MSC_DY_FAQ_100815.pdf.

Suskie, L. (2009). *Assessing student learning: A common sense guide.* Jossey-Bass.

Walvoord, B. (2010). *Assessment clear and simple: A practical guide for institutions, departments, and general education.* Jossey-Bass.

Appendix A. University Studies' Holistic Critical Thinking Rubric[3]

4	➤ Identifies and develops a compelling question or problem that meaningfully recognizes context. ▲ Demonstrates a systematic approach to exploring a topic, problem, or issue through research, documented experimentation, and/or other methodologies. ◆ Analysis integrates a diverse range of relevant considerations and/or points of view. ● Conclusions and related outcomes reflect student's informed evaluation and ability to assess and weigh evidence and perspectives. ▣ Creates a novel or unique idea, question, format, or product, and incorporates new directions or approaches in the final product. ✪ Evaluates own strengths, challenges, and/or assumptions and identifies important areas for further exploration, learning, or understanding.
3	➤ Identifies and develops a question or problem that acknowledges context. ▲ Demonstrates awareness of methodology, though the approach is not always thorough or fully developed. ◆ Analysis represents a range of relevant considerations and/or points of view. ● Conclusions and related outcomes follow from the evidence and reflect student's evaluation and ability to assess and weigh evidence and perspectives. ▣ Experiments with creating a novel or unique idea, question, format, or product, and considers new directions or approaches to the final product. ✪ Identifies own strengths, challenges, and/or assumptions and some areas for further exploration, learning, or understanding.

---

3.   The University Studies Critical Thinking Rubric was updated in 2016. This is the updated version of our rubric, but it reflects the structure of our previous holistic rubric. For a copy of our previous rubric, please contact either of the authors.

2	➤ Identifies a question or problem with limited understanding of context 🔲 Demonstrates some awareness of methodology, but the approach is neither thorough nor in-depth. ◆ Analysis represents a limited range of considerations and/or points of view. ● Conclusions and related outcomes reflect student's attempt at evaluation and ability to assess and weigh evidence and perspectives. ▣ Reformulates a collection of available ideas, and may acknowledge alternate, divergent, or contradictory perspectives or ideas. ✪ Mentions own strengths and/or challenges, with little recognition of own assumptions or the possibility of further exploration, learning, or understanding.
1	➤ Does not clearly identify a question or problem. Shows little understanding of context. 🔲 Demonstrates little awareness or understanding of methodology. ◆ Analysis represents no range of considerations and/or points of view. ● Conclusions are not connected to evidence. ▣ Primarily summarizes or repeats available information. ✪ Minimal acknowledgment of own strengths, challenges and/or assumptions.
0	➤ Demonstrates no attempt to identify a question or problem and shows no understanding of context. 🔲 Demonstrates no awareness of methodology. ◆ Demonstrates no analysis. ● The student reaches no conclusions, and evidence is either missing or inaccurate. ▣ Does not identify relevant information. ✪ No acknowledgment of own strengths, challenges and/or assumptions.

Appendix B. AAC&U Integrated Learning VALUE Rubric

Integrative Learning VALUE Rubric

for more information, please contact value@aacu.org

The VALUE rubrics were developed by teams of faculty experts representing colleges and universities across the United States through a process that examined many existing campus rubrics and related documents for each learning outcome and incorporated additional feedback from faculty. The rubrics articulate fundamental criteria for each learning outcome, with performance descriptors demonstrating progressively more sophisticated levels of attainment. The rubrics are intended for institutional-level use in evaluating and discussing student learning, not for grading. The core expectations articulated in all 15 of the VALUE rubrics can and should be translated into the language of individual campuses, disciplines, and even courses. The utility of the VALUE rubrics is to position learning at all undergraduate levels within a basic framework of expectations such that evidence of learning can by shared nationally through a common dialog and understanding of student success.

Definition

Integrative learning is an understanding and a disposition that a student builds across the curriculum and co-curriculum, from making simple connections among ideas and experiences to synthesizing and transferring learning to new, complex situations within and beyond the campus.

Framing Language

Fostering students' abilities to integrate learning—across courses, over time, and between campus and community life—is one of the most important goals and challenges for higher education. Initially, students connect previous learning to new classroom learning. Later, significant knowledge within individual disciplines serves as the foundation, but integrative learning goes beyond academic boundaries. Indeed, integrative experiences often occur as learners address real-world problems, unscripted and sufficiently broad, to require multiple areas of knowledge and multiple modes of inquiry, offering multiple solutions and benefiting from multiple perspectives. Integrative learning also involves internal changes in the learner. These internal changes, which indicate growth as a confident, lifelong learner, include the ability to adapt one's intellectual skills, to contribute in a wide variety of situations, and to understand and develop individual purpose, values, and ethics. Developing students' capacities for integrative learning is central to personal success, social responsibility, and civic engagement in today's global society. Students face a rapidly changing and increasingly connected world where integrative learning becomes not just a benefit . . . but a necessity.

Because integrative learning is about making connections, this learning may not be as evident in traditional academic artifacts such as research papers and academic projects unless the student, for example, is prompted to draw implications for practice. These connections often surface, however, in reflective work, self-assessment, or creative endeavors of all kinds. Integrative assignments foster learning between courses or by connecting courses to experientially-based work. Work samples or collections of work that include such artifacts give evidence of integrative learning. Faculty are encouraged to look for evidence that the student connects the learning gained in classroom study to learning gained in real life situations that are related to other learning experiences, extra-curricular activities, or work. Through integrative learning, students pull together their entire experience inside and outside of the formal classroom; thus, artificial barriers between formal study and informal or tacit learning become permeable. Integrative learning, whatever the context or source, builds upon connecting both theory and practice toward a deepened understanding.

Assignments to foster such connections and understanding could include, for example, composition papers that focus on topics from biology, economics, or history; mathematics assignments that apply mathematical tools to important issues and require written analysis to explain the implications and limitations of the mathematical treatment, or art history presentations that demonstrate aesthetic connections between selected paintings and novels. In this regard, some majors (e.g., interdisciplinary majors or problem-based field studies) seem to inherently evoke characteristics of integrative learning and result in work samples or collections of work that significantly demonstrate this outcome. However, fields of study that require accumulation of extensive and high-consensus content knowledge (such as accounting, engineering, or chemistry) also involve the kinds of complex and integrative constructions (e.g., ethical dilemmas and social consciousness) that seem to be highlighted so extensively in self reflection in arts and humanities, but they may be embedded in individual performances and less evident. The key in the development of such work samples or collections of work will be in designing structures that include artifacts and reflective writing or feedback that support students' examination of their learning and give evidence that, as graduates, they will extend their integrative abilities into the challenges of personal, professional, and civic life.

Glossary

The definitions that follow were developed to clarify
terms and concepts used in this rubric only.

- Academic knowledge: Disciplinary learning; learning from academic study, texts, etc.
- Content: The information conveyed in the work samples or collections of work.
- Contexts: Actual or simulated situations in which a student demonstrates learning outcomes. New and challenging contexts encourage students to stretch beyond their current frames of reference.
- Co-curriculum: A parallel component of the academic curriculum that is in addition to formal classroom (student government, community service, residence hall activities, student organizations, etc.).
- Experience: Learning that takes place in a setting outside of the formal classroom, such as workplace, service learning site, internship site or another.
- Form: The external frameworks in which information and evidence are presented, ranging from choices for particular work sample or collection of works (such as a research paper, PowerPoint, video recording, etc.) to choices in make-up of the ePortfolio.
- Performance: A dynamic and sustained act that brings together knowing and doing (creating a painting, solving an experimental design problem, developing a public relations strategy for a business, etc.); performance makes learning observable.
- Reflection: A meta-cognitive act of examining a performance in order to explore its significance and consequences.

- Self Assessment: Describing, interpreting, and judging a performance based on stated or implied expectations followed by planning for further learning.

Integrative Learning VALUE Rubric

for more information, please contact value@aacu.org

Definition

Integrative learning is an understanding and a disposition that a student builds across the curriculum and co-curriculum, from making simple connections among ideas and experiences to synthesizing and transferring learning to new, complex situations within and beyond the campus.

Evaluators are encouraged to assign a zero to any work sample or collection of work that does not meet benchmark (cell one) level performance.

	Capstone 4	Milestones 3	Milestone 2	Benchmark 1
Connections to Experience *Connects relevant experience and academic knowledge*	Meaningfully synthesizes connections among experiences outside of the formal classroom (including life experiences and academic experiences such as internships and travel abroad) to deepen understanding of fields of study and to broaden own points of view.	Effectively selects and develops examples of life experiences, drawn from a variety of contexts (e.g., family life, artistic participation, civic involvement, work experience), to illuminate concepts/theories/frameworks of fields of study.	Compares life experiences and academic knowledge to infer differences, as well as similarities, and acknowledge perspectives other than own.	Identifies connections between life experiences and those academic texts and ideas perceived as similar and related to own interests.
Connections to Discipline *Sees (makes) connections across disciplines, perspectives*	Independently creates wholes out of multiple parts (synthesizes) or draws conclusions by combining examples, facts, or theories from more than one field of study or perspective.	Independently connects examples, facts, or theories from more than one field of study or perspective.	When prompted, connects examples, facts, or theories from more than one field of study or perspective.	When prompted, presents examples, facts, or theories from more than one field of study or perspective.

	Capstone 4	Milestones 3	Milestone 2	Benchmark 1
Transfer *Adapts and applies skills, abilities, theories, or methodologies gained in one situation to new situations*	Adapts and applies, independently, skills, abilities, theories, or methodologies gained in one situation to new situations **to solve difficult problems or explore complex issues in original ways.**	Adapts and applies skills, abilities, theories, or methodologies gained in one situation to new situations **to solve problems or explore issues.**	Uses skills, abilities, theories, or methodologies gained in one situation in a new situation **to contribute to understanding of problems or issues.**	Uses, in a basic way, skills, abilities, theories, or methodologies gained in one situation **in a new situation.**
Transfer *Adapts and applies skills, abilities, theories, or methodologies gained in one situation to new situations*	Adapts and applies, independently, skills, abilities, theories, or methodologies gained in one situation to new situations **to solve difficult problems or explore complex issues in original ways.**	Adapts and applies skills, abilities, theories, or methodologies gained in one situation to new situations **to solve problems or explore issues.**	Uses skills, abilities, theories, or methodologies gained in one situation in a new situation **to contribute to understanding of problems or issues.**	Uses, in a basic way, skills, abilities, theories, or methodologies gained in one situation **in a new situation.**
Integrated Communication	Fulfills the assignment(s) by choosing a format, language, or graph (or other visual representation) **in ways that enhance meaning,** making clear the interdependence of language and meaning, thought, and expression.	Fulfills the assignment(s) by choosing a format, language, or graph (or other visual representation) **to explicitly connect content and form,** demonstrating awareness of purpose and audience.	Fulfills the assignment(s) by choosing a format, language, or graph (or other visual representation) that **connects in a basic way** what is being communicated (content) with how it is said (form).	Fulfills the assignment(s) (i.e., to produce an essay, a poster, a video, a PowerPoint presentation, etc.) **in an appropriate form.**

continued on next page

	Capstone 4	Milestones 3	Milestone 2	Benchmark 1
Reflection and Self-Assessment *Demonstrates a developing sense of self as a learner, building on prior experiences to respond to new and challenging contexts (may be evident in self-assessment, reflective, or creative work)*	Envisions a future self (and possibly makes plans that build on past experiences that have occurred across multiple and diverse contexts).	Evaluates changes in own learning over time, recognizing complex contextual factors (e.g., works with ambiguity and risk, deals with frustration, considers ethical frameworks).	Articulates strengths and challenges (within specific performances or events) to increase effectiveness in different contexts (through increased self-awareness).	Describes own performances with general descriptors of success and failure.

Integrative Learning VALUE Rubric
for more information, please contact value@aacu.org

Appendix C. Example Assessment Report

Inquiry and Critical Thinking Assessment

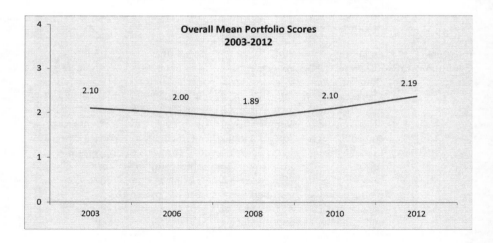

Overall

Number of student work samples: 229
Mean Score: 2.19 on a 0 to 4 scale.
Number of papers per score.

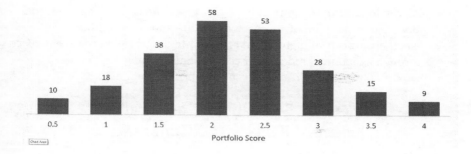

Team 1.

Number of student work samples: 26
Mean Score: 2.21 on a 0 to 4 scale.
Number of papers per score

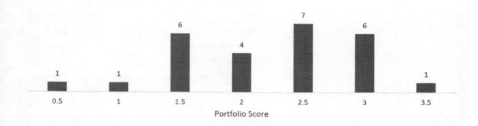

Inquiry and Critical Thinking Discussion. Inq & CT Rubric Data

- Look at the holistic rubric. Where would you expect your students to score? How does the distribution of rubric scores for your theme compare with those expectations?
- Given these scores and your experience with your students, do you identify areas in need of improvement? What aspects of critical thinking do your students do well? struggle with?
- What actions will you take as a team or as individual faculty to further enhance inquiry and critical thinking in your courses?
- Is there support the UNST program can offer you to assist in addressing those areas?

Favorite Assignment

- Share a description of an assignment related to this goal with each other.
- Look at the inquiry and critical thinking rubric. Which of the criteria is most relevant to the assignment?

- As you look across assignments in your group, does your theme emphasize a particular kind of approach to inquiry and critical thinking?
- Are there aspects of inquiry and critical thinking that you could enhance through assignment redesign or course adjustments?
- Do the rubrics provide ideas for modifying the assignment?

Appendix D. Adaptive Comparative Judgment Ranking and Comments

Port. No.	Rank	ACJ Score	Theme	Comments
68	1	17.4	1	Strong research project in Portfolio A and it's even listed under Critical thinking!
				A is more reflective; uses analysis and synthesis in his/her thinking. Also, included various pieces of evidence.
				Beautiful voice; applies concepts well to self and other texts/experiences. I am biased in favor of voice, which may have influenced by very slight preference for B
				The author of portfolio A used critical thinking in all aspects of the assignments presented. There was just a lot more detail about that process than in B
86	2	16.5	3	B makes connections to other classes; also, comparative and analytical approaches are highlighted.
				Both portfolios were good. Portfolio A had some great short writing exercises, which were a less formal assignment, which helped me make my decision.
57	3	14.7	1	Portfolio B has a fully realized research paper with an original thesis
				Though A demonstrated the process of inquiry and learning, B did so more proficiently and with more gusto.
				A had more depth and development of the students' own ideas.
78	4	13.3	6	Both portfolios were quite thoughtful but I chose B because it offered more samples each one accompanied by a reflective part. As total, it was more nuanced
				Really just a bit more sophisticated than B, but a tough distinction for me, as I am impressed by both.

Continuing through the rankings to the lowest ranked portfolios

Port. No.	Rank	ACJ Score	Theme	Comments
74	97	−8.1	5	Merely supporting a conclusion.
				Very little was shown of any substance in this portfolio. This was a difficult decision because neither portfolio was very robust or displayed assignments calling for risk and critical thinking.
				Material in A was mostly summary.
8	98	−8.8	3	Really doesn't move beyond presentation of discovered information. Very basic
				This portfolio did not really include any examples of critical thinking. There was a lot of description but little evidence of engaging.
				A was informative, but lacked depth or critical inquiry.
7	99	−9.5	7	Lacking work samples to assess, so could only go by the final reflection, which lacked depth compared to the analysis paper in the other portfolio.
				This was tough, because neither portfolio had much evidence in terms of students' work. I picked B since there was a little more evidence and the students referred to other sources and connected them to their ideas.

Chapter 12. Electronic Portfolios: Scaling Up from Programmatic to Inter-Institutional Articulation and Assessment

Michael Day

Northern Illinois University

Electronic portfolios are widely regarded as a high impact practice (Eynon & Gambino, 2017; Kahn & Scott, 2013) that helps students integrate their assignments, courses, and co-curricular experiences, as well as to write the story of how they learned and how they developed a professional identity. In so doing, ePortfolios help students to make a meta-cognitive move (Kinsman et al., 2014; Reynolds & Patton, 2014; Rickards & Guilbault, 2009) that has been demonstrated to lead to transferable written communication (Bowman, 2016; Whithaus, 2013; Yancey, 2017), critical thinking (Reynolds & Patton, 2014), and information literacy skills (Whithaus, 2013) needed for integrated lifelong learning (Chen, 2009; Eynon & Gambino, 2017; Reynolds & Patton, 2014), reflective practice as career professionals (Eynon & Gambino, 2017; Reynolds & Patton, 2014), and engaged citizenship (Johnson & Kahn, 2013).

This chapter tells the story of one first-year composition (FYComp) program's 15-year development of an electronic portfolio *assessment* to show how a single program can cooperate with other campus stakeholders to "scale up" to a meaningful, outcomes-based general education assessment (Day, 2009, 2015). The FYComp portfolio has been used not only for instructors' assessment of individual student progress in meeting FYComp outcomes, but also for programmatic assessment and institutional assessment of written communication, critical thinking, and information literacy general education outcomes (see Carpenter & Labissiere, this collection).

Like other U.S. universities, Northern Illinois University has been responding to the need to make general education requirements more relevant. Over the past several years, our electronic portfolio has been evolving into a longitudinal learning record that students can work on every semester of their college experience, allowing them to understand how courses that make use of our ePortfolio system are helping them learn and grow. Not only can they collect *artifacts* of their learning, select those artifacts that demonstrate their achievement of baccalaureate outcomes, and reflect in detail to discover the trajectory and pattern of their learning, they can also connect the artifacts and *reflections* to their co-curricular, life, and job experiences (see Coleman et al., this collection). Finally, through a professional *showcase electronic portfolio* that they can use to apply for graduate school or jobs, the students can project from their undergraduate experiences to

DOI: https://doi.org/10.37514/PRA-B.2020.1084.2.12

a professional identity that will emerge toward the end of their college career (see Polly et al., this collection).

To provide context for scaling up, I will first review models and strategies for scaling up at the national level. I will then describe the process and outcomes of Northern Illinois University's (NIU's) first-year composition electronic portfolio and discuss the intra-university consensus-building and stakeholder analysis needed to move to the next level: scaling up to a longitudinal general education electronic portfolio that requires students to demonstrate written communication, critical thinking, and information literacy skills, among others, at every level from first-year to capstone experiences. Further, I will sketch the outlines of a regional community college and university partnership based on sharing electronic portfolio practices, with the goal of making it easier for students to transfer among area higher educational institutions. Finally, I will discuss the opportunities and roadblocks to our process of scaling up, suggesting that we add three dispositions—collaboration, persistence, and *kairos*—to the Catalyst for Learning's excellent Core Strategies for Scaling Up.

Scaling Up Models and Examples: What is Scaling Up and Why Do It?

Some champions of ePortfolio at colleges and universities—excited and encouraged by smaller-scale success with their ePortfolio efforts and becoming increasingly aware of implementations on other campuses that are changing the culture of learning—want to share what they are doing with colleagues across their campuses, pooling their efforts to create more relevant learning environments for their students. They are aware of external demands for assessment, accreditation, and accountability, and want to be pro-active, perhaps pushing back against the culture of standardized, high-stakes testing (see Carpenter & Labissiere, this collection). These are just a few of the reasons that stakeholders may want to scale up.

To provide context for this local-regional story of scaling up, I rely upon two sources of information: the international dialogue on scaling up with ePortfolios so carefully framed by the Connect to Learning (C2L) Project, and relevant models of scaling up provided by other institutions.

The Catalyst for Learning Project

The Catalyst for Learning website (http://c2l.mcnrc.org/) created by 24 universities with ePortfolio programs that collaborated in the Connect to Learning Network to "advance the transformative capacities of ePortfolio for teaching, learning, and assessment," outlines the scaling up practice and provides a set of ten "Core Strategies for Scaling Up." Bret Eynon and his co-authors (2014a) explain: "By Scaling Up, we mean the strategies and approaches by which ePortfolio projects begin within small segments of an institution and then expand, as additional faculty, courses, and programs begin to work with ePortfolio" (p. 1). As such, scaling up[1] refers to the process of bringing together isolated pockets of ePortfolio use to make ePortfolio—along with the processes of engaged, integrated learning it implies—a more integral part of an institutional culture.

The previous paragraph defines the "what" of scaling up, but for more about the "why," we can look to Randall Bass's "Scaling Strategies and ePortfolio as a Catalyst for Change" (2014). Bass (2014) sees scaling up in the context of an emerging paradigm of higher education, that is, how, in the current climate of educational research and socioeconomic change, higher education must move from a paradigm of "curricular design that is generally atomistic, linear, and built on inputs" to a paradigm that "comprehends the importance of both curriculum and co-curriculum, focuses on student learning as an outcome, and understands learning to be fundamentally integrative and iterative" (p. 1) (see Terry & Whillock, this collection). To Bass and proponents of Catalyst for Learning, ePortfolios can provide a bridge from one paradigm to the other, by providing

> a network of connections—among students and faculty, and programs and majors, and integrating with institutional initiatives, such as General Education, outcomes assessment, and high-impact practices. Through these connections, ePortfolio initiatives inform and deepen emerging pedagogical practices and introduce increasingly rich views of student learning into the everyday flow of teaching, assessment, and curriculum design. (Bass, 2014, p. 1) (see Summers et al., this collection)

To provide a backdrop for this paradigm shift, Bass (2014) describes a few of the larger changes in the higher education landscape in the last few decades, including "online learning, adaptive learning systems, learning analytics and granular certification," all of which value "access to learning, alignment of outcomes and personalization of learning," but "threaten to advance the paradigm in disintegrative ways, unbundling education into a series of disparate and disconnected experiences" (p. 1). This unbundling "creates challenges for efforts to advance local institutional value, the impact of community on learning, and the holistic dimensions of education" (Bass 2014, pp. 1–2). In Bass's view, ePortfolio can catalyze change and growth by helping institutions "shape a more intentional and integrative strategy for negotiating the potential disruptions of the higher education landscape" (2014, p. 2).

These ePortfolio scaling up strategies usually involve moving "beyond knowledge areas to skills and dispositions" (Bass, 2014, p. 2), broadening the view of student success through first-year experiences and increasing opportunities for integrative and experiential learning. According to Bass (2014), they also foster

---

1.   More recently, Eynon and Gambino (2017) use "scaling" and "scaling up" to refer to the same process. Since I am specifically referring to expansion, I prefer to use "scaling up."

intra-institutional connections, by providing "a context for bringing together stakeholders from across boundaries, creating a network of connections that respond to the ecosystemic nature of institutions" (p. 2). This notion of an institutional ecosystem, in which stakeholders reflect on the relationships between the pieces and players with an eye toward coherence and complementarity, provides the background for the scaling up case study I present in this chapter. Bass (2014) notes that "on some campuses, ePortfolio provides the apparatus that links First-Year Experiences, General Education programs, and outcomes assessment," and, "by providing data and *authentic* evidence of student learning, [helps ePortfolio proponents] leverage support from allies in administration, the faculty governance structure, or the strategic planning process" (p. 3) (see Carpenter & Labassiere, this collection). As we shall see, the NIU scaling up story fits this model well, but the institution still struggles to develop the "network of reinforcing connections" through ePortfolio that "helps to create and catalyze an institutional ethos of learning" (Bass, 2014, p. 3).

Relevant Core Strategies

After members of C2L submitted their 2011–2012 Activity Reports, the "Core Strategies for Scaling Up" emerged as a way of summarizing and comparing scaling up approaches from various campuses. These ten core strategies are available on the Catalyst for Learning website, but there are four that stand out as most relevant to the process of scaling up at NIU:

#1 Developing an Effective Campus ePortfolio Team

#2 Connecting to Programs

#6 Building Strategic Connections to Outcomes Assessment

#9 Aligning with Institutional Planning

After providing a few scaling up examples from other institutions, I will show how, without knowledge of the Catalyst for Learning Core Strategies, stakeholders at NIU made use of a different but related set of strategies.

Setting the Context: Examples of Scaling Up

In the 1990s, when the World Wide Web became widely available, several universities, such as Indiana University-Purdue University Indianapolis (IUPUI), the University of Minnesota, Portland State University, and Alverno College, among others, began piloting ePortfolio programs. Encouraged by the visionary work of early adopters and theorists such as Helen Barrett, Trent Batson, Barbara Cambridge, Darren Cambridge, Helen Chen, Peg Syverson, and Kathleen Blake Yancey, groups of collaborators—many of whom would later form such organizations as the Open Source Portfolio (OSP) initiative, Sakai, the Inter/

National Coalition for Electronic Portfolio Research (I/NCEPR), and the Association for Authentic, Experiential, and Evidence-Based Learning (AAEEBL)—began to compare notes. Emerging from their work, as well as important new findings in assessment and faculty development research, ePortfolio programs of varying scale and design began to pop up at the institutions mentioned earlier. NIU learned much from the challenges and successes of these early models for scaling up.

Indiana University-Purdue University Indianapolis (IUPUI)

According to Susan Kahn and Susan Scott (2013), IUPUI was "an early adopter of ePortfolios"; it "began its ePortfolio initiative without a roadmap or example to follow. Enthusiastic leaders were not enough; early efforts fell short. [They] retrenched and revamped, listening carefully to the needs of [their] campus stakeholders and attuning [their] strategy to the variety of disciplinary cultures." It is important to note that instead of a single "ePortfolio initiative with a unified approach," IUPUI has had over 40 different ePortfolio projects, ranging from professional accreditation portfolios to capstone projects, but involving only about 15% of the student body. What unites the projects is the focus on high impact practices facilitated by ePortfolios—practices such as *integrative learning* and reflective learning that deepen student engagement. Further, the ePortfolio projects have multiple aims, and each project "defines success in its own terms."

Starting in about 2000, IUPUI developed new outcomes, their Principles of Undergraduate Learning (PUL) (Kahn & Scott, 2013). A faculty committee endorsed by the executive vice chancellor decided to implement an ePortfolio "spanning the undergraduate experience," using the Open Source Portfolio (OSP), which had just merged with the Sakai Project. They also created a set of First-Year Seminars (FYS) within Themed Learning Communities (TLC) in which to introduce the OSP ePortfolio, beginning in 2004 (see Terry & Whillock, this collection). What they discovered, however, was that they had underestimated the "magnitude of the paradigm shift that ePortfolios represented," and, as a result, they had not prepared adequately with faculty development and other support needs. Therefore, many instructors "did not understand the rationale for the portfolio and treated it as an add-on rather than as an integral part of the FYS [see Dellinger & Hanger, this collection]. Not surprisingly, these faculty members experienced the ePortfolio as time-consuming, and students perceived it as busy work." Moreover, the OSP software was not ready for launch, and did not live up the grand claims made about its functionality. Consequently, from auspicious beginnings in an energized faculty committee, within a year or so, the FYC/TLC ePortfolio pilot was viewed as a failed, top-down imposed initiative.

Despite these difficulties, however, ePortfolio proponents at IUPUI, including a very supportive upper administration, did not give up. They recognized that learning from mistakes and regrouping would allow them to fine-tune their efforts. As they regrouped and moved ahead, they spent much more time "working with programs to help them chart their own course with ePortfolio," listening to stakeholders' needs, offering incentives to departments and programs, and strengthening faculty development through collaboration with the Center for Teaching and Learning. These scaling up strategies—1) listening to stakeholder needs and 2) reflecting on discoveries—allowed proponents to conduct a kind of grounded research in which the categories and approaches were generated from the data, not predetermined. By this time, IUPUI had already participated in the first cohort (2003—2006) of the National Coalition for Electronic Portfolio Research (NCEPR, now I/NCEPR to reflect its international growth), and had both learned about grounded ePortfolio research from other schools (such as Alverno College) and participated in such research through the coalition's study of reflection in the context of ePortfolio learning. After another key step—hiring an ePortfolio coordinator in 2009—IUPUI ePortfolio proponents returned to I/NCEPR for Cohort VI in 2010, deepening their collaboration with other institutions and improving their ability to learn from stakeholders and pilot projects. Kahn and Scott (2013) note that their work with I/NCEPR and AAEEBL (which had its first conference that year in 2010) were crucial steps in scaling up: "These developments . . . allowed us to engage a larger group of IUPUI faculty, staff, and students in intensive ePortfolio inquiry and work, while helping us validate the importance of this work with internal constituencies." As other researchers have noted, the convergence of local institutional needs with higher-level concerns in educational research can be a strong motivator for ePortfolio researchers and practitioners (CCCC, 2015; Day, 2009; Yancey et al., 2009), and therefore can provide a catalyst for scaling up.

There is no single recipe for scaling up, since all institutions are different, but Kahn and Scott (2013) conclude their IUPUI scaling up story with these helpful tips, which have been instructive to NIU and should be helpful to other institutions interested in scaling up:

- Start small.
- Attune your strategy to your institutional context and culture(s).
- Start with the needs your faculty, administration, and student stakeholders perceive now; once they begin with ePortfolio, approaches and uses will broaden and deepen.
- Understand that ePortfolios represent and require a paradigm shift.
- Develop advocates in key areas of the institution.
- Give the people who will use the technology as much control as possible over selection of a platform. (see Richardson et al., this collection)
- Expect to provide professional development assistance and resources.
- Expose instructors and others to national and international ePortfolio work.

- Align with your campus' strategic goals: most campuses are seeking to improve student success and to generate meaningful assessment information. (see Carpenter & Labissiere, this collection)

Clemson University

Gail Ring and Barbara Ramirez (2012) note similar challenges and opportunities with scaling up to a university ePortfolio requirement at Clemson University. Clemson initiated its ePortfolio program in 2006 "out of a need to evaluate [its] recently revised general education program," requiring all undergraduates to "create and submit a digital portfolio as a record of academic and experiential mastery" (p. 87) of the general education competencies. In 2003–2006, under the leadership of I/NCEPR leader Kathleen Blake Yancey, Clemson was a host institution for several meetings of I/NCEPR. To some degree, the design of their ePortfolio program reveals the careful thinking about reflection, integrative learning, Yancey's concept of "making learning visible" (Ring & Ramirez, 2012), and student-centered assessment that went on in I/NCEPR research meetings.

After the first year, Clemson hired a director (Ring) to oversee the ePortfolio program, and, through surveys and interviews, the director discovered "issues that needed to be addressed, including: 1. Overall confusion and misunderstandings regarding the ePortfolio Program; 2. Limited support available to students; 3. A lack of exemplars . . .; 4. A lack of [student] motivation . . .; and 5. Uneven integration of the ePortfolio throughout the undergraduate curriculum" (Ring & Ramirez, 2012, p. 89). Over the last decade, proponents of the ePortfolio at Clemson have used this analysis of shortcomings to redesign the program into an iterative process that has included more and more stakeholders and focuses on the ePortfolio's support system, evaluation, reflection, and improvement (Ring & Ramirez, 2012). Further, like many other institutions, Clemson discovered that faculty development, exemplars, awards, and surveys helped to "deepen faculty understanding and buy-in" (Ring & Ramirez, 2012, p. 90) in the process of redefining goals and scaling up to greater campus involvement (see Richardson et al. and Summers et al., this collection).

Far more than a simple assessment tool, ePortfolio at Clemson has become a focal point for campus discussion and qualitative evaluation of larger institutional goals: "using the ePortfolio as a catalyst for dialogue contributes to new ideas, new learning and broader thinking" (Ring & Ramirez, 2012, p. 91). That focus on campus-wide reflection and dialogue, observe Ring and Ramirez (2012), is critical to Clemson's success in scaling up. They hope that "the University community will see ePortfolios as a forum through which expertise may be developed during the undergraduate years, providing the 'value–added' experiences found only in the university setting" (2012, p. 94). Ring and Ramirez (2012) remind us that ePortfolio assessment is most valuable when it is formative, not just summative, and agree with Margaret Heritage (2007) that this sort of ePortfolio assessment then "becomes a moving picture—a video stream of achievement, rather than a periodic snapshot" (p. 94; Heritage, 2007, p. 141).

Other institutions report similar experiences with scaling up. The University of Iowa has had marked success—particularly in the area of helping newly certified teachers from all disciplines get jobs—with its now over 20-year-old Iowa ePortfolio in the College of Education (Achrazoglou et al., 2002). Portland State University, LaGuardia Community College, Boston University, and many others among the Catalyst for Learning scaling up model institutions report steady progress in the move to university-wide ePortfolio initiatives. As will become evident in the next section, NIU has made some progress scaling up from individual and class ePortfolios to programmatic assessment, but, like many other schools (Donahue, 2017; Thurman, 2017), has struggled to take scaling up to the next level: a university-wide general education initiative.

The Northern Illinois University (NIU) FYComp ePortfolio

Course and Program-based ePortfolios and I/NCEPR

As a composition teacher, I have always been a fan of the authentic assessment opportunities afforded by portfolios (see Carpenter & Labissiere, this collection), and, as a digital rhetorician, I saw great possibilities for putting those portfolios online and making use of the linking power of hypertext to create online learning records and professional showcase portfolios (see Summers et al. and Polly et al., this collection). In the year 2000, I had teacher certification students creating online portfolios, and in 2001 I hosted a regional faculty development workshop on ePortfolios at my university and supervised two undergraduate teacher certification candidates in creating an informational web page on ePortfolios. In 2002, I was asked to become the director of first-year composition, but it took me some time to figure out how I would address the "elephant in the room" of any large college program: assessment. From what I knew about ePortfolios, they seemed like the best option, but, within the program, all stakeholders had to come together to define what we value in writing—encoding these values in a set of outcomes based on the Council of Writing Program Administrators' Outcomes Statement. We managed to accomplish that goal in my first year as program director, and by 2003 I was working with my FYComp colleagues to develop the ePortfolio pilot. When I saw the call for participants in the first cohort of the National Coalition for Electronic Portfolio Research that year, I was so excited that I contacted my chair, dean, and provost in charge of assessment almost immediately, and with their support, sent in a proposal.

Designing the FYComp ePortfolio

Once the proposal was accepted, the ten schools in Cohort I began working on our research questions about reflection, comparing notes, and, most importantly, designing and/or refining our own ePortfolio implementations. Predictably, my project was to work with my two NIU colleagues to develop a robust pilot assessment for FYComp (see Terry & Whillock, this collection). With guidance from the coalition leaders, we put the pilot into motion in fall 2004 by requiring certain sections of FYComp to create ePortfolios in Mozilla Composer. By and large, those sections were the ones taught by a "captive audience": the new teaching assistants who were required to take my Seminar in the Teaching of College Writing class. Eric Hoffman, the co-instructor of that class, happened to be the coordinator of Networked Writing and Research (NWR), a digital teaching support center for FYComp, and was also a member of the NCEPR Cohort I team. As a result, we had ample technology support for ePortfolios through the staff, hardware, and software in the NWR.

The NIU FYComp Electronic Portfolio in Practice

At NIU, we break our ePortfolio assessment process into five stages: Preparation, Calibration, Scoring, Leader Debriefing, and Closing the Feedback Loop (see Figure 12.1). As part of the Preparation stage, the assessment office prepares a student profile that reflects the diverse demographics of NIU students. They send us between 100 and 300 student identification numbers. We send these numbers to the instructors, who collect the student ePortfolios electronically.

Figure 12.1. The FYComp ePortfolio assessment process.

Calibration involves two steps. First the 10 or so group leaders read two student ePortfolios (chosen because they exemplify different performance levels and a number of traits that might need to be discussed), score the ePortfolios individually on the computer, then discuss why each reader assigned particular scores, and other features they noticed, in terms of the *rubric* (see Figure 12.2) and program outcomes. Each of the group leaders repeats this process with their group (of about 10), and, in both cases, the scores are projected on an overhead screen so that everyone can see the relative agreement and qualitative comments. This process helps group members give consistent scores when they read other ePortfolios, because they have come to a better agreement on what each rubric category means and the level of performance being measured in each category. Group leaders must encourage discussion, as the discussion sometimes is a more valuable assessment activity than any of the numbers (see Carpenter & Labissiere, this collection).

In the Scoring process, group members use a template, pre-populated with NIU's FYComp rubric, to read, score, and comment on their assigned ePortfolios. Instructors do not read ePortfolios from their own classes (they evaluate each of their students separately for the class grade), and each ePortfolio is scored by at least two different readers. Groups debrief at the end of the session, discussing strengths and weaknesses they noticed in the ePortfolios they scored, as well as strengths and weaknesses in the overall process (see Carpenter & Labissiere and Sanborn & Ramírez, this collection).

Group leaders also meet after the final scoring session to debrief and record their observations about the ePortfolios, the calibration session, and the scoring process. They take detailed notes on strengths, weaknesses, and the overall process. These notes become part of the qualitative report on that semester's assessment.

To close the feedback loop, we aggregate and graph all the scores to show change between semesters and achievement by categories of student and types of instruction. We use both the qualitative and quantitative reports to plan future assessments, curricular changes, textbook selection, and faculty development activities, among many other program improvement activities. Mindful of external pressures for assessment and accountability inside and outside of our university, we also report regularly to the Office of Assessment Services and the University Assessment Panel, so that our data can be part of the larger institutional picture. Our program assessment was featured as an exemplar at the NIU 2014 Assessment Expo, and has been presented as a model at the 2015 Conference on College Composition and Communication (CCCC), the 2015 Computers and Writing conference (C&W), the 2012 Council of Writing Program Administrators conference (CWPA), and in invited presentations at California State University, Northridge; Governor's State University; Iowa State University; and Kumamoto and Osaka Universities in Japan.

Holistic Impression	Excelling (4)	Accomplishing (3)	Progressing (2)	Developing (1)
Audience & Style	Through a compelling voice and style, writer demonstrates thorough understanding of audience and task.	Through an appropriate voice and style, writer demonstrates adequate understanding of audience and task.	Writer's voice and style may not demonstrate understanding of audience and task.	Writer's inappropriate voice and style fails to demonstrate understanding of audience and task.
Focus & Development	Writer clarifies major aims, arranges material to support those aims, and may show insight into problematic or provocative aspects of the topic.	Writer clarifies major aims, arranges most material to support those aims, and provides adequate material.	Writer does not always make major aims clear, arrange material to support those aims, or provide adequate material.	Writer confuses readers about major aims or develops no major point adequately.
Analysis	Writer carefully and consistently evaluates the relevance of contexts and/or rhetorical strategies when presenting a position.	Writer evaluates the relevance of contexts and/or rhetorical strategies when presenting a position.	Writer identifies some relevant contexts and/or rhetorical strategies when presenting a position, but may not evaluate consistently and carefully.	Writer fails to identify contexts and/or rhetorical strategies when presenting a position.
Source Integration	Writer understands and eloquently articulates his/her ideas as they relate to those of others and effectively integrates source material.	Writer frequently understands and articulates his/her ideas as they relate to those of others and integrates source material.	Writer sometimes understands and articulates his/her ideas as they relate to those of others and attempts to integrate source material.	Writer rarely understands and articulates his/her ideas as they relate to those of others and ineffectively integrates source material.
Format & Editing	Writer shows mature command of format conventions and sentence-level features of written language (grammar, spelling, punctuation, and usage).	Writer controls format conventions and sentence-level features of written language.	Writer may not adhere to conventions of format, and loses control of one or more elements of written language at the sentence level without significantly impeding communication.	Writer does not adhere to format conventions and loses control of one or more elements of written language at the sentence level, impeding communication.
Reflection	Writer evaluates growth and composing processes in detail, and cites compelling evidence within portfolio.	Writer describes growth and composing processes, citing evidence within portfolio.	Writer describes growth and processes superficially, or may not adequately develop ideas or provide evidence.	Writer fails to describe growth and processes.

Figure 12.2. The FYComp ePortfolio scoring rubric.

Scaling UP: Intra-institutional Progress

Once FYComp had shown that we could use our ePortfolio assessment for meaningful program improvement and curricular change, we focused on the possibilities for using ePortfolios for learning and assessment campus-wide, with the idea that faculty and departments could learn a great deal about students and their learning by having students keep longitudinal, cross-disciplinary ePortfolios. Some of the institutions in our I/NCEPR cohort and later cohorts, including IUPUI, Clemson, and University of Georgia, actually had such campus-wide implementations in effect, and I hoped that NIU could learn something from them. In 2005, we hosted Kathleen Blake Yancey to give an ePortfolio keynote at our conference on portfolio integration, and members of the campus community seemed to be energized by the palpable excitement about ePortfolios. But we learned the hard way that unless higher administrators embrace and support changes in curriculum, pedagogy, and assessment, busy faculty will continue "business as usual" and not take on the hard work of making the changes in their own practices (see Summers et al. and Castaño & Novo, this collection).

In 2008 and 2011, the NIU president rolled out strategic planning initiatives to gather good ideas for productive changes in the way we "do" higher education to better support our student population and regional mission. Since I was still a strong believer in ePortfolio learning and assessment, in both years I put forth strategic planning proposals for a longitudinal general education ePortfolio (see Summers et al., this collection). Of course, I had to contact and get letters from stakeholders in key campus support offices such as Faculty Development and Instructional Design, Writing Across the Curriculum, the Office of Assessment, and many more, and these stakeholders were effusive in their support. In 2008 there was really no response to my strategic planning proposal beyond silence, but in 2011, there was a hopeful tone to the upper administration's response, along the lines of: "We are not ready, but this is a good idea."

Collaboration with General Education

Behind the scenes, however, forces were moving in a more positive direction. We had been through a two-year cycle of Foundations of Excellence in the First Year of College (a national program run by the John N. Gardner Institute for Excellence in Undergraduate Education), and the General Education Revisioning Task Force had begun collecting data on campus opinions about what general education (Gen Ed) and the baccalaureate should become in the future. Gen Ed goals and outcomes were being rewritten and there seemed to be more incentive for change.

Enter, in 2013, a brand-new president and a brand-new provost with good ideas about jumpstarting collaboration and changing the outlook of the university based on what all stakeholders—students, faculty, administrators, staff, alumni, and local citizens—could agree on. The new initiative, the Bold Futures program, brought stakeholders together to decide on what actions they could take to make change in the university and the relationship between the university and the city. General education revision and retention were at or near the top of the list, and finally stakeholders from many campus departments and offices began meeting to explore how they could work together. For example, the associate vice-provosts for assessment and general education took a keen interest in the example set by the FYComp ePortfolio assessment, and soon picked up on the fact that I had proposed a Gen Ed ePortfolio program a few years earlier.

Collaboration with Office of Assessment

The director of the Office of Assessment Services began collaborating with FYComp on incremental steps to make our program ePortfolio a more integral part of the university's assessment landscape by offering us help with tabulating ePortfolio scores and correlating them with other important demographic information such as gender, race, socioeconomic background, and standardized test scores. These correlations allow us to find out how well we are serving diverse populations and give us a footprint of student abilities in written communication, critical thinking, and information literacy that we use as part of our annual Voluntary System of Accountability (VSA) report. With an eye toward a campus-wide writing rubric that could be used at any level in any department, the director of assessment also funded the FYComp assessment subcommittee to work for a semester to revise the ePortfolio scoring rubric to align it with the American Association of Colleges and Universities (AAC&U) VALUE rubrics for written communication, critical thinking, and information literacy (see Carpenter & Labissiere, this collection). Our most recent program outcomes statement and scoring rubric reflect changes that allow comparability of writing scores across the disciplines and from students at every level of undergraduate studies.

The Longitudinal General Education ePortfolio

In our discussions about the future of general education at NIU, we agreed on a key point mentioned frequently in current research: as a high impact practice, ePortfolio could become a cornerstone and hinge-pin of the undergraduate student experience (Eynon & Gambino, 2017; Hubert et al., 2015; Watson et al., 2016). Currently, NIU students begin their ePortfolios in FYComp classes, but we agreed that the ePortfolio should really be an integral part of a student's introduction to general studies, and thus it was implemented on a trial basis in UNIV 101: Introduction to the University classes (see Terry & Whillock, this collection). At the time of writing, perhaps 60% of NIU students take this class, but within a few years, we hope that the class will be mandatory for all first-year students, and transfer students will need to take UNIV 201, a similar introductory course that takes notice of their previous academic experience and channels it into what NIU can provide.

Of course, assessment of student general education outcomes is one main purpose of the NIU ePortfolio, but those of us who use portfolios know that they can enable much more than evaluation or assessment. In short, ePortfolios are a focal point for conversations about our trajectories and growth as students and professionals. Like most portfolio users, we want to harness some of the integrative, iterative, and synthesizing power of *folio thinking* to deepen and enrich the educational experiences of our students. As a "meta high impact practice" (Kahn & Scott, 2013), the ePortfolio process itself—not just the eventual assessment of the portfolio—can make the biggest difference in whether students feel connected to their learning and able to create and maintain first a learning identity, then a professional identity through the stories they tell in their online portfolios. And as Trent Batson (2015) points out, ePortfolios are a discourse form, a dialogic literate practice through which reflective lifelong learners invent and reinvent themselves.

Platform Decisions

The longitudinal Gen Ed ePortfolio is still in its infancy, and we have many, many challenges to overcome. For example, the question of what software platform to use comes up frequently (see Richardson et al., this collection). Inevitably, every program, department, college, or university has different needs and local circumstances. In FYComp we had no budget for commercial software solutions such as Livetext or Digication, two popular platforms in the US, so we taught students to use Mozilla Composer, which is now called Seamonkey, to create their ePortfolios. This pedagogical choice proved time consuming in terms of faculty development and supporting students, but since we are a technology-rich writing program, we have been able to provide that support from within our program infrastructure. About seven years ago, we discovered that the Google Sites platform was free and much easier to use, and, coincidentally, our school migrated all student email to Google around the same time. So Google Sites allowed us to require ePortfolios of all students in the program—about 2,000 per semester.

However, when we joined forces with Assessment and General Education, we had to face the fact that all NIU students use the Blackboard course management system for almost all of their other classes, and Blackboard offers its own ePortfolio tool. My colleagues across campus, including support staff in Faculty Development and Instructional Design, were fairly insistent that FYComp needed to use the Blackboard ePortfolio tool in order to allow students to maintain continuity across the semesters and years of their undergraduate education. This position is understandable, since the chronology of learning development is one of the most helpful features of a longitudinal ePortfolio, and viewing the history of one's own learning offers students rich opportunities for finding patterns in their own growth and extrapolating toward professional identities. Using the same platform to develop the ePortfolio helps avoid confusion and promotes continuity (see Dellinger & Hanger, this collection). However, without more progress on the institution-wide portfolio as of the present moment (2020), we are seriously considering moving beyond Blackboard and/or allowing more student and instructor choice.

Scaling up often means sacrificing local concerns so that artifacts and data are comparable, but local iterations can persist. For example, even though snapshots of all of our students' FYComp ePortfolios are officially accessible through Blackboard, we allow for students to link out from Blackboard to live versions of their ePortfolios in Google, Wix, Squarespace, or whatever platform they prefer. When they graduate, of course, despite all the promises to the contrary by Blackboard about portability of student portfolios, students will most likely keep and maintain their portfolios on these other platforms.

Scaling Up: Inter-institutional Progress

For the past few decades, national and international organizations have facilitated large-scale collaborations among individuals and institutions interested in ePortfolios (see Figure 12.3), as discussed above. But in a time of dwindling travel budgets and support for membership fees, some educators are not able to join forces with these national and international organizations. Further, local and regional needs may not reflect larger national and international trends. More to the point, regional higher education institutions, since they share an increasingly mobile population of students and potential students, have a vested interest in sharing resources to make it easier for those students to transfer among regional community colleges and universities.

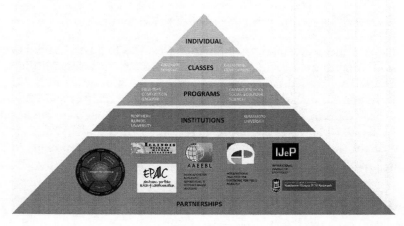

Figure 12.3. Scaling up from individual ePortfolios to international partnerships.

Collaborating with Community College Partners

When the partners at my regional institution—Assessment, General Education, and FYComp—announced the changes to Gen Ed to the Council of Deans, we were met with a lot of questions, among them the problem of transferability. Since our community college partners have an established system of facilitating transfer of general education credits to our university, they asked, how could NIU guarantee that transfer students would continue to get credit under the new system? Moreover, if we made the Gen Ed ePortfolio part of our degree requirements, how would students at community colleges prepare to fulfill this requirement? Partially to address these concerns, NIU sent delegations to our main "feeder" schools to meet with faculty and administrators there and discuss ways of moving forward together. At these meetings, as part of our introduction to the new Progressive Learning in Undergraduate Studies (PLUS) general education program,[2] we brought up the Gen Ed ePortfolio idea, and found that many of the schools either already had a portfolio serving some assessment purpose, or desired to create or improve one.

Based on these contacts, three of us—the former associate vice provost for general education, the former associate vice provost for outcomes assessment, and myself—developed an informal network of regional colleagues who expressed an interest in working with each other to figure out how ePortfolios might help with transferability in two ways. First, to help community colleges and universities better understand shared learning outcomes and ePortfolio practices, and second, to better facilitate the transfer of credit by allowing students to create portable records of their learning, along with personal statements about what that learning means to them (see Carpenter & Labissiere, this collection).

The Northern Illinois ePortfolio Symposium

Our first step in harnessing some of that interest was to host a regional ePortfolio summit and invite faculty and administrators from across northern Illinois to join us. We had generous support through a grant from the Illinois Board of Higher Education to cover keynote travel expenses and honoraria, and to provide refreshments and lunch to attendees. Our keynote speakers were nationally known ePortfolio experts Bret Eynon and Laura Gambino, who brought the audience up to speed with the latest developments in both the theory and the implementation of ePortfolios across the country. Since the

---

2.   Progressive Learning in Undergraduate Studies (PLUS) is NIU's revised general education program. Not only does it include foundational, breadth, and diversity requirements, it also offers students academic/career pathways in a variety of cross-disciplinary fields, such as sustainability, social justice, and global connections. For more information, see http://niu.edu/plus/.

Catalyst for Learning site had only that year been rolled out, they showcased some of the powerful examples and resources for higher education ePortfolio initiatives and provided a thorough rationale for the higher education ePort-folio movement.

Energized by the keynote, my colleagues and I moved to presentations and discussions of exemplars from NIU and two community colleges, covering the disciplines of FYComp, nursing, educational technology, and two different general education exit portfolio requirements, one currently digital and the other aspiring to go digital soon. The keynote speakers provided a thoughtful response, discussing the ways in which these diverse programs might work together to provide a powerful interdisciplinary, inter-institutional framework for students to document their learning in several areas.

About 30 colleagues from 15 different northern Illinois higher education institutions stayed for the final meeting, which focused on planning a regional ePortfolio partnership. As local planners at NIU, our goals were fairly modest. First, we wanted to investigate possible roles for ePortfolios to help students in the process of transferring general education credit and documenting both institutional and extra-curricular learning experiences, and second, we wanted to create a sharing network for ePortfolio practices among our regional institutions. Despite our attempts to limit the scope of the partnership, several of the attendees brought up less attainable goals, such as having all institutions adopt the same ePortfolio platform, or unifying general education goals and outcomes across all institutions. But we agreed that we would like to collaborate, and gave ourselves the name Illinois Regional ePortfolio Partnership (IREP). See Appendix A for our objectives and project goals.

IREP: A Wobbly Beginning

Since one of the NIU ePortfolio partners took a job elsewhere, and the other two of us were busy running our separate programs, it took many months to make any progress on IREP.[3] However, I presented on IREP at the ePortfolio Forum at the AAC&U conference in January 2015 with the faculty chair of assessment

---

3. As most of the IREP planning was taking place, I was in conversation with the I/NCEPR leaders about the possibility of proposing a cohort that would focus precisely on the needs IREP had identified: the role of ePortfolio in facilitating transfer among institutions in a specific region. In 2014, IREP leaders put out several emails to faculty and staff at partner schools mentioning the possibility of such a cohort and asking partners to express interest. A few did express interest, but as is typical with those who do the "heavy lifting" work of institutional assessment and change, most were overcommitted, and many became confused about the relationship between the two opportunities, the IREP regional group and the I/NCEPR potential cohort. At a certain point late in 2014, we had to make a choice about our priorities, so we postponed the I/NCEPR proposal and focused only on getting IREP up to speed. If and when the time is right, we will revisit the idea of creating a new coalition cohort to model the process of regional ePortfolio collaboration.

from one of our community college partners, and we were encouraged by the Northern Illinois P–20 Partnership of high schools, community colleges, and universities to work with their organization. This was especially helpful since the NIU president and the presidents of most of the regional community colleges are already members of the P–20 Network; with their endorsement in February 2015, we were able to identify faculty and staff to represent each institution at IREP meetings.

After months of planning and getting endorsements from higher administration at our partner institutions, we hosted a "kickoff" meeting in May 2015. About 30 faculty and staff from 12 institutions attended. We affirmed a basic set of goals and purpose statement (see Appendix A) and discussed some "what-if" scenarios: some that seemed helpful for transfer, but others that seemed to some of the community college stakeholders as if NIU would be creating a new, extra entrance requirement very difficult for community college transfer students to fulfill. We tried to assuage that concern by guaranteeing that any new initiatives would only be pilot projects, meant to test ideas but not to create new hurdles for transfer.

At the end of the day, the IREP group did agree on at least two action items. First, the nursing programs from the partner schools agreed to be in touch to discuss ways to coordinate their nursing portfolios so that students from each institution could bring a portable learning record that would be acceptable and recognized by the transfer institution. And second, the partners agreed that a good initial step would be to put up an IREP website stating our history, goals, purpose, and objectives, as well as showcasing ePortfolio practices from partner institutions.

However, leadership (and therefore enthusiasm and motivation) changed in NIU's nursing program, and early proponents seemed doubtful that we could run a pilot after all. We agreed to shift our focus to FYComp for the pilot, and accomplished significant work on the IREP web site. Then, we hit a wall when budget cuts led to enrollment drops and drastic reduction in personnel through attrition.

Budget and Enrollment Worries: When Scaling Up Gets Put on Hold

Timing isn't everything, but just as opportunities and complementary institutional needs can emerge quickly, they can disappear just as fast when conditions change. In November 2014, Illinoisans elected a new governor, whose first order of business was to try to fix a very broken state budget and pension system. This "fix" resulted in a stand-off over the state budget, which led to state university funding being withheld. At the same time, a combination of low numbers of college-aged students and parents with more savvy higher education shopping strategies resulted in dropping enrollments: from a high of over 25,000 students in 2006, enrollments fell to 18,000 in 2016. The then-new president and provost had made their best efforts to address student retention issues in their early years, but by 2015, the combination of budget shortfalls and lowered enrollments produced a hiring freeze. NIU survived by not hiring new faculty and staff when people retired or moved elsewhere, and this meant that everyone had to work harder, and many innovative (but potentially costly in terms of money and time) programs were put on hold. Such was the fate of IREP, and it "took the wind out of the sails" of our efforts to work on a longitudinal general education portfolio for all students.

Program Prioritization: Opportunities for Transformation?

However, even in the midst of a budget crisis, our institution followed through on another strategic planning process, Program Prioritization (PP), which allowed NIU to reallocate resources to departments and programs with a demonstrated record of serving students well, in cost-effective ways. English and FYComp fared well in the PP process, and transformation plans should have allowed us to proceed with efforts to coordinate FYComp with UNIV Introduction to the University classes and integrate the longitudinal general education ePortfolio in UNIV 101 classes as outlined above. One sticking point—that not all first-year students were taking UNIV 101—was addressed in the report, which recommended that UNIV 101 be required for all first-year students and be housed in an academic department or college. When drafting this chapter in 2015, I thought that the planets might be aligning again, and though busy with running my FYComp program, I was ready to collaborate again on making meaningful institutional change to benefit our students. But the budget crisis continued into a third year, enrollments dropped again, and the NIU president, who had been an ally to FYComp, came under fire for improper hiring practices during his efforts to remake the university in his first few years. Planets come into alignment, but they also fall out of alignment, so the conditions for change that follow must be considered both in their presence and their absence.

What are the Conditions for Change?

To affirm and expand upon the groundbreaking work of the C2L group, I will here discuss three strategies—collaboration, persistence, and *kairos*—that stakeholders need to embrace to meet the kinds of paradigm shifts in education brought on by recent socioeconomic changes affecting higher education (see Figure 12.4).

Collaboration

At every level—individual, course, program, institution, and inter-institutional partnership—the key to progress depends upon looking beyond individual classes and programs to find and build relationships with stakeholders in other campus departments and offices, and at our partner institutions. Randall Bass (2014) and the other authors represented in the C2L literature recognize this collaborative element in almost all ten of their Core Strategies for Scaling Up. Not only must institutions develop an effective ePortfolio team (#1), that team must represent key stakeholders from across the campus (see Richardson et al., this collection), connect to academic and co-curricular programs (#2), involve students (#4), use professional development to advance the ePortfolio initiative (#5), and align with institutional planning (#9) (see Dellinger & Hanger and Summers et al., this collection). What's more, to be effective, collaboration must advance from both ends of the spectrum: bottom-up with student exemplars and forward-thinking faculty, and top-down through the efforts of higher administrators (president, provost, deans, chairs) who understand and have the authority and resources (C2L Core Strategy #9) to enact the vision for higher educational change articulated so well by the AAC&U, AAEEBL, I/NCEPR, and other groups. Our collaborations with the higher administration in the offices of Assessment, General Education, and Faculty Development have created a feeling of trust, and a strong hope that we can accomplish much together (see Summers et al., this collection). When we work together, we stay focused on the goal of helping students succeed in their studies, become engaged, critical-thinking citizens, and embark on enriching professional pathways.

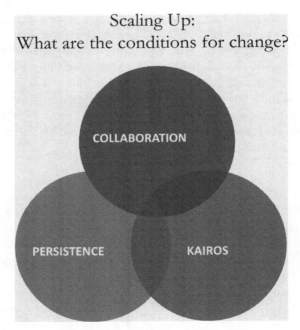

Figure 12.4. Strategies for change.

Persistence[4]

In the context of institutional and inter-institutional needs, state and national initiatives, and educational research, meaningful change can be glacial. An organization's ability to change can depend upon many factors such as: accreditation of the university and its programs, the ability of students to transfer easily between colleges and universities, state and national requirements, retention issues (remember that NIU enrollments are down by thousands of students), and stakeholders' reluctance to try new (possibly risky) initiatives. In the face of such institutional inertia, ePortfolio proponents have to be patient and work with colleagues to think ahead, and must always be ready for change. Persistence means continually, but gently, reminding stakeholders of both the need for change and the pathways for doing so. It means not only recognizing internal and external catalysts for change, but also *being* a catalyst. It means keeping alive and pursuing Bass's (2014) vision for "a set of practices and connections that enable an institution to carry out an unshakeable focus on student learning and a shared responsibility for educational quality and student success" (p. 5). In my case, remember that I started proposing Gen Ed ePortfolios over nine years ago (see timeline, Appendix B); it took many years and many tries for me to find collaborators in Faculty Development, Assessment, and General Education who would listen to and enact initiatives with me. Sometimes, as in current years of budget impasse, declining enrollments, and the departure of our president, we must not expect speedy change, but instead stay patient, active, and involved (see Summers et al., this collection).

Kairos

Kairos is a Greek term that means at the right or appropriate time or a propitious moment for decision and action. Change doesn't happen overnight, but sometimes many catalysts or enabling conditions (rhetoricians call these exigencies) appear at the same time, and it becomes clear that it is time to act. Institutional priorities with common or complementary interests often emerge simultaneously, like an interplanetary alignment. With the dispositions of persistence and a collaboration firmly entrenched in our institutional cultures, we can be ready when *kairos* emerges, when the conditions for change come about. We need to have relationships in place with other stakeholders, so that we can act strategically at the right moment, when the interests dovetail and the need is clear. Being aware not only of *what* and *how* is important, but as Dànielle DeVoss, Ellen Cushman, and Jeff Grabill (2005) point out, the policies and systems

---

4. Note that in the context of this chapter, by "persistence," I mean the willingness of institutional stakeholders to pursue institutional change in the face of challenging circumstances, not "persistence" as used by some educational theorists to refer to students remaining at an institution from one semester/year to the next.

that make up institutional infrastructures "might best be thought of as a 'when' and not a 'what'" (p. 37), so recognizing *when* to wait and *when* to act is also crucial.

Letting the Light Shine on Grassroots: Top-Down and Bottom-Up

Advocates for change need to be good collaborators, they need to be persistent, and they need to be in touch with both local and global contexts so that they can recognize *kairos* when conditions arise. To some degree, they must be able to see through the eyes and experiences of many stakeholders, grasp the significance of changing social and educational trends, understand policy and strategic planning, and know how to share the urgency or exigency with others. And they need to come from different points on the spectrum of experience and expertise: from students and faculty, to supportive professional staff, deans, provosts, and presidents. But, as emphasized in the Core Strategies for Scaling Up (Eynon et al., 2014b), no matter how strong the grassroots efforts may be, they probably will not survive if top administrative leaders aren't involved and providing the curricular, pedagogical, financial, and merit (e.g., tenure and promotion) support that allows the light to shine in to encourage the grassroots. Unfortunately, the current NIU leadership has been too busy with the budget impasse, enrollment worries, and the change in top-level leadership to consider providing that support, but I feel confident that the situation will soon improve.

Conclusion

Since I first drafted this chapter, Catalyst for Learning leaders Bret Eynon and Laura Gambino (2017) have published an update on the C2L project entitled *High Impact ePortfolio Practice: A Catalyst for Student, Faculty, and Institutional Learning*, which includes an even more succinct statement on scaling up (Chapter 7, pp. 134–152), and an updated statement from Randall Bass on scaling up ePortfolio's role in rethinking and rebuilding higher education (Chapter 8, pp. 153–160). On the book's cover, it is noted that "over half of U.S. colleges are employing ePortfolios" so "the time is ripe to develop their full potential to advance integrative learning and broad institutional change." In Chapter 7, Eynon and Gambino (2017) admit that "scaling any technology-based innovation in higher education is challenging" (p. 134) and that even though "64% of U.S. colleges use ePortfolio at their institution . . . very few of them have most or all of their students using ePortfolios" (p. 135). Like some of NIU's efforts to take ePortfolios campus-wide, "many ePortfolio projects remain at the pilot stages and never fulfill their promise" (Eynon and Gambino, 2017, p. 135). And yet, as I hope I have made clear, as a programmatic initiative, ePortfolio pedagogy, curriculum, and assessment efforts have matured in NIU FYComp. In times of better funding and enrollments, with forward-thinking leadership and support for grassroots efforts, we made significant progress toward campus-wide ePortfolio integration by forming strategic partnerships with the Offices of Assessment, General Education, and Faculty Development, and at the very least, we have an effective tool for comparing written communication, critical thinking, and information literacy in all undergraduate programs and levels. Through the creation of IREP, we demonstrated that in a better economic climate, higher education institutions from a regional area could collaborate to improve the changing educational and assessment landscape for students who, more frequently than ever, transfer among these institutions. At both the institutional and interinstitutional level, along with the partners left standing, I remain committed to Bass's (2014) claim that by connecting "often-marginalized centers of innovation," ePortfolio initiatives "inform and deepen pedagogical practices campus-wide and introduce increasingly rich views of student learning into the everyday flows of teaching, learning, assessment, and curriculum design" (p. 153). But until at least two conditions emerge—a stable state budget and new campus leaders who accept and can build on the findings of Eynon, Gambino, Bass, and others through local action—we are left in a holding pattern: persistent to the end, and ready to collaborate when *kairos* dictates.

References

Achrazoglou, J., Anthony, R., Jun, M. K, Marshall, J. & Roe, G. (2002). *A white paper on performance assessment in teacher education: The Iowa ePortfolio model.* University of Iowa College of Education.

Bass, R. (2014). Scaling strategies and ePortfolio as a catalyst for change. http://c2l. mcnrc.org/wp-content/uploads/sites/8/2014/01/Scaling_Strategies.pdf.

Batson, T. (2015. September 2). The ePortfolio as archetypal literate form. AAEEBL. http://www.aaeebl.org/blogpost/1008436/225678/The-ePortfolio-as-Archetypal-Literate-Form.

Bowman, J., Lowe, B. J., Sabourin, K. & Sweet, C. S. (2016). The use of ePortfolios to support metacognitive practice in a first-year writing program. *International Journal of ePortfolio, 6*(1), 1–22.

Chen, H. L. (2009). Using ePortfolios to support lifelong and lifewide learning. In D. Cambridge, B. Cambridge & K. B. Yancey (Eds.), *Electronic portfolios 2.0: Emergent research on implementation and impact* (pp. 29–36). Stylus,

Conference on College Composition and Communication (CCCC) (2015). Principles and practices in electronic portfolios. http://www.ncte.org/cccc/resources/positions/electronicportfolios.

Day, M. (2009). Influencing learning through faculty- and student-generated outcome assessment. In D. Cambridge, B. Cambridge & K. B. Yancey (Eds.), *Electronic portfolios 2.0: Emergent research on implementation and impact* (pp. 83–86). Stylus.

Day, M. (2015, October 13). Scaling up: Moving from class and program to institutional and inter-institutional ePortfolios for assessment and articulation [Keynote address]. Kumamoto University's E-Learning Forum, Kumamoto, Japan. Slides available at https://slideplayer.com/slide/10896597/.

Devoss, D., Cushman, E. & Grabill, J. (2005). Infrastructure and composing: The *when* of new-media writing. *CCCC, 57*(1), 14–44.

Donahue, P. (2017, June 12). RE: General education portfolio assessment [Comment on online forum post General education portfolio assessment]. WPA-L Listserv. https://lists.asu.edu/cgi-bin/wa?A2=ind1706&L=WPA-L&F=&S=&P=137639.

Eynon, B. & Gambino, L. (2017). *High impact ePortfolio practice: A catalyst for student, faculty, and institutional learning*. Stylus.

Eynon, B., Gambino, L. & Torok, J. (2014a). Core strategies for scaling up: 1–10. http://c2l.mcnrc.org/scaling/scaling-analysis/.

Heritage, M. (2007). Formative assessment: What do teachers need to know and do? *Phi Delta Kappan, 89*(2), 140–145.

Hubert, D., Pickavance, J. & Hyberger, A. (2105). Reflective ePortfolios: One HIP to rule them all? *Peer Review, 17*(4), 15–18.

Johnson, K. R. & Kahn, S. (2013). What are you going to do with that major? An ePortfolio as bridge from the university to the world. In K. V. Wills & R. Rice (Eds.), *ePortfolio performance support systems: Constructing, presenting, and assessing portfolios* (pp. 89–108). The WAC Clearinghouse; Parlor Press. https://wac.colostate.edu/books/perspectives/eportfolios/.

Kahn, S. & Scott, S. (2013, December 13). Scaling up ePortfolios at a complex urban research university: The IUPUI story. Indiana University-Purdue University Indianapolis. http://iupui.mcnrc.org/scaling-story/ .

Kinsman, R. P., Kahn, S. & Scott, S. (2014, January 25). Social pedagogy: Working together to develop metacognition and professional identity. Catalyst for Learning: ePortfolio Resources and Research. http://c2l.mcnrc.org/soc-practice-2/.

The Making Connections National Resource Center (2020). Catalyst for Learning: ePortfolio Resources and Research

Reynolds, C. & Patton, J. (2014). *Leveraging the ePortfolio for integrative learning: A faculty guide to classroom practices for transforming student learning*. Stylus.

Rickards, W. & Guilbault, L. (2009). Studying student reflection in an electronic portfolio environment: An inquiry in the context of practice. In D. Cambridge, B. Cambridge & K. B. Yancey (Eds.), *Electronic portfolios 2.0: Emergent research on implementation and impact* (pp. 17–28). Stylus.

Ring, G. & Ramirez, B. (2012). Implementing ePortfolios for the assessment of general education competencies. *International Journal of ePortfolio, 2*(1), 87–97.

Thurman, J. (2017, June 12). General education portfolio assessment [Comment on online forum post General education portfolio assessment]. WPA-L Listserv. https://lists.asu.edu/cgi-bin/wa?A2=ind1706&L=WPA-L&F=&S=&P=81881.

Watson, C. E., Kuh, G., Rhodes, T., Light, T. P. & Chen, H. L. (2016). Editorial: ePortfolios—The eleventh high impact practice. *International Journal of ePortfolio, 6*(2), 65–69.

Whithaus, C. (2013). ePortfolios as tools for facilitating and assessing knowledge transfer from lower division, general education courses to upper division, discipline specific courses. In K. V. Wills & R. Rice, (Eds.), *ePortfolio performance support systems: Constructing, presenting, and assessing portfolios* (pp. 205–220). The WAC Clearinghouse; Parlor Press. https://doi.org/10.37514/PER-B.2013.0490.2.11.

Yancey, K. B., Cambridge, B. & Cambridge, D. (2009). Making common cause: Electronic portfolios, learning, and the power of community. The Academic Commons Issue #6: Case Studies on Digital Collaboration and Blended/Hybrid Learning. http://www.academiccommons.org/making-common-cause-electronic-portfolios-learning-and-the-power-of-community/.

Appendix A. Illinois Regional ePortfolio Partnership (IREP)

Purpose/Objectives

- Explore ways in which ePortfolios can be used to facilitate students' transfer across institutions in the Illinois higher education system
- Demonstrate the use of ePortfolios as a means of assessing college and career readiness and as a way to complement/supplement the use of standardized tests
- Share successes and develop a compelling case for the adoption of ePortfolios within the Illinois higher education system
- Share lessons learned in the implementation and use of ePortfolios
- Explore ways that ePortfolios can foster inter-institution articulation at all levels
- Establish a nationally recognized model for the integrated use of ePortfolios across the Illinois higher education system.

IREP Project Goals

- Demonstrate a viable alternative to standardized testing for assessing common core competencies by sharing and collaborating on a mindset of "folio thinking" that requires iterative reflection on learning and professional pathways
- Clarify the issues (technical, procedural, and pedagogical) that need to be addressed in order to facilitate the transfer of student portfolios across institutions
- Determine whether an ePortfolio can help to better assess incoming students' educational needs as they move across institutions
- Show how an ePortfolio could help students feel better prepared to transition to a new school or the marketplace

Appendix B: NIU ePortfolio Timeline 2001–2015

2001

INDIVIDUAL AND CLASS-BASED EPORTFOLIOS

• Faculty development workshop on eportfolios

THE POWER OF COLLABORATION: CONNECTING WITH STAKEHOLDERS

2002

• Society for Technical Communication workshop on professional eportfolios

• Undergraduate Research Apprenticeship Program on eportfolios

• Collaboration with Faculty Development Office at NIU resulted in NIU eportfolio workshops and conferences

FIRST-YEAR COMPOSITION PROGRAM EPORTFOLIO PILOT

2003

• Professional electronic teaching portfolios for pre-certification teachers

• Collaboration between College, Provost, English Department allowed NIU to join the Inter/National Coalition for Eportfolio Research (I/NCEPR)

• Program Outcomes Development: One year process working from Council of Writing Program Administrators Outcomes Statement

2004

INTER/NATIONAL COALITION FOR ELECTRONIC PORTFOLIO RESEARCH (I/NCEPR)

• Pilot 1: Online discussion board posts with reflections in new TA sections

ELECTRONIC TEACHING PORTFOLIOS FOR ALL FIRST-YEAR TEACHING ASSISTANTS

2005

• Ten US institutions in I/NCEPR cohort one, with intense collaboration and sharing on the role of reflection in the eportfolio

• Portfolio Summit with keynote Kathleen Blake Yancey

• Pilot 2: Mozilla Composer (Sea Monkey) web pages with templates (2005-2010) in new TA sections

• Major requirement for English 600, Seminar in the Teaching of College Writing, a yearlong course

2006

• Support and guidance for developing NIU's First-Year Composition (FYComp) program eportfolio

• Includes teaching philosophy, assignments, example strategies and assignments, and lots of reflection

2007

• Google Sites is the default, but students can use any platform (E.G. WIX, Wordpress, Squarespace) they like

2008

LONGITUDINAL GENERAL EDUCATION EPORTFOLIO PLANNING

• Draft version due fall semester, final version due in spring

2009

• NIU Strategic Planning Proposal

2010

• Assessment, Gen Ed, and FYComp collaborations

2011

FYCOMP FULL-PROGRAM IMPLEMENTATION

• General Education Revisioning

• Workshop with Helen Barrett

2012

• Google Sites with templates and required reflections

• Collaboration with Office of Assessment Services and General Education Committee

2013

• Aligning FYComp eportfolio rubric to AAC&U VALUE Rubrics for campuswide writing assessment

2014

• Establishing the eportfolio as a cornerstone of PLUS Gen. Ed. Assessment, beginning in UNIV 101 (Intro to Integrated Studies) & continuing in UNIV 301 (Intro to Careers)

ILLINOIS REGIONAL EPORTFOLIO PARTNERSHIP (IREP)

• Common Core and College Readiness (PARCC), 2014

• Deans concerned about general education transfer, March 2014

• Visits to community colleges, May-June 2014

• Northern Illinois Eportfolio Symposium, September 2014

2015

• Blackboard eportfolios with templates

• PLUS UNIV 101, 301 Eportfolio model

• The idea for the Illinois Regional Eportfolio Partnership (IREP)

• IREP presentation at AAC&U Conference, January 2015

• Community college presidents endorse IREP, February 2015

Glossary

Active learning: "Students' efforts to actively construct their knowledge" (Carr et al., 2014) through activities, discussions, and peer interaction.

Adaptive Comparative Judgment (ACJ): "The ACJ approach asks ePortfolio reviewers only to compare two portfolios and make one choice. Each portfolio is then compared with several others over the course of the day and each portfolio is read by more judges than in a standard holistic rubric scoring approach" (Carpenter & Labissiere, this collection).

Analytic rubric: "An analytical rubric provides a list of detailed learning objectives, each with its own rating scheme that corresponds to a specific skill or quality to be evaluated using the criterion. Analytical rubrics provide scoring for individual aspects of a learning objective, but they usually require more time to create. When using analytical rubrics, it may be necessary to consider weighing the score using a different scoring scale or score multipliers for the learning objectives" (Hall, 2014,).

Anchor ePortfolios: Examples of students' ePortfolios that exemplify the attributes at each performance level (see Carpenter & Labissiere, this collection).

Artifact: Tangible evidence of a student's knowledge, skills, experience, achievements, and values. ePortfolio artifacts can be work samples, media, feedback provided by supervisors, teachers, or peers, résumés, reflections, etc.

Assessment (of learning): The process of observing, evaluating, and documenting students' performance in accordance with a set of criteria such as learning outcomes, goals, short-term objectives, and the like.

Authenticity; authentic learning/assessment: Any product or process that connects to or simulates real-world situations.

Back-end/front-end collaboration: Cooperation and coordination between IT specialists (back-end) and faculty or staff (front-end) involved in ePortfolio development, implementation, instruction, and/or assessment.

Backward design: An approach to curriculum planning in which instructors and administrators begin with learning targets (outcomes) and benchmarks, then identify the assessment tool to measure and document students' performance as meeting or not meeting those targets, and finally plan daily classroom activities that align with those targets (Wiggins & McTighe, 1998).

Badges: "Badges 'were created to capture learning whenever and wherever that learning occurs: formal, informal, public, private, group, individual' and Open badges 'can be designed to represent a small thing, such as fundamental principle or a single competency or to represent a large thing like a competency set, license, or a degree.'" (Castaño & Novo, this collection)

Calibration: The "process of peer review carried out by members of a disciplinary and/or professional community who typically discuss, review and compare student work in order to reach a shared understanding of the academic standard which such work needs to meet." (Advance HE, 2018,).

Constructivism/Constructivist: "An approach to learning that holds that people actively construct or make their own knowledge and that reality is determined by the experiences of the learner." (Elliott as cited in McLeod, 2019).

Conversational Framework: The conceptualization of teaching/learning as an ongoing dialogue that supports learning through communication, adaptation, reflection, and "goal-oriented actions with feedback" (Laurillard, 2008; see Castaño & Novo, this collection).

Curation: The process of collecting, selecting, categorizing, and reflecting on artifacts.

Design thinking: A methodology for problem-solving that includes empathy, collaboration, creativity, reflection, and discovery.

Evidence-based learning/assessment: Conceptualizations, decisions, or methods based on or informed by empirical evidence.

Folio thinking/portfolio thinking: A habit of mind; "a process of exploring, establishing touchstones (artifacts, experiences), and extrapolating into one's future based on past and present experiences" (Lutz et al., 2016)

Holistic rubric: A scoring tool that identifies three to five levels of performance and indicates the general traits for each to assess a student as a whole.

HTML: A protocol for displaying data. (Balthazor et al., this collection).

Hyperlink: A word, phrase, or image that provides direct access from one electronic document to another or from one section to another within a single document.

Inquiry-based learning/assessment: A problem-solving approach that presents learners with questions, problems, or scenarios.

Integrative learning: "Integrative learning is an understanding and a disposition that a student builds across the curriculum and co-curriculum, from making simple connections among ideas and experiences to synthesizing and transferring learning to new, complex situations within and beyond the campus" (American Council of Colleges and Universities, quoted by Carpenter & Labissiere, this collection).

Learning path: The succession of activities and experiences that facilitates the learner's creation of knowledge or cultivation of a particular skill.

Metacognition: Thinking about thinking; "the processes used to plan, monitor, and assess one's understanding and performance." (Chick, 2020).

Metafolio: "An array of resources about ePortfolio, which can feature videos, tips, walk-throughs, prompts, and suggestions concerning the what, why, and how of ePortfolios at an institution, in a program, or a course." (Terry & Whillock, this collection).

Multimodal: Conveying meaning or imparting information through a variety of modes or multiple literacies.

Outcome-based learning/assessment/design: An approach through which instruction, assessment, and organization relate to specified learning outcomes that are both observable and measurable.

Reflection: In the framework of ePortfolio, reflection can be "the action of curation as reflection, the reflection of intent, and . . . an artifact (a piece of evidence) or something else altogether." (Coleman et al., this collection).

Rubric: An assessment tool that identifies levels of performance and performance descriptors (see "analytic rubric" and "holistic rubric").

Scaffolding: ". . . instructional techniques used to move students progressively toward stronger understanding and, ultimately, greater independence in the learning process" (Scaffolding, 2015)

SMART goals: Goals that are Specific, Measurable, Attainable, Relevant, and Time-bound (Doran, 1981).

Showcase ePortfolio: "ePortfolio as Showcase/Product – Selection/Reflection + Direction + Presentation" (Barrett, 2013).

Standards-based: Learning designed in accordance with a set of standards established/published by a recognized organization, institution, or government agency.

XML (Extensible Markup Language): "XML is a protocol for marking the structure of documents, and is designed to store, transport, and exchange data (rather than display data, like html). XML is used for organizing data of any kind in a systematic manner by creating descriptive markup tags (e.g., an essay might include tags for marking paragraphs, sentences, introductions, thesis statements, etc.)." (Balthazor et al., this collection).

Workspace: The unpublished repository of evidence (e.g., artifacts, feedback, reflections).

Workspace ePortfolio: "ePortfolio as Workspace/Process – Collection + Reflection"(Barrett, 2013).

References

Advance HE (2018). *What is calibration?* https://www.heacademy.ac.uk/project-section/what-is-calibration.

Barrett, H. (2013). Balancing the two faces of ePortfolios. https://electronicportfolios.org/balance/#2.

Carr, R., Palmer, S. & Hagel, P. (2015). Active learning: the importance of developing a comprehensive measure. *Active Learning in Higher Education, 16,* 173–186.

Chick, N. (n.d.) *Metacognition.* Vanderbilt University. https://cft.vanderbilt.edu/guides-sub-pages/metacognition/.

Doran, G. T. (1981). There's a S.M.A.R.T. way to write management's goals and objectives. *Management Review, 70*(11), 35–36.

Hall, M. (2014, November 21). *Creating rubrics. Innovative Instructor Blog.* Johns Hopkins University. https://ii.library.jhu.edu/tag/analytical-rubric/.

Lutz, B., Blakely, B., Rose, K & Ballard, T. M. (2016). Learning and reflecting with ISUComm ePortfolios: Exploring technological and curricular places. *The Journal of Interactive Technology and Pedagogy, 10.* https://jitp.commons.gc.cuny.edu/learning-and-reflecting-with-isucomm-eportfolios/.

McLeod, S. (2019). Constructivism as a theory for teaching and learning. https://www.simplypsychology.org/constructivism.html.

Scaffolding. (2015). The glossary of education reform. https://www.edglossary.org/scaffolding/.

Wiggins, G. P. & McTighe, J. (1998) *Understanding by design.* Association for Supervision and Curriculum Development.

Contributing Authors and Editors

Ron Balthazor served as an academic professional at the University of Georgia and has recently retired. He taught composition and environmental literature and was the lead developer of Emma. His continuing interests include Thoreau, honeybees, chickens, sheep, fungi, worms, and the rich ecosystem of the backyard garden.

Denise Bollenback is Assistant Professor in the Department of Management and Technology at Embry-Riddle Aeronautical University. At ERAU she has developed and taught several courses, including IT Management, Strategy, and Governance, Business Intelligence and Data Analytics, and Business Analytics for Managers.

Rowanna Carpenter is the Director of Assessment and Upper Division Clusters for University Studies, the interdisciplinary general education program at Portland State University. She works with faculty across the University Studies program to encourage assessment of student learning and an understanding of the student experience with an emphasis on using data to implement change. Currently she leads a project which is creating online general education pathways for students and has been conducting research into online students' success. Rowanna earned her B.A. from the University of Hawaii and an M.P.A. and Ph.D. in Public Administration and Policy from Portland State University. She conducts research, writes and presents on student learning assessment, students' experiences with ePortfolios, and the use of data to improve and support student success.

Andrea Ximena Castaño Sánchez received her doctorate at Rovira i Virgili University with an emphasis in Technology Applied to Education and Knowledge Management. She worked as a researcher and professor in subjects related to educational technology at Rovira I Virgili University and the Universidad Nacional de Educación (Ecuador). Dr. Castaño Sanchez's research focuses on meaningful learning, instructional technology, and the design of technology-based learning.

Helen L. Chen is a research scientist in the Designing Education Lab in the Department of Mechanical Engineering at Stanford University. She serves on the board for the Association for Authentic, Experiential and Evidence-Based Learning, is a co-author of *Documenting Learning with ePortfolios: A Guide for College Instructors* and co-executive editor of the *International Journal of ePortfolio*. Her current research interests focus on engineering and entrepreneurship education; applications of design thinking for curricular change; the pedagogy of portfolios and reflective practice in higher education; and redesigning how learning is recorded and recognized in traditional transcripts and academic credentials.

Kathryn Coleman is an artist, researcher, and teacher based in Melbourne. She is the Australasian representative on the Board of Directors of Association of Authentic, Experiential and Evidence Based Learning (AAEEBL) and World Council Representative for the South-East Asia Pacific Region for the International Society for Education though Art (InSEA). Her work focuses on the integration of digital pedagogies and digital portfolios for sustained creative practice and assessment. Kate's praxis includes taking aspects of her theoretical and practical work as a/r/tographer to consider how practitioners, teachers and students use site to create place in the digital and physical. Her Ph.D. was the first fully online thesis as digital portfolio submitted at The University of Melbourne, where Kate is a lecturer in Visual Arts and Design Teacher Secondary Education at the Melbourne Graduate School of Education.

Elizabeth Davis is the Coordinator of the interdisciplinary Writing Certificate Program (WCP) at the University of Georgia. She teaches rhetoric and composition courses in the Department of English, and conducts the capstone ePortfolio workshop for the WCP. She is the co-author, with Nedra Reynolds, of the Third Editions of *Portfolio Keeping: A Guide for Students* and *Portfolio Teaching: A Guide for Instructors* (Bedford/St. Martin's, 2014).

Michael Day is Professor of English at Northern Illinois University (NIU), where he directs the first-year composition program and teaches rhetoric, composition, teaching of writing, technical writing, and writing for electronic media. He has presented and published widely on topics ranging from intercultural and digital rhetoric to electronic portfolio assessment. A member of the first cohort of the Inter/National Coalition for Electronic Portfolio Research, Day is a past chair of both the Conference on College Composition and Communication (CCCC) Committee on Computers in Composition and Communication and the National Council of Teachers of English Assembly on Computers in English. His awards include the 2006 *Computers and Composition* Charles Moran Award for Distinguished Contributions to the Field and the 2011 CCCC Technology Innovator Award.

Thomas Fath is Deputy Director of the Dementia Research Centre and Professor in the Department of Biomedical Sciences, Faculty of Medicine and Health Science, at Macquarie University (Australia). His research team investigates the actin cytoskeleton as a potential drug target to provide protection and promote regeneration in the injured or diseased nervous system.

Deidre Anne Evans Garriott is the Director of the Writing Center at the University of South Carolina in Columbia, SC. Her current research includes inquiry into reforming writing center practices through social justice pedagogy. She also studies sites of public memory through a cultural rhetorics framework.

Kelly Whealan George is Associate Professor in the College of Arts & Sciences and Worldwide Liaison for Accreditation at Embry-Riddle Aeronautical University. Her research projects center on the interrelationship of the aviation/aerospace industry and economic impact of a Research Park. Dr. George has received multiple honors for research excellence in the ERAU Worldwide Campus.

Laurin Hanger joined Virginia Military Institute in 1998 as the Help Desk Coordinator providing the VMI community with computer hardware and software support as well as training workshops for faculty and staff. In 2008, she assumed the responsibility as the administrator of the LMS (Learning Management System). Laurin holds a B.S. in Automated Technology Management from James Madison University.

Rachel Kow completed her undergraduate studies in liberal studies and mathematics and her Master's in Secondary Education at San Francisco State University. She worked with Academic Technology at San Francisco State as a student ambassador for ePortfolios and testing new ePortfolio platforms.

Yves Labissiere, a social psychologist by training, is Associate Professor at Portland State University where he directs PSU's award-winning University Studies program. For 20 years he has developed curricular innovations supporting student transitions to higher education. These interventions focus on engaging changing self-perceptions and beliefs that inform and shape identity and motivation in underrepresented students at high schools and universities. Dr. Labissiere is an experienced assessment specialist, and program evaluator.

Sophie McKenzie is a lecturer in the School of Information Technology at Deakin University and is experienced in teaching across a broad range of areas in IT. Her areas of expertise include game design, 3D content creation, web design and emerging technologies. Her research interests lie in the scholarship of teaching and learning in higher education, specifically in the area of career development learning and employability.

Deborah Church Miller, longtime Associate Director of First-year Composition (FYC) at the University of Georgia, recently retired. She served as Interim Director of FYC in her final year. In addition to overseeing the day-to-day administration and management of a large FYC program, she also developed curricula for the program and upper division writing courses. She taught first-year composition, advanced composition, composition theory and pedagogy, the graduate teaching practicum, and the occasional Medieval lit course.

María Teresa Novo Molinero is Associate Professor and Coordinator of Science Education at Rovira i Virgili University (Spain). Her research is focused on the application and assessment of learning methodologies in STEM disciplines and the development of scientific competence in learners. Her projects are aimed at promoting scientific vocation in at-risk children, scientific reasoning in early childhood education, and professional development for classroom teachers in STEM settings.

Deb Perry is an Instructional Designer and Information Technology Consultant at San Francisco State University. In her current role, she consults with faculty one-on-one, introducing instructors to technological efficiencies that save them time. With her colleagues in Academic Technology and the Teaching and Learning with Technology Leadership Team, she enjoys designing new faculty development workshops.

Patsie Polly is Scientia Education Fellow in the Department of Pathology at the University of New South Wales (Australia). She has led reflective ePortfolio implementation to develop deep learning of teamwork and communication competencies in students, contextualizing these skills for their future as medical researchers and health professionals. Professor Polly has held three competitive international and national fellowships to conduct her research on gene regulation.

Jenny Ramirez is an adjunct professor of art history at James Madison University and Mary Baldwin University. She has taught courses on the history of Asian art, Chinese art and culture, Japanese art and aesthetics, as well as a course on *Japonisme* (East & West interactions in the nineteenth century). Dr. Ramirez has co-published several articles on pedagogy, reflection, and ePortfolios.

Tracey M. Richardson is Associate Professor of the College of Business and Assistant Dean for Performance Excellence & Accreditation at Embry-Riddle Aeronautical University. Her research centers on project management—her field of expertise—and the role of planning in students' success.

Howard B. Sanborn is Professor of International Studies & Political Science at the Virginia Military Institute. He has taught courses on the comparative politics of East Asia, and his research has been published in a number of highly-respected journals, including the *British Journal of Political Science, Political Behavior, Political Research Quarterly, European Political Science Review,* and the *Asian Journal of Comparative Politics.* Dr. Sanborn served as director of the VMI ePortfolio Project from 2012–2014.

Sara Steger is Senior Lecturer and Assistant Director of First-Year Writing at the University of Georgia, where she teaches Romantic and Victorian literature, digital rhetoric, and first-year writing classes. She is also a researcher and developer for the Emma project, a digital writing environment.

Teggin Summers is Director of Teaching and Learning Programs and Services of the Teaching and Learning, Center for Equity and Excellence in Teaching and Learning, at San Francisco State University. She has broad experience with tools and techniques for engaging faculty around technology-enhanced, student-centered learning, including affordable and open educational resources, academic integrity, ePortfolio assessment, and Quality Learning & Teaching (QLT) peer review and certification, among others.

Daniel Terry is Director of Yes/And Initiative, Office of Academic Affairs, and Assistant Professor, Cato School of Education, at Queens University of Charlotte. In his former position, he served as the Director of ePortfolio in the Office of the Provost at Texas Christian University. In this role, he directed the strategy, implementation, and evaluation of the TCU's ePortfolio initiative. His research interests and publications include cognitive science, ePortfolio pedagogy, higher education and spirituality, educational philosophy, leadership development, curriculum theory, and moral and intellectual development.

Thuan Thai is Senior Lecturer in the School of Education, University of Notre Dame Australia, Sydney campus, where he teaches mathematics and science pedagogy in both primary and secondary education programs. He has more than 15 years of experience as an education consultant, advising on mathematics curriculum and design as well as the integration of educational technology to enhance learning. Prior to becoming a teacher educator, Dr. Thai was a heart researcher and taught Pathology at the University of New South Wales (Australia).

Constance Ulasewicz is Professor Emerita of Apparel Design and Merchandising at San Francisco State University where she continues to be at the foreground of online learning opportunities and workshops offered at SFSU. Her research interests include, transparency in supply chain management of sewn products manufacturing from fiber to finished product information to the consumer, and product reuse.

David Whillock, is Associate Provost and Dean of the Academy of Tomorrow at Texas Christian University. He teaches courses in History of the Cinema, Film Theory and Criticism, National Cinemas, American Culture in Film and Myth, Media, and Message: The Evolution of the Blues. Dr. Willock has published in international and national journals of film and media. His research interest includes film and history, the Vietnam War in American cinema, and new technologies in our way of knowing.

Cai Wilkinson is Associate Professor of International Relations at Deakin University (Australia). She joined Deakin in February 2012 from the University of Birmingham, UK, where she was a lecturer in the Centre for Russian and East European Studies and taught International Relations and Russian language. Her research focuses on societal security in the post-Soviet space, with a particular focus on LGBTQ human rights and "traditional values" in Kyrgyzstan and Russia, as well as on interrogating the role of genders and sexualities in international politics.

Crystal O. Wong works in a variety of faculty positions at San Francisco State University. She is a lecturer in the English Department, an Open Educational Resource ambassador, and a faculty fellow with the Center for Equity and Excellence in Teaching and Learning. Her work includes teaching undergraduate composition courses, mentoring faculty to share best practices, and leading professional development workshops.

Jia-Lin Yang is Associate Professor in the Prince of Wales Clinical School at the University of New South Wales (Australia), where he teaches oncology and carcinogenesis. His research interests also include cell biology and gene regulation, preventative medicines, and biostatistics. In addition to his medical research, Dr. Yang has co-authored numerous papers on ePortfolios, integrative learning, and career skills.

Editors

Mary Ann Dellinger is Professor (emerita) of Spanish Language and Cultures at the Virginia Military Institute and served as the Institute's first Director of the VMI ePortfolio Project. Her research focuses on second language acquisition, language learning technology, and Peninsular cultural studies, particularly the official culture and counterculture during the Franco dictatorship. Dr. Dellinger's latest publication, *Indagaciones. Introducción a los estudios culturales hispanos* (Georgetown University Press), co-authored with Professors Ellen Mayock and Beatriz Trigo, is the first textbook on cultural studies for students of Spanish as a second language. Also with Dr. Trigo, she co-edited *Homenaje a la profesora L. Teresa Vadivieso. Ensayos críticos* (Juan de la Cuesta, University of Delaware, 2008) and *Entornos digitales. Conceptualización y praxis* (Universitat Oberta de Barcelona University Press, 2017) The latter figures among the first scholarly collections on the digital humanities written in Spanish.

D. Alexis Hart, Director of Writing at Allegheny College, is the editor of *How to Start an Undergraduate Research Journal* (CUR, 2012), and her published work has also appeared in *CUR Quarterly, Pedagogy, Writing on the Edge, Composition Forum,* and several edited collections. She was the co-recipient, with Roger Thompson, of a Conference on College Composition and Communication (CCCC) research grant to study veterans returning to college writing classrooms; Hart's and Thompson's *College Composition and Communication* article based on this research earned the 2017 Richard Braddock Memorial Award and appears in the *2018 Best of the Journals in Rhetoric & Composition* collection. Their co-written book, *Writing Programs, Veterans Studies, and the Post–9/11 University: A Field Guide* was published in 2020. Hart also serves on the editorial boards of *The Peer Review, Journal of Veteran Studies,* and *International Journal for ePortfolio,* among others.